UNTIL WE MEET AGAIN

UNTIL WE MEET AGAIN

A True Story of Love and

Survival in the Holocaust

MICHAEL KORENBLIT

AND

KATHLEEN JANGER

Miracle Press
Edmond, Oklahoma

**Call 405/359-0369 to book a speaking engagement with
Michael Korenblit or to interview him via FaceTime or
telephone. See Facebook.com/Until/We/Meet/AgainBook.
Also available on Kindle, Nook, and iTunes.**

Earlier editions of this book were published as follows: In
2000, a school market edition by Scholastic, Inc.; in 1995 by
Charles River Press; and in 1983 by G. P. Putnam's Sons.

Permissions appear on pages iv, 24, 62, 188, and 256.

Library of Congress Cataloging-in-Publication Data
Korenblit, Michael
Until We Meet Again: A True Story of Love and Survival in the
Holocaust/
Michael Korenblit and Kathleen Janger.
        p.cm.
        ISBN 978-0-929889-08-5 (paperback)
        1.   Holocaust, Jewish (1939-1945)—Poland—Hrubieszow—
Biography. 2. Jews—Persecution—Poland—Hrubieszow. 3.
Korenblit, Meyer. 4. Korenblit, Manya. 5. Nagelsztajn, Chaim.
6. Hrubieszow (Poland)—Ethnic relations. I. Janger, Kathleen.
II. Title.
DS125.P62H74   1995
940.53'18'094384—dc20   95-35382
                                         CIP
Design by Bonnie Campbell
Manufactured in the United States of America
Printed on recycled paper.
20   19   18   17   16   15

DEDICATED TO:
Adam
Andrea
Bill
Brian
Caitlin
Gemma
Hanah
Hayley
Jay
Jennifer
Jordan
Joshua
Kimberly
Kristin
Lianne
Luke
Margi
Matte
Megan
Megan Ruth
Michelle
Molly
Morgan
Paul
Peter
Sadie
Sarah
Stephen
Todd
Will
and children everywhere:

May you make—and be—friends like Josef Wisniewski, John and Janek Salki, Franiek and Henrik Gorski, and others whose actions altered destiny.

OF BLESSED MEMORY:
Meyer Korenblit (1923-2012)
Harry "Chaim" Nagelsztajn (1928-2010)
Manya Nagelsztajn Korenblit (1924-2008)
Baby Girl Nagelsztajn-Korenblit
Motl Korenblit
Adam Herling
Wolf Danziger

"Oh, to climb into a corner, well-hidden under the coal, and to stay there quiet and still in the dark, to listen endlessly to the rhythm of the wheels, stronger than hunger or tiredness; until, at a certain moment, the train would stop and I would feel the warm air and the smell of hay and I would get out into the sun; then I would lie down on the ground to kiss the earth, as you read in books, with my face in the grass. And a woman would pass, and she would ask me 'Who are you?' in Italian, and I would tell her my story in Italian, and she would understand, and she would give me food and shelter. And she would not believe the things I tell her, and I would show her the number on my arm, and then she would believe...."

Contents

Preface

At the age of six, most kids are inquisitive little people, and I was no exception. I remember, at that age, noticing the strange blue letters that seemed to be painted on my parents' arms. I asked a lot of questions, and my parents explained that the markings were called tattoos. I recall trying to rub them off, but they were permanent—as permanent, I was to learn, as the memories associated with them.

My mother and father sat me down and explained very gently that they had the tattoos because they had been imprisoned in concentration camps during World War II. I sensed that they were trying not to scare me, because they spoke very softly as they described the catastrophe that had decimated their families. I could tell that the subject was very difficult for them to discuss, and I remember feeling sad and hurt. I didn't understand a lot of what they said, but what I did learn was that this tragedy was the reason my brother, Sam, and I had only one uncle, one aunt, and one cousin.

This lack of extended family haunted me throughout my early years. When I was in elementary school, every Monday morning the teacher would start class by asking, "What did you do this weekend?" I would sit there and listen to my classmates tell how they had visited their grandparents' farm, or gone to Tulsa or Oklahoma City to see their aunts, uncles, and cousins. Sometimes they'd mention that all their relatives had come to our town, Ponca City, for a family reunion. I felt deprived and envious. I'd never known what it was like to have grandparents or to attend a reunion of relatives; in fact, I could just about count the members of my family on one hand.

In the years that followed, I became more aware of the very

ix

special status of my parents and our family. In high school and college, my interest in the Holocaust grew. I learned that from 1941 to 1945 Adolf Hitler and the Nazis had tried to erase the Jews, my people, from the face of Europe. By the end of that period, six million Jews had been systematically murdered. Yet my parents had survived. I developed a dedication to learn all the details about what had happened to them during this time and to preserve their story for my own and future generations. After all, if I didn't, who would?

I married in 1974, and my wife, Joan, felt as strongly as I that we should learn all of my parents' story so that someday we could pass it on to our own children. But, in the following years, Joan took it a step further. Feeling we had the makings of a book, Joan queried publishers, and the onus shifted to me.

I had no idea if I would be able to write a book about my parents. How would they react when I asked them about their experiences—with anger, hatred, bitterness? Could I reopen their wounds? Should I? What would it do to them—and to me? This apprehension on my part was why I asked my close friend Kathie Janger to write the book with me.

Next I did the hardest thing I had ever done: I called my parents and asked them to tell me their story. At first, there was silence on the phone, then two deep sighs. They were sighs of relief. At the age of twenty-nine, I was finally asking them about their experiences during the Holocaust. During all those years, they had thought I was not interested—while I had thought they didn't want to talk about it. Nothing could have been further from the truth.

In March of 1980, I flew to Oklahoma from Washington, D.C., to listen to my parents tell their story from beginning to end. By opening a door they had kept locked for more than thirty-five years, they were about to relive the darkest time of their lives. For the next two years, during numerous visits, I asked them thousands of questions.

The answers came painfully. One of many jarring exchanges took place late on a Saturday afternoon. We had been talking for a number of hours, but I wanted to cover one more area before we took a break. Until then, my father had spoken in a normal tone of voice. When he paused before responding, I looked up from my yellow pad. His eyes were glistening and ringed in red. His voice grew hoarse, dropped to a whisper, then faded altogether. He's tired, I thought. After all, he's been talking for two hours. I wanted to urge him to speak up so that the tape recorder wouldn't miss his words, but something told me to keep quiet.

He blinked rapidly and repeatedly. I didn't want to take my eyes off him, but I was compelled to see my mother's expression as she sat next to him. In that moment, I saw her live and die her past life. She knew what Dad was about to say. The memories were written all over her face. For a second, I wondered if any of us was breathing.

I looked back at my dad. Tears were running down his cheeks. Then his voice boomed in the silent room. "That was the last time," he shouted, "the last time we saw your mama's family alive!" His whole body shook as he put his head in his hands and sobbed. Mom, also weeping, softly stroked his head. I placed my hand on my dad's shoulder and squeezed it.

I felt helpless to console such enormous grief. I felt a profound sadness about the family members and friends who had been described to me in such loving terms and for whom I had come to care so much. And I felt resentment as I pictured them so vividly in my mind, because that was the only place I would ever see them.

Alone, later that night, I replayed the scene again and again. If Dad got this upset about my mother's family, I wondered what would happen when we talked about *his* parents?

Many, many conversations followed, as my parents patiently relived and recounted their past for our use in this book. While parts of the narrative and dialogue in these pages have been imaginatively reconstructed, scenes, characters, and impressions are based on the direct experiences of my mother and father. Descriptions of the few scenes in which my parents were not involved are drawn from their recollections of what others told them. Information from the interviews with my parents was supplemented, in some cases, by conversations with other surviving friends and family members who appear in the book.

learned a lot through the experience of writing this book—not only about my parents, but also about myself. I now understand the origins of my values and the passion I have about intolerance and suffering anywhere in the world. These traits are shared by many children of Holocaust survivors.

I have always admired and been very proud of my parents. To me, they and other survivors are the embodiment of the words "hero" and "courage." They walked out of the darkness of those years—from the camps, from hiding, and from fighting with partisan groups—to start life anew. With barely a glance at the past, they grabbed the present hungrily. They had a clear perspective on what was hard and what was doable, so that beginning again, alone and with nothing, was—to them—possible. As a population group, no matter where they settled after the war, these survivors' achievements and contributions to society have been nothing short of miraculous.

My parents taught me to love, not hate. They taught me about justice, not revenge. And maybe the most important thing my parents taught me was to care about all human beings.

There are two wonderful Jewish sayings I've come to embrace because of my mother and father: "When one human being is suffering, it is as though we are all suffering," and "When you help save one person, it is as though you saved the world." I will teach my children the meaning of these words, as will many children of survivors. If we do not, we will have failed in what my parents' and other survivors' very existence demonstrates: that we each must strive every day to make this world a better place.

I love my parents as much as any son can, and I have often wished that I could do something to compensate them for their years of sacrifice and love. Well, I am a very fortunate person, for I was able to give back to my parents a part of life they thought was gone forever. While doing the research for this book, we took a number of trips to Europe and Israel. During one of those trips an amazing discovery was made.

It was January 25, 1982, and I was sitting in a room at the British Embassy in Washington, D.C., holding the last of a stack of telephone directories of Scotland in my lap. I flipped through the pages as quickly as I could, looking for where the Ms stopped and the Ns started. Spread out over the floor were another twenty directories, some open, others with pieces of paper sticking out, marking places. I had carefully gone through page after page, my finger and eyes moving together slowly down each column. N-a-g-e-l, N-e-g-e-l, N-i-g-e-l, N-o-g-e-l.

I had come to the embassy on the basis of a rumor we'd heard in Israel that my mother's brother had survived the war and could be living in Scotland or perhaps England. I had felt sure somehow that I'd be able to locate my mother's family name of Nagelsztajn in one of these directories. However, so far, I'd found nothing even similar to the correct spelling. Maybe I was hoping for too much; after all, for thirty-nine years my mother had thought every other member of her family was dead.

I fanned through the pages so quickly I was at the Ps. I turned back. My finger started down the page. Not a single N-a-g in the directory. I tossed it down to the floor to join the others that had given me so much hope only an hour ago.

As I bent over to retrieve the books to look through them one more time, I saw Neil Matthews, the embassy official who'd been helping me, coming down the stairs. He was balancing an open directory across the palm of his left hand.

When I saw his face, I couldn't help but shout out, "You found it!" I was only vaguely aware that my outburst had startled the small group of security guards and visitors in the adjacent reception area. I leaped out of my chair and rushed to Neil's side, my eyes widening as I too saw the listing to which he was pointing.

Although Neil cautioned me that the spelling was a little different, I could hardly contain my excitement as I copied the number in my notebook, then the address as well. Neil said I could try to phone from there, but I decided to go back to my office, thinking that the call might not go through at first and I would need to be somewhere I could wait for a call back.

After thanking Neil, I decided to call my wife from the embassy. I remember well that in my nervousness, I first dropped all over the floor the coins taken from my pocket, and then having retrieved a nickel and a dime, dropped them into the slot, misdialed, and dialed again.

"Hello?"

"Joan! I found him! I've got his phone number!"

"I *knew* you would," answered Joan. "Where is he?"

"Newcastle—he lives in Newcastle, England."

"Well, call him!"

"I will, I will, but I want to do it from the office. It's going to be a shock, Joan. Maybe I should wait and get my thoughts together. I feel tingly all over—excited, but scared. Maybe he has a bad heart or something." I was having trouble just putting words together to tell my wife.

"Mike, you have to call him right away!" Joan urged.

"Okay, you're right. I'll go back to the office and call him from there. And I'll call you as soon as I've spoken with him."

I replaced the receiver and bent over to gather the coins from the floor. As I hurried to the door, I called out more thank-yous to the amused guards. My cheeks hurt from the wide grin frozen on my face, as I headed across the snow toward my car.

Driving to my office in Arlington, Virginia, seemed to take half a lifetime as I encountered every possible red light and casual driver en route. Finally inside, I threw off my coat, fumbled for my notebook, and walked down the hall to find Kathie Janger. We had been working on the book, living and reliving the story for a year and a half, and I wanted her with me when I made the call.

When I walked around Kathie's partition, I discovered she was on the phone. I paced back and forth in front of her, clutching the notebook and making "Hang up!" gestures. Finally, as I headed back to my office, she hung up and followed. I showed her the notebook where I had written "Nageisztajn, C." She looked at me and put one hand over her mouth. I closed the door behind her and told her that I was going to call him right now.

"Operator, I would like to place an international credit card call, please."

"For what country?" came the response.

"England, I'm calling Newcastle, England," I said, giving the number.

"I can do that for you," said the operator. "One moment, please."

"It's ringing," I said to Kathie, and crossed my fingers.

"Hello?" A woman's voice. I froze. How could the call have gone through so quickly? Why didn't the operator say something? Was it Newcastle? I had expected an exasperating delay — at least a couple of hours or more. Surely it couldn't happen this fast. But I had to say something; the woman might hang up.

"Uh, hello?" I stammered. "Is this Newcastle?"

"Yes," said the woman.

My carefully constructed plan for how to ease into the conversation fell apart. Better to plunge right in.

"Is this the residence of C. Nagelsztajn?" I asked.

"Yes, it is," said the woman.

"Does the 'C' stand for Chaim?" I asked.

"Yes," she said.

I took a deep breath and looked at Kathie.

"Is Chaim Nagelsztajn from Hrubieszow, Poland?" I asked.

"Yes, he is," said the woman, only now there was a slight uncertainty in her voice. "He is here; let me call him to the phone."

"Hello?" A voice came over the line after a couple of minutes.

"Is this Chaim Nagelsztajn?" I asked.

"Yes, yes, what is it?"

"I think you had better sit down, because what I'm going to say will shock you. My name is Mike Korenblit. My mother is Manya."

"Who? I don't understand."

Oh, God, I thought, it couldn't be a mistake, could it? "Was your father Shlomo?" I asked.

A noticeable pause was followed by "Yes, my father was Shlomo."

"And your mother was Mincha?"

"Mincha? Yes, my mother was Mincha."

"And you had a sister, Manya?"

"Manya? No, I had a brother Ely, another brother Joshua, a sister Gittel, a sister Matl—"

"Matl! Yes, that's her Polish name. In America we call her Manya."

"But no, she's— That's not possible."

"Please, sir, listen to me. Do you remember Meyer Korenblit?"

"Korenblit?"

"Yes, Meyer Korenblit. As a boy he came to your house to see your sister before the war?"

"Meyer—you mean Mayorek?"

"Mayorek! Yes! Mayorek is my father!"

"He's alive?"

"Yes, he's alive. He and Matl are married. They live in Oklahoma."

"Matl? She's alive? My sister is alive?"

"Yes, Chaim. My mother is your sister. You both survived!"

This book is the story of my mother and my father and the unimaginable things that happened to them.

By telling their story, I was finally able to get to know the rest of my family. I found my uncle in England; the others, only but always, in my parents' hearts.

—MICHAEL KORENBLIT
EDMOND, OKLAHOMA
MAY 1995

The Nagelsztajn and Korenblit Families
(ages in 1942)

The Nagelsztajns
Shlomo, 48
Mincha, 44
      (Ely, killed in 1940 at age 21)
      Manya, 17
      Gittel, 16
      Chaim, 14
      Joshua, 12
      Letty, 10
      Pola, 8
      (Aunt Zlaty, killed in 1942 at age 58)

The Korenblits
Avrum, 43
Malka, 43
      Shuyl, 22
      Motl, 19
      Meyer, 17
      Toba, 14
      Minka, 11
      Cyvia, 8

CHAPTER ONE

Decisions and departures

As the Nazi wave of destruction rolled over Europe in 1942, the 8,000 Jews of the town of Hrubieszow, Poland, faced three possible fates. If convinced that the situation they faced was hopeless, they could abandon their homeland for uncertain exile. Some had earlier gone to their ancestral lands of Palestine or to other countries. More had gone to Russia, then part of the Soviet Union, especially because as a consequence of the German-Soviet pact of 1939, Poland had been divided, and Soviet-occupied territory now began at the River Bug, three miles away. Tightening immigration restrictions and reports of hardship in Russia, however, were fast foreclosing this path.

Other Jews of the town, especially those who believed they had merely to outlast the menace, chose a second path: building or seeking out hiding places for themselves and their families to occupy until the danger was past. The third path, however, would be the fate of most. On two occasions—June 1 and 7, 1942—Jews had been gathered in the town square, divided into groups, and deported to concentration camps, never to be heard from again.

OCTOBER 27, 1942

It was half-past five in the morning when Avrum Korenblit quietly wakened his son. "Meyer," he whispered, shaking the groggy seventeen-year-old. "Meyer, wake up."

With eyes only half open, the young man quickly rose from the bed and pulled on his trousers. He followed his father into the kitchen, trying to button his pants and hold on to his boots as he walked.

Avrum turned to his shivering son, now seated on a wooden chair, sliding his cold feet into the boots. The two had been up late the night before. Although needing to discuss the latest developments in Hrubieszow, they had waited to talk until the rest of the family was in bed so as not to alarm them. Now, the older man's face was gaunt, lined with the effects of too little sleep and too many worries. He seemed reluctant to begin.

"How long have you been up?" asked Meyer. "Why didn't you wake me sooner?"

"Shh, you'll wake the others." His father spoke in a low voice. "Now, listen carefully. There are some things you must do. It's important that you find out what's happening in town, but first you must go to Josef's to make sure everything is prepared."

"Yes, Papa, I'll run there as fast as I can."

"No! You must not appear to be in a hurry. They would surely stop you. Walk calmly. If you're stopped, tell them you're going to the bakery for your mother. On your way back from Josef's, go to Salki. He'll tell you everything we should know."

Meyer saw the concern on his father's face and knew that Avrum would prefer to check on the arrangements himself. But sometimes older people went out and never came back. It was up to Meyer this time.

"Don't worry, Papa. I'll be fine."

"I know, Meyer, I know. But remember, come straight back here. Do not stop anywhere else, do you hear me? Don't go anywhere else."

Meyer put on his jacket and ripped off the yellow armband. He went to the door, opened it quietly, and slipped out into the cold Polish dawn. Through the window Avrum watched as his son walked casually down the street, kicking a loose stone here and there to confirm the innocence of his errand to any other possible observers. A half-smile crossed Avrum's face. He'll go to Manya's, Avrum thought; no matter what I say, he'll go to Manya's.

Avrum sat down at the small kitchen table and put his hands to his head. He was weary and anxious to act, but he knew that Meyer would not return for some time. He reached for his prayerbook and fingered the worn pages, forcing himself to follow the lines of Hebrew, to control his thoughts with prayer. But his eyes skimmed the page without reading and landed instead on his tattered yellow armband with its Star of David lying on the table.

They should have left Poland and gone to Russia, Avrum thought. His two oldest sons, Shuyl and Motl, had left for Russia three years ago and were, he hoped, safe. Avrum knew now that he should have taken the rest of his family as well. He looked at the photographs on the wall, sent by relatives who had journeyed to Palestine years ago. Perhaps somehow from Russia he, his wife, and children could have made their way there too.

Like many Jews of Poland, Avrum had settled into the alien routine established by the Germans more than two years before, sustained by his religion and the conviction that this hardship was God's will—indeed, His commandment—to atone for the inadequacies and indiscretions of others. If this was his test, Avrum thought, he would strive to be equal to it. He had chosen to suffer the indignities and injustices inflicted on the Hrubieszow Jews: armbands, curfew, food rationing, loss of property and assets, suspension of religious services, desecration of synagogues. His acceptance stemmed not so much from fear as it did from devotion to his God. This was the one thing the Nazis could never take from him: his commitment to believe in God as a Jew. He was not yielding to terror; he was surrendering himself to God's justice.

Avrum supposed that Meyer had reached Josef Wisniewski's house on the edge of town by now. They had met Josef years ago when he brought wheat from his farm to Avrum's flour mill. Avrum had been awed by the man's strength: Josef would pick up two hundred-pound sacks of flour at once and toss them about with ease. Standing six-feet-two and weighing two hundred pounds, Josef was a powerfully built, good-natured man with smiling dark eyes, a reverence for life, and a zest for living. Although he wouldn't harm the smallest of living things, neither would he run from a fight as the scar on his left cheek attested. In many hours at his favorite tavern, it wasn't unusual for him, his ego swollen with drink, to issue or accept challenges from fellow patrons. What had begun as a flirtation with alcohol soon grew into a serious dependence, so that now, at twenty-eight, Josef was never without a cork-topped pint of vodka in his hip pocket.

But Avrum had seen another side of Josef. The wheat farmer had always taken time to talk with Meyer during his visits to the flour mill, and before long, Meyer cautiously ventured over to Josef's farm to help him with chores: milking cows, pitching hay, threshing wheat. Although Avrum needed Meyer to work at the mill as well, he encouraged the friendship between his son and Josef and, as it developed, found himself surprisingly at ease in business dealings with the farmer. Over the years, Avrum's respect and affection for Josef grew into a bond of trust. But whatever the past, a chilling question gnawed at his soul: Could he trust their *lives* to Josef? Avrum knew that many Poles had turned in Jews for a pound of sugar, the bounty offered by the Germans. Trusting a Pole couldn't help but trouble him.

Avrum brought himself up short. He felt ashamed as he thought of the many Catholic Poles who had helped his family. The Polish foreman at the brick factory, at Meyer's urging, had falsified his manpower requests to the Germans, sometimes doubling the number of people he needed to complete available work. Avrum might have been taken away long ago had it not been for the foreman's cooperation in giving him a job.

Franiek Gorski, the chief of police in Hrubieszow, had hidden Avrum's family in his attic a few months before. John Salki, the commissioner of roads, provided them with information, assistance, and once, even a place to hide. Antonio Tomitzki and Isaac Achler in Mislavitch, a small town eleven miles away, had offered Avrum and his family a place to stay. These men were all Poles, but more than that, they were human beings who were risking their own safety and that of their families by helping Jews.

As the morning dragged on, Avrum reviewed his options. He considered, as he had before, taking his family to Mislavitch, but it was too late for that now. The recent arrival of massive numbers of SS reinforcements, now encamped around Hrubieszow, had eliminated that option. He couldn't go back to Gorski or Salki; enough had been asked of them already. They'd simply have to place their trust in Josef Wisniewski.

When Avrum and Meyer had visited Josef to seek his help, he had agreed, without reluctance, to devise a plan. Avrum even remembered Josef's words: "Not to worry, my friends, I will take care of you," uttered with a big, warm smile on his face. In the weeks that followed, Avrum and Meyer learned little of their benefactor's activities, because spending time with him might have aroused suspicion. When Josef was finally satisfied that the preparations were complete, he revealed his plan. Only the three of them knew of its existence—that is, Avrum thought wryly, unless Josef had blurted it out in a fit of revelry at the tavern or bellowed out a song about it as he lurched home from an evening's drinking. "My mouth has a lock on it," Josef had soberly assured Avrum, but even John Salki, who knew Josef was helping them, had questioned Avrum's reliance on the farmer. "Josef's a good man, but if he goes on a binge--"

That was yesterday. Today the turmoil and rumors intensified. Today the dazed Hrubieszow Jews milled about, reaching out to one another, their instincts confused, their resolve undermined. Today they all felt that something terrible was going to happen. And so today, Avrum's plan for escape would be implemented.

On the other side of town, Shlomo Nagelsztajn stood silently in the sparsely furnished main hall of Hrubieszow's Jewish Center. The room was more crowded than on his two earlier trips that day, and the mood more tense. What had once been the center of a thriving network of Jewish social and religious activities had been transformed by German occupation into the dreary source of mandated work orders and SS dictates. Shlomo had little faith in the ability of the Jewish Council set up in the Center to provide direction or shelter for the town's desperate Jews, managed as it was by men no less trapped than he. But on this day he'd been driven to its doors by a compulsion to confirm or deny the rumors that had engulfed the community since daybreak.

Shlomo wasn't sure what he expected to learn. It had been years since he'd seen Jews clustered together on the streets, but today they were everywhere, nervously sharing bits of information. In the noise and turmoil, people were running about begging for answers—some crying, others walking silently, locked in their own fears. The SS troops were conspicuously absent, and open shops stood empty in mute testimony to the omnipresent danger. All had noted the mounting German reinforcements that had begun to arrive earlier in the week. Now the enemy encircled the town, choking its inhabitants in confusion and indecision.

Behind a cluttered desk, the Council's chief spoke quietly, his voice taut yet uncertain, as he patiently acknowledged the questions of the crowd. Listening to the rote responses, Shlomo realized that this man could offer little more than empty words. The real truth was written on the faces of those around him. Shlomo could see his own growing fear in their eyes, hear his own uneasiness in their voices as they posed the same queries over and over: What does this troop buildup mean? What will happen to us? Why do they hate us so? Where can we hide?

Shlomo left the Jewish Center, stepping out into the sunshine without feeling its warmth. There was nothing more he could learn here. Two men outside the door of the Center looked up expectantly as he passed. When Shlomo smiled grimly and shook his head, the men returned to their whispering.

Shlomo felt a strong need to be alone with his thoughts but knew his family waiting at home would be concerned if he was gone too long. He wondered if his daughter Manya had seen Meyer Korenblit in the last few hours and if Meyer had brought any news. He knew that when all this was over and if they all survived, he'd be giving his daughter's hand in marriage to this sometimes brash but always thoughtful boy.

A soft breeze ruffled his brown hair, and he pulled his light coat about him. To reassure himself, he concentrated his thoughts on the secret hiding place he'd built with his own hands to try to provide safety for the ones he loved.

Shlomo had decided early on that the only way he could hope to protect his family during the unpredictable German raids was to build a hideout. A bricklayer all his life, he determined to construct a concealed room in his own home. In the basement he would build a brick partition to serve as a false wall, with an opening just large enough for an adult to crawl through.

For weeks after making the decision, Shlomo had searched for bricks to fit his needs. They had to be the right size and color, worn and aged to the same degree as the other bricks in the room. A single mismatched piece, he knew, could arouse suspicion and cost his family their lives. The stolen bricks, at first hidden under his masonry tools, were later stuffed inside the waistband of his trousers, then concealed under his coat, for the journey to his basement. He could still feel the rough texture of the bricks chafing at his skin as day after day he smuggled them home.

Shlomo had risen early on the day he'd chosen to build the wall. He knew that he would only have the daylight hours to work, for the glow of a candle in the basement window would have brought a suspicious German sentry to investigate. Because he couldn't risk a half-finished wall being discovered during a raid, the job would have to be accomplished in one day. With clay and straw carefully collected and hidden for weeks, he mixed a sturdy mortar to weave the rows of bricks into a solid fortress behind which his family would hide. When he finished, he carefully positioned an old mattress, potatoes, and other vegetables to hide the opening. At dusk, the exhausted craftsman stepped back to survey his handiwork. It was a masterful job.

Thinking back as he walked along, Shlomo could almost recall the sense of accomplishment he felt when the wall was completed and then a few months later when he and his family used the hideout successfully during a raid. But months of harassment and stress had taken their toll, and although Shlomo still felt that his hiding place was a good one, disquieting pictures formed in his mind. The hideout was in the center of town—a risk in itself. And there was the question of food and water. Their stockpile of vegetables would sustain them for a while, but water would have to be replenished often. How was he to manage that? This proud but simple bricklayer, who usually walked with an air of assurance, was now slouched, hands thrust deep in his coat pockets, the burden of decision on his shoulders. How safe or long-term could any hideout be? Shlomo shivered with the sudden thought that instead of walling the Germans out, he might be walling his family in.

Shlomo crossed the road and turned into a street dotted with familiar sights. He passed the baker and the tailor shop, both previously owned by Jews forced out of business at the start of the war. Scenes from the past raced through his mind, taunting him with both pain and pleasure. He recalled hours spent discussing business and politics with those merchants and many occasions shared with them and their families in the synagogue. Weddings, bar mitzvahs, and holidays had been celebrated with vodka, cake, and wine.

He'd seen some of them today at the Jewish Center, nodding recognition to each other but not coming to talk. A few men had asked him what he was planning to do, where he would hide his family. Shlomo hadn't mentioned the basement hideout, telling them instead that he would take his family to relatives in the nearby towns of Zamosc or Kreliv. Despite his longing to band together with his friends, he couldn't tell even them the truth.

Many cleverly disguised hideouts had been revealed to the Germans, who had many informers and followed up every rumor.

He fought off the nagging sadness that the lies to his friends had caused. He hated the Nazis most for bringing him to the point at which, in order to survive, he had to deceive the very people who shared his life.

His steps brought him to the edge of an empty soccer field in the park. Stopping for a moment, he recalled the spirited contests of happier days when he had been to this field many times to watch his eldest son, Ely, play. In his imagination, he heard the cheers of a long-ago crowd, their voices building to a crescendo: "Ely! Ely!" Shlomo remembered that his son was always careful not to give the spectators too much attention, concentrating instead on the black-checkered ball as he kicked it confidently to the goal. But once home, there were hugs and warm praise for the young man with the talent to become a professional. How proud Shlomo had been of his son—especially considering that the boy had been born without a right hand or forearm. What a fine handsome face; what brightness and spirit. But that was over now: Ely had been killed over a year ago in Russia, where he'd gone to escape the German invasion. Shlomo turned his back on the field in a futile effort to shut out the past.

His thoughts drifted to Aunt Zlaty. Shlomo could see her as clearly as he had on the night she disappeared, her face almost serene in the decision to stay upstairs while the rest of the family retreated to safety in the hideout. It must have been hard for her to say goodbye to them, especially to the children, and yet Zlaty had shown no fear. Shlomo liked to imagine that she'd worn the same expression when the Germans found her that night. He wasn't sure why. Like so many of his friends, the only steps he'd taken to fight back were defensive ones—building the basement hideout, for example—yet his own sense of himself and that of those he loved begged for the image of dignity if their worst fears were realized.

As he approached his block, Shlomo puzzled over what had brought him to this point: Why hadn't he listened to Ely's pleas for them to leave Poland? How many times since Ely's departure had he been forced to compromise? Although he'd exhausted his limited influence in search of freedom for his family, had he really believed that it would ensure their survival? In some ways, Shlomo realized that he had determined his own fate by denying his fears for so long. It was in his nature to abhor violence, but this enemy was relying on his pacifism to destroy him. Still he wouldn't make it easy. He'd put his trust in the only weapon at his disposal: a stubborn will to live. Anxious but undefeated, he reached his home.

Slowly, Shlomo climbed the steps that led above the shop. A small man, he put his shoulders back to present a look of confidence to his family. They would need his strength. Crossing over the threshold, Shlomo touched his fingers to his lips and placed them on the mezuzah nailed to the right side of the doorpost. Despite his agony, Shlomo believed in the words written on the parchment inside the tiny religious symbol: "Hear, O Israel: the Lord our God . . ."

Avrum Korenblit shifted in the hard wooden chair as he read: ". . . the Lord is One."

He felt the sting of restored circulation as he lowered his stiff arms and closed his prayerbook. For the first time in hours, he focused on the room. His three daughters were pressing against their mother, Malka, who hardly seemed to notice the moans of hunger coming from her daughters. Avrum wanted to offer them some hope by telling them about his plans, but he knew he must wait for Meyer to return to be sure that this was the time.

Avrum felt powerless to protect his family. He wanted to shake his fists and roar his anguish. He wanted to—

The sound of footsteps climbing the outside stairs caused the huddled figures to stiffen, their eyes riveted to the door. There was a brief fumbling with the latch, and then the door swung open. Meyer burst into the room, his shirt dark with sweat, his chest heaving. So intent was he on reporting to his father that he didn't see the terror on the faces before him.

"Papa, it's true—it's all true!" he gasped. "I've just talked to Salki, and he confirms it. He says we must either go away or hide, for the Germans are going to take all the remaining Jews away this time. I've been to Manya's house, and they're ready to hide. It's all so terrible. People are wandering around, talking and crying. There aren't any soldiers in town; Salki says they're all at the encampment. No one knows what to do. They kept asking me what we were going to do—"

"You didn't tell them—" interrupted Avrum.

"No, Papa, no. I said only that we might go to Mislavitch," Meyer reassured him.

"Tell them what, Avrum?" asked Malka, trying to comprehend the flurry of words.

Meyer acknowledged his mother's question with a glance, then shifted his gaze to his father. Avrum rose heavily from the table.

"Listen to me carefully," he said slowly to his wife and daughters. "We have a hideout."

Avrum weighed every word as he searched each anxious face, trying to measure their reactions. He kept his voice low and even. "Meyer and I made all the arrangements with Josef Wisniewski long ago, but we wanted to keep it secret. Meyer spoke with Josef again today. He is expecting us."

"Wisniewski!" exploded Malka. "Wisniewski?! You went to a drunk for help? You told a drunk where we would hide and kept it secret from your own family? What can you be thinking? We can't trust him." She shook her head fiercely in frustration.

Avrum was shocked. He'd meant for this announcement to ease his family's fears and give them confidence in the hours ahead. But he'd forgotten his own struggle with the decision to trust Josef. Avrum reached out and caught one of Malka's hands and held it in his, seeking to give her some of his strength. She drew his hand to her cheek in an unspoken apology for her doubts.

Eleven-year-old Minka and fourteen-year-old Toba approached their mother shyly, gripping the folds of her skirt. Meyer saw Cyvia, his youngest sister, look away from the doll that had held her attention until now. At eight, she could hardly be expected to understand what had caused her mother's outburst. But her usually bright round face clouded with fear as she scrambled off the floor to hold on to Malka.

Time was slipping away, and Meyer wanted to urge them all to action. Then his father spoke again.

"I know I always said we would go to Mislavitch, but it's too late for that now. If we were going to Mislavitch, we should have gone six months ago. Or to Russia—we could have gone to Russia."

Almost as if Avrum realized that his rambling confession was alarming his family, he turned imploring eyes to his son.

Meyer's words came without hesitation. "There's no time to look back. There's no time for more talk. We have to go."

"We're going to a hiding place where we'll be safe." Avrum spoke with renewed authority. "No one will find us in this hideout, I promise you. Then maybe in a few days we will go to Mislavitch." He looked intently at his wife. "Malka, have the girls put on extra socks and underwear; we mustn't carry too much, it would look suspicious. We'll take a little food. No need to carry water; we can get that from Josef."

Malka stood transfixed.

Avrum sharpened his tone. "Malka! Quick! We're leaving now!"

Meyer saw his mother's trancelike gaze snap into focus. She released her hold on her daughters and spun around. For a moment, her eyes darted about, her hands reaching out uncertainly. Then, she swooped up two straw baskets and began packing what little food they had. She instructed Toba, Minka, and Cyvia to fetch some extra clothes and denied their requests to take dolls and playthings. She looked at their drawn faces and fought down the impulse to relent.

"No, my little ones, we'll take only what we need," she said gently but firmly, "and we don't need dolls. Get your clothes as Papa asked. Toba, help your sisters; be sure to put on jackets, too." Toba ushered the two upstairs, and soon Malka herself was running up to the bedrooms, calling to Meyer over her shoulder to change his shirt.

Meyer stood back as the preparations for departure swirled around him. The time had come. He'd rehearsed it in his mind so often, and now he stood watching, almost as if it were happening to someone else. He knew what was causing his sense of distance: he was thinking about Manya. Meyer was sure he couldn't go to Josef's without her, but how was he to tell his father? Avrum picked up his prayerbook and tucked it safely in his pocket.

Meyer knew he couldn't delay any longer. "Papa," he started, "I have to see Manya."

Avrum turned to him. "Manya! Why? You've seen her already today. Besides, they're probably closed up in their hideout by now. You could cause them trouble by going over there again. Someone may follow you."

"Papa, I can't leave without letting her know that we have a place to hide, that we'll be safe. I don't even know if I can leave her. Maybe I'll hide at her house."

"No, that's no good," said Avrum. "Their place is in town; you won't be safe there. You'll come with us. You can check on her later. She'll understand, Meyer."

"I'm going to Manya, Papa," Meyer repeated. "I have to see her; I want her to be with me. There's room in our hideout. I'll go get her and bring her to Josef's."

"We have enough to worry about with our own family," Avrum retorted, annoyed. "There might not be enough room at Josef's for anyone extra. Please, Meyer, be sensible. Help me get the flashlights."

It was difficult for Meyer to argue with his father, but he persisted. "I'm going to Manya's. I can make it—I've sneaked over there after curfew hundreds of times. I'll be all right. I'll come back to the house, and if you're gone, I'll meet you at Josef's barn."

"Even if you'd gone a thousand times, it wouldn't matter," begged Avrum. "It's too dangerous to go to town now. And your clothes. . . ."

"Tell Mama to bring something for me" came the reply. Meyer turned to the door and saw his mother standing on the stairs, one arm laden with a tangle of clothing, the other slipped inside one sleeve of a coat. Their eyes met and he could read the message, but before she could add her objections to his father's, Meyer started for the door. He knew she deserved an explanation, but he couldn't spare any more time.

"I'll be back, Mama. Don't worry." That was all he could say as he closed the door behind him. He hoped she would understand.

Malka and Avrum stared at the emptiness where their son had been. "They'll catch him this time, I just know it," Malka said. "He's the only son we have left, and they'll catch him."

"He said he'd be back, Malka, and he will," Avrum reassured his wife even while urging her to finish packing.

Outside in the early evening air, Meyer stood holding the latch. Although the darkness held dangers, over the preceding months he'd become accustomed to it. The night with all its challenges allowed him to be strong. He turned and surveyed his route. Everything seemed to be quiet. He went down the steps by twos, landing hard in the dirt at the bottom, adding yet another layer of dust to his damp skin. After all the times he'd traveled this route, he'd have to be more careful this time than ever before. He must not allow familiarity to trip him up. He couldn't tell whether he felt fear or elation—perhaps a mixture of both—but he had to remain calm, to reach his destination quickly, to make no movement that would betray his family or himself.

He knew his father was right: he was taking a big chance. But logic and reason were impotent adversaries against the urgings of his heart. He smiled to himself when he thought of the rather offhand way he had treated Manya only a few years before. His young manhood had been boosted by Manya's instant warmth at his briefest look or word. He'd even been pleased by the hint of jealousy she showed when he was attentive to other girls. Over the last months, he'd found himself wanting to be with her all the time. And so, night after night, he risked the unthinkable to steal away to her house after curfew. He was proud that he'd never been caught. The sense of daring satisfied his starved ego, as each successful journey represented a small rebellion against the Germans.

He had known that he would never leave without Manya. He had ached to tell her about their hideout, to smooth away the worried lines on her face with this comforting antidote. He'd come close to blurting it out several times, but his father had sworn that he would tell no one and Meyer could do no less.

In place of sharing their plans with Manya, he had reassured her again and again that he would take care of her. In addition, he had tried to sharpen his senses, observing and storing away everything he saw, knowing that the time would come when he'd need it. Meyer picked up his pace and hurried to Manya.

Avrum descended the stairs from the second floor. The beds were stripped, contents of drawers scattered about. He paused halfway down to use the slight elevation as a vantage point. He was quite calm now, confident of his ability to get his family away. He scanned the lower floor with an objective eye. They'd done a good job here, too: no pictures on the walls, a rolled-up carpet that looked as if it had been abandoned in a hasty departure. In a few minutes they'd be gone. As the group reassembled in the kitchen, it was very quiet. Malka checked over each of the little girls carefully, then looked down at her own body—almost as if she could step out of herself. She was ready. Avrum sensed the bubble of fear that expanded with each second's inactivity.

"We go," he announced. He opened the door and motioned them out. As they crossed the porch, he looked over the room. He was glad there had been no cooking that day; there would be no stale odors or warm stove. He was satisfied that the house would appear to have been deserted for some time. His eyes moved to the kitchen table. His armband! No, he thought, he didn't need that anymore. He stepped quickly outside and closed the door.

The family made their way as casually as possible across the fields in the direction of Josef Wisniewski's farm. The determined rhythm of movement accentuated the grim silence. They didn't look back, but proceeded intently toward their destination. Avrum led the way, constantly glancing over his shoulder to make sure everyone was staying close to him, and taking special care to urge his young daughters to move along quietly.

Josef was in his barn, tending his horses and waiting. His talk with Meyer only hours before had set their plan in motion. Josef wasn't concerned about his personal safety, but he didn't want to endanger his mother and sister. For this reason, he and Avrum had agreed that, if the Korenblits were discovered in the hideout, Josef would deny any knowledge of their presence.

Josef hadn't told his mother about the hideout. He knew she'd be upset, not because he was aiding Jews but because she would fear the possible consequences for her own family. Everyone knew what happened to Poles who helped Jews; the Germans had made it very clear. But Josef feared his mother's wrath almost as much as he hated the Germans, and he'd have to be resourceful in unveiling the secret. After all, he had planned for her to prepare food for the hidden family.

Keeping his eyes on the path to the barn, Josef continued to watch for the Korenblits. He hadn't intended to be here when they arrived. The plan was for them to enter the barn and climb into the loft on their own. But it was taking longer than usual for his mother and sister to milk the cows. Tonight of all nights, the cows were uncooperative. Even though the stalls were on the other side of the barn, he had to wait and warn the Korenblits to be careful.

For what seemed like the fiftieth time, Josef looked through the barn door into the fields. There they were at last: two, four, five. Five! There should be six! Meyer wasn't with them. Josef leaned outside and motioned the family in, holding his finger to his lips and gesturing toward the cows. He pointed to the ladder leaning against the loft.

As Avrum came close, Josef whispered, "Where's Meyer?"

"He'll be coming soon," Avrum replied.

Malka climbed up first, then reached down to assist Toba, Minka, and Cyvia. Finally Avrum scaled the ladder and pulled it into the loft behind him. They settled in with as little movement as possible.

After a moment Malka leaned over to Avrum. "So this is the wonderful hiding place where no one will find us?" she hissed. "In a barn right by the fort, with hundreds of German soldiers. There couldn't be a more obvious place for Jews to hide!"

"Hush, Malka," Avrum whispered. "Rest a bit. This is temporary. We must wait until it's late. Then you'll see how safe we'll be." He turned away from her to show the finality of his words.

Soon he could hear the sounds of deep breathing around him, but he couldn't sleep. To him this was the most perilous stage of the plan. Malka was right: they were vulnerable in a barn, subject to routine searches by the Nazis, for barns were common hiding places for Jews. But if this was a weak link in their escape, it was necessary to safeguard the location of their final destination. No, Avrum couldn't rest. First he'd listen for Meyer's arrival; then he'd listen for the Germans.

It was a little more than a mile from his house to Manya's, and Meyer made better time than he'd expected. He was close now, only a few more blocks, straight ahead, turn left, through the alley, cross the street, past the baker, turn right, past the shoemaker, the tailor, the dressmaker, through the narrow doorway, and up the steps.

The building was quiet, with no sign of activity, as he proceeded down the hallway to the sliding doors of the small bedroom adjacent to the kitchen. He threw the doors open and peered in.

Manya's family, frozen with alarm, stared back at him.

"Meyer!" Manya exclaimed in a tone of disbelief. She thought he would be hiding with his family and had resigned herself to not seeing him for some time.

"Meyer, what is it?" asked Shlomo. "Do you want to hide with us? Has something happened to your family?"

Meyer shook his head, gasping for air. "I've come because I want Manya and me to be together. My family is going away to hide, but I had to see Manya."

"We were just going down to the basement hideout," Shlomo told him. "Come with us; we'll be safe."

Delaying for breath and time, Meyer leaned against the wall. He was strangely comforted by Shlomo's confident tone. It was true that the basement hideout had been tested. Perhaps he would be better off staying here. Meyer wiped the sweat from his face with the back of his arm, grateful to shield his eyes from the stares for even a second, and wished that his resolve was as firm as it had been when he left his father's house. But he remembered his final promise to his mother. He'd have to go to Josef's. Meyer couldn't bear to have his parents think that he'd been caught. He shifted his weight back onto legs still shaky from running. Meeting Shlomo's look, he groped for the strength to make himself understood.

"No, I don't want to be in town; too many people have been caught here. I want Manya to come with me—you can all come with me—we have a good hiding place."

Manya looked away from Meyer and sought her father's strong face. The expression alone was enough to tell her that he wouldn't accept Meyer's offer. She saw Shlomo's lips part, and then heard his reply: "No, we can't leave; we'll be safe here."

She squeezed her eyes shut and shook her head as if to throw off the burden of Meyer's offer and her father's answer. Manya could feel them all looking at her.

She would have to choose between staying with her family and going with Meyer. She hadn't expected to have to make a decision like this, and now she just wanted to run and shut herself away. Everything was happening too quickly. A few minutes earlier she'd been wishing for Meyer to be here with her. Now Meyer was standing only a few feet away, but the distance to him could be bridged only by choosing one love over another.

"Will you come with me, Manya?" Meyer's voice was pleading. Only then did she look up. His eyes beseeched her for a response as his hand reached out to her urgently, his look loving and vulnerable, his attitude impatient. He loved her so, and yet couldn't indulge this delay, this reluctance. What was the matter with Manya? he thought. There was no time for debating, no time for more tears—no time.

Helplessly Shlomo watched his daughter's struggle. There was a time when seventeen-year-old Manya would have looked to him for permission. But that time had passed. He wanted to ask Meyer where they would hide, to demand some assurance that his daughter would be safe, but he knew it was useless. If she went with Meyer, she might be safe or she might be caught; if she stayed with them, the same was true. In these days, when one came to expect nothing and everything, even the smallest chance was worth the risk. The pain was in the choosing.

"It's all right, Manya," Shlomo finally said, seeming to give his approval to her departure.

Manya turned to face her mother.

"Manya, if you're coming, we must leave immediately!" Meyer demanded.

"You go ahead, Manya," Mincha whispered, holding her arms out to her eldest daughter. "I know Meyer will take good care of you. If you go, maybe one of us will survive."

The words rang in Mincha's head, and the dark memory of her son's departure years before came on her in a rush. She had given her blessing to her son to leave; she could do no less for her daughter. But Ely was dead . . . . No! She wouldn't think those thoughts. Letting Manya go was the right decision. She knew it.

Manya tried to form words with her lips but failed. Mother and daughter clutched each other, crying. Manya finally pulled herself away and knelt to embrace her brothers and sisters, then stood before her father.

"We'll be safe, Manya, don't worry about us. This will be over soon. We'll see each other again, I'm sure of it," he said, clinging to her. Manya nodded hopefully.

She quickly assembled a few belongings to take with her, then turned to Meyer. The tears running from his eyes made small rivulets in the dust on his face. He understood. The hand he held out to her was gentle now, promising comfort.

"Come," he said quietly.

Manya moved toward him and grasped his hand tightly, then reached up and tenderly touched his cheek.

Manya looked at each member of her family again. Her eyes met her younger brother Chaim's and held. Then she turned her back and started with Meyer from the room.

"I want to come too," said Chaim. Manya spun around and looked at her brother, then at Meyer.

"You're welcome to come—you're all welcome to come," said Meyer.

Mincha couldn't believe her ears. She wanted to scream out: No, Chaim! Her world revolved around her family, and it was splintering away before her eyes. Though she accepted Manya's departure and believed she'd be safe with Meyer, Mincha was not prepared for separation from yet another of her children. Her knees buckled.

Shlomo moved to brace his wife. "It will be good for Manya to have him with her," he whispered.

Manya stared dumbstruck as Chaim said his goodbyes. Somehow this quiet fourteen-year-old had made his own decision.

Then her father spoke. "Go with God, Chaim, but know we will feel your absence." Pair by pair, the hands released Chaim and formed a new chain among those who would stay.

As Chaim turned to go, he felt a touch on his shoulder. With growing force, his mother pulled him to her once more, her arms encircling his body. Manya saw her brother wince and was surprised at the strength within her mother. Mincha finally loosened her grip, taking Chaim's face in her trembling hands.

"Be strong, Chaim, and care for your sister. I love you." Then she kissed his forehead and let her fingers trace the outline of his face.

Without a word, Meyer guided Manya and Chaim out the door.

CHAPTER TWO

The hiding place

"I see the eight of us with our 'Secret Annexe' as if we were a little piece of blue heaven, surrounded by heavy black rain clouds. The round, clearly defined spot where we stand is still safe, but the clouds gather more closely about us and the circle which separates us from the approaching danger closes more and more tightly. Now we are so surrounded by danger and darkness That we bump against each other, as we search desperately for a means of escape. We all look down below, where people are fighting each other, we look above, where it is quiet and beautiful, and meanwhile we are cut off by the great dark mass, which will not let us go upwards, but which stands before us as an impenetrable wall; it tries to crush us, but cannot do so yet. I can only cry and implore: 'Oh, if only the black circle could recede and open the way for us!'"

From THE DIARY OF A YOUNG GIRL THE DEFINITIVE EDITION by Anne Frank, edited by Otto H. Frank and Mirjam Pressler, translated by Susan Massotty, translation copyright © 1995 by Doubleday, a division of Random House, Inc. Used by permission of Doubleday, a division of Random House, Inc.

Night had fallen during the time Meyer had been in the Nagelsztajn house. He was glad that darkness would help cover the trek he, Manya, and Chaim must make to the barn to join his family. Meyer knew it was unlikely that the Germans would launch the final evacuation of Hrubieszow's Jews at night, for night raids generally were used only as terror tactics to keep the Jews off balance. The first two deportations had taken place in the daytime, and tomorrow, October 28, it was said that the last third of the town's Jews would be taken away.

Meyer had spent all day gathering information. Like everyone else, he knew that the regular SS sentries were no longer posted in town: they'd been pulled back to the encampments around the city. His visit that morning with their family friend, Commissioner of Roads John Salki, had confirmed that fact and more. Salki had outlined the German plan in detail, giving Meyer the location of the encampments as well as the specific circuit of the patrols and recommending a safe route for the Korenblits to take out of the city.

After leaving Salki, Meyer had tracked down another friend, Franiek Gorski, the chief of police. "What more can you tell me about the Germans' locations? What about the fort?" Meyer had asked.

"Stay away from the fort. There aren't many soldiers, but the SS could make reassignments," Gorski had said. "Polish informers are dispersed throughout the city. Their orders are to report any Jews attempting escape. These places must be avoided as you leave town," he had added, giving Meyer the locations of the Polish lookouts. Only the police chief, who had chosen and positioned them, had this vital information.

Now, leading Manya and Chaim quickly through the dark

streets, Meyer shook his head in an effort to stay alert. They were nearing the tavern where German enlisted men sneaked drinks, and he mustn't let down his guard. He had to concentrate on getting them through the maze of streets undetected.

As they crept along, Manya looked back over her shoulder. She couldn't remember the last time she'd been outside under the stars because, for nearly three years, her home had become a prison at the six o'clock curfew each evening. She strained to see her house as long as she could, then took a deep breath and reached for Chaim's hand. They moved along, blindly following Meyer's signals and whispered instructions.

Suddenly she realized that she had no idea where they were going. "Where is this hiding place?" she asked Meyer.

"Trust me, Manya. I can't explain now."

No, of course he couldn't, Manya thought, watching Meyer's head turn left, right, then to the rear, his practiced eyes checking again and again that their route was clear—pausing to listen before striking out once more in the darkness, then freezing in mid-stride. Hush! What was that? Whirling around as a leaf crunched underfoot; flattening themselves against a wall, then darting for the next alley. On and on they crept, passing the edge of town, then crashing through marsh grass, where a frenzy of chirping crickets suddenly became silent as the trio passed, seeming to announce their escape. As they entered open fields, Manya heard Meyer curse the moonlight that flooded the pastures and threatened to expose them.

But wait! That was Meyer's house just ahead. She felt Chaim break stride as he too recognized their location, but she tightened her grip on his hand and firmly pulled him along.

As they reached the Korenblit house, Meyer motioned Manya and Chaim to stay in the bushes nearby while he crawled up the stairs. He lay across the top steps and part of the porch, getting as close to the door as possible, then cupped his hands and called very softly, "Papa?" He listened a moment, then eased himself down backward.

"They've gone," he whispered. "Come, follow me."

He paused, surveying the landscape for a moment, then

steered his companions toward the fields. They had almost three miles to go. He had traveled this route alone many times, but in the dark it looked different and this time there were three figures scurrying through the night. In addition to the fact that the fields offered no shelter, they would have to pass close to the German-occupied fort. Even though Meyer knew there were only a few soldiers left in the building, Gorski's warning rang in his ears.

With the fort straight ahead of them, Meyer pulled Manya and Chaim into a crouch and signaled them to wait. He crawled a few yards to the left, then past them again and to the right, trying to see around both sides of the structure. He spotted only two guards, and they seemed to be taking their duty lightly, standing relaxed facing the building. There was a brief flare as one of them lit a cigarette. Meyer scooted quickly back to Manya and Chaim.

"Keep low," he whispered, pulling them up and on their way again.

The guards didn't turn around as the three figures crept past. As they approached Josef's barn, Meyer drew Manya and Chaim close. "Be very quiet now," he whispered, "we're going into Josef's barn and up into the loft. My family is there already."

"Is that the hiding place?" asked Manya.

"We'll stay in the loft for a few hours," came the reply, "and then we'll go to the hiding place."

"But where is it?" she persisted.

"It's very close by. You can almost see it from here," Meyer assured them. "Come, we must get inside!"

Manya peered into the night, but all she saw was emptiness. She didn't understand why Meyer wouldn't share the secret of the hideout with her, but she knew they must not delay any longer in the open. They entered the barn, and once again Meyer called to his father. As if by magic, a ladder appeared from the loft and slipped silently to the floor.

"Up you go," said Meyer to Manya and Chaim, giving them a boost.

At the top, Manya collapsed in the hay. Too weak to crawl, she rolled aside to make room for Meyer and Chaim. Her head pounded and her eyes burned. Without the moonlight, she had difficulty seeing, but soon she could make out other forms lying in the hay. Meyer pulled the ladder up and fell alongside her; Chaim was on her other side.

As they lay so close to each other, their heartbeats seemed to settle into a common cadence. Then the rhythmic beats slowed.

The darkness, the cradling hay, warm bodies, and exhaustion spun a cocoon and lulled her into the escape of sleep. She dreamed:

She was working at the brick factory, the heat of the ovens making her sweat. The bricks she carried were heavy, but she was strong. Her father's bruised and bleeding face appeared; the Nazis had beaten him up at work. Scores of people were being pushed through the streets, all so tired, so frightened, so thirsty. She tried to give them some water. The Gestapo shoved her away and she fell down, scraping her hand on the bricks. Then there were no more soldiers. She was a little girl at school, and the teacher was scolding her, telling her to hold out her hand. She didn't want to be hit with the ruler. She wanted to go home.

Then it was market day in Hrubieszow. Nine-year-old Manya was thrilled to be going to market with her mother. The noisy, smelly streets were choked with people, loaded wagons, and animals. The stalls brimmed with succulent fruits and shiny vegetables, vats of pickles, frothy milk, pungent cheeses. Plucked chickens, ducks, and geese were hanging like clothes on a line. There were mountains of crusty loaves of bread and delicate sweet pastries, crockery, scrub brushes, soap, harnesses, and horse blinders.

Mincha ignored the hawking of the vendors, and Manya knew better than to touch anything. Nothing would be purchased on impulse. Mincha knew exactly what she wanted: they would buy half a chicken, three or four eggs—broken ones would save a few pennies—a few ounces of tea and sugar, a half-jar of milk, flour, oil, and maybe fruit.

Later, at home, Mincha would stretch the food to feed her family of nine, while Manya minded the new baby. One part milk would be diluted with three parts water. The clusters of fat and bits of fatty skin would be removed from the chicken, cut into small pieces, and heated slowly. When they melted, she would add sliced onions, cooking them until they were brown. Then she strained the liquid from the solids. The whole house was full of the aroma, tantalizing the family and bringing Manya to the kitchen to snitch a morsel, pop it into her mouth, and suck on it. "Make it last," she told herself, "savor the taste."

The precious cracklings and liquid fat were reserved to lend flavor to baked noodles, thick kasha melanges, soups, and vegetables. Mincha made bread: rye for every day, white for the Sabbath. The chicken itself was reserved for the Sabbath meal. Manya's father often said, "Even a poor family is rich on the Sabbath." One or two of the precious eggs were mixed with rye flour to make dark, rich noodles—a family favorite, eaten in a bowl with a splash of milk.

As Manya and her mother proceeded through the narrow streets, each purchase was carefully placed in their straw shopping basket. Mincha had bargained well; there was enough money left to stop at the fruit stand. Mincha guided her daughter firmly past the Polish merchant with his strings of spicy sausages, slabs of bacon, and rosy hams, for somehow even pausing to take in the aroma of these forbidden foods was an indiscretion.

Manya obediently skipped along, hardly noticing that her toes threatened to burst through her tight shoes. As her eyes stole a curious glance at the pork vendor, she felt her mother's touch on her arm. But she wanted to watch the merchant cut the thick slices of ham and chunks of bacon for his Polish customers. She wasn't ready to leave yet. Just a little while longer—there was so much to see, and her mother said they might stop at the shoemaker's to arrange for a new pair of shoes. But the pulling on her arm was more insistent now, and she couldn't ignore it.

Manya opened her eyes. Where was she? Meyer's face was next to hers. He had awakened her as he gently released their entwined arms.

She finally responded. "What is it?"

Meyer lifted his finger to his mouth. "Shh! It's almost time to go. I'll be right back."

Her eyes followed him as he slowly stood and moved away. She watched him pick his way around the others, trying not to waken them. He stopped next to a dark figure standing at the edge of the loft. As her eyes adjusted to the darkness, she recognized Avrum's silhouette.

Rustling sounds from below diverted her attention. Who could that be, she wondered, as her eyes darted back to Avrum and Meyer, now quietly making their way down the ladder. She rolled over onto her stomach and crawled to the edge of the loft, being careful not to push hay over the side.

She watched intently as Avrum and Meyer joined a man who towered over them.

"Josef," she heard amid muffled words.

So that's Josef. Manya nodded to herself, remembering stories Meyer had shared with her about his Polish friend.

The whispering stopped. Josef turned and walked out the door. Meyer and Avrum moved toward the ladder, then climbed up. Manya's mind raced. Do we have to leave? Meyer did say that this isn't the hiding place. She had to see what was happening. She got up and inched her way to the ladder. Her eyes met Meyer's as he stepped from the last wooden rung. "What's going on?" she asked him quietly.

"Josef says it's time for us to leave for the hideout. We must waken everyone."

Avrum gently nudged Malka. "We must go now," he whispered to his wife.

Meyer quickly turned when he heard Cyvia whine, "I don't want to get up. I'm sleepy!"

"I know, my little darling, but we must go now. You'll have time to sleep later."

"Chaim, Chaim, it's time to get up," Manya said, shaking her brother gently. Chaim jumped to his feet. All eyes turned toward Avrum.

"Josef has been keeping watch for the past two hours. He says there has been no activity nearby; everything is quiet. He's sure it's safe for us to go to the hiding place. We'll be walking across a large open field, so we must go very quickly and stay close together. Nobody, *nobody*, should utter a sound. Malka, follow me down with the girls."

Manya carefully edged down the ladder, then joined Malka and her daughters in a corner of the barn. As they waited, Manya saw Malka's lips moving silently. She knew Malka was asking God to see them safely to their hideout.

Meyer used his hands to sweep bits of straw away from the edge of the loft and did his best to fluff up the flattened areas where they had slept. Then, he slid to the barn floor.

Avrum inhaled deeply, then sighed. Only one mile between us and safety, he thought, just one mile. In God's name, let us make it. In a hushed voice he spoke. "Josef is outside. We should hear his signal any moment." Again he emphasized, "Quiet now! Nobody should speak." Even the cows and horses followed Avrum's command and were silent.

They waited tensely for the signal from Josef, and then picked up faint noises: a tiny squeak, then a pop, then the squeak again. Meyer knew immediately what it was. He smiled to himself, and Manya looked at him. He pressed his mouth to her ear and whispered, "It's the cork in Josef's vodka bottle."

Avrum looked toward him sternly, then returned his attention to the barn door. There came a muffled "Avrum! Avrum!"

Avrum leaned down to grab Cyvia's hand, then motioned for the others to follow him outside. Keeping pace with Josef's long strides, Avrum turned his head only long enough to be sure that the others were following. Cyvia struggled to keep up with him, her short legs taking three steps to each of his.

They had walked some two hundred yards when Josef stopped. Confident that Avrum had his bearings, Josef moved aside and wordlessly held out his hand. The older man gripped the outstretched hand with both of his, then looked squarely into Josef's face. The farmer swung his free arm around his friend's shoulders in a powerful, bracing hug.

Cyvia, clinging to Avrum's coat, moved closer to the two men. She reached up her tiny hand and gave Josef a shy pat. He smiled down at her in the silence of the night and gently dropped a big hand to stroke her hair.

Avrum took a deep breath, nodded, and turned to lead his family into the darkness.

By twos, the procession filed past Josef. When Meyer stopped in front of him, the Pole reached into his back pocket, extracted the half-pint bottle, and held it toward Meyer in a salute. The characteristic gesture made Meyer grin and warmed him as if he had taken a shot of the liquor himself. Josef popped the cork, leaned back, and drew a long swig. As he did, the moonlight flashed on the crucifix hanging from his neck.

"Dziekuje, Josef," Meyer smiled.

"We will drink together again in happier times, my friend."

Meyer turned away, pulling Manya along in a half-run to catch up with the others. He could sense her silent suffering and knew that there was similar anguish in the Nagelsztajns' basement. He could only hope and pray that her family's hideout would again outwit the Germans.

Meyer looked up. The moon beamed its soft yellow light, and thousands of stars sparkled in the black velvet sky. How could the beauty of this night be party to such evil, he wondered. He tightened his grip on Manya's hand.

She was thinking deeply too as they moved along. Should I have come with Meyer? Oh, I wish Papa had come! I should have stayed at home. I am the oldest. I could be helping with the little ones. God, please watch over my family and keep them safe.

Keeping pace with Meyer's quick steps, Manya searched for a clue to their destination. Meyer had said it was only a short distance from the barn, but where? The flat landscape stretched on and on, with not even a tree to break the monotony. Just as she thought she could go no further, Meyer pointed straight ahead.

"There's the hiding place," he whispered, giving her a congratulatory squeeze.

Manya blinked her eyes, trying to focus on the looming, shadowy object. What was it? It couldn't be another barn—that would be too obvious a place.

She squinted. "Where?" she asked.

"Right in front of us," he said, pointing once more.

The dark shape got bigger and bigger until she could see nothing else. Suddenly she knew what it was although she'd never seen one this large before. It was taller than her house. They stopped in front of it. She put her arm around Chaim and looked at Meyer.

"This is where we are going to hide? Behind this . . . this mountain of hay?"

"Not behind it," came the exultant reply, "*in* it!"

"What do you mean, *in* it?" asked Manya. "A haystack is a haystack. There's no 'in'; there's just hay. What are you talking about?" She tried to set her face disapprovingly, to show Meyer that if he was joking, she didn't find it very amusing.

Meyer moved to face her. "Manya, listen. Josef has dug out the inside. The Germans will never think to look for Jews in a haystack! Look at my father. He's trying to find the small wire that marks the entrance."

As they stood in the damp predawn cold, Avrum whispered to Malka to take everyone quietly to the nearby cornfield, for that would be their latrine. There were more whispers and some reluctant looks, but soon they stumbled off in pairs into the furrowed area with its dry stalks of camouflage.

Manya watched Avrum as he crawled around the base of the haystack. She saw him draw his hands slowly along the circumference, pausing here and there to run his fingertips back over a section. His searching fingers beat out a faint rhythm — pat, pat, pat, brush, pat, pat, pat. She could see Avrum's frustration at trying to find the spot in the dark. But even though they had flashlights, he wouldn't dare use them.

Then she heard a break in the pattern. Avrum stiffened, and with great effort tugged at the base of the haystack: once, and again, and then very slowly a chunk of hay slid away from the pile. Manya caught her breath, expecting the mountain to topple, burying them in its avalanche. But it held.

The group came back from the cornfield. Meyer went to Manya and propelled her toward the entrance, but Avrum put out his hand.

"You go in first, Meyer. Make sure it's safe and hasn't caved in. Be careful, but go quickly. We've been out in the open too long."

All eyes were focused on Meyer as he dropped to the ground and crawled into the entrance. In an instant he was out of sight, swallowed up by the haystack.

As Meyer pulled himself along the ground, he reached out to feel the sides of the narrow passage, testing to make sure the walls of hay would hold. Then he felt nothing. He scooted in a little farther and turned 360 degrees on his hands and knees to make sure the area was cleared out. Slowly he stood up, finally reaching full height. His head didn't touch the top, so he raised his arms, and his fingers met the sturdy ceiling of hay. He wanted to yell out: hurrah, Josef, you did it! Instead, he quickly scurried back through the passage to tell the others.

Nobody had moved. All eyes were still fixed on the opening as Meyer came popping out, grinning from ear to ear. Avrum helped Meyer up.

"Papa, Josef did it! There's plenty of room for all of us. We can even stand up."

Avrum sighed deeply in relief. "Good, let's go in."

One by one, they lay on the ground and crawled through the tunnel of hay, clawing the ground for traction, so afraid were they of pulling the straw down on top of them. Avrum slid in last, backward, stopping to sprinkle bits of hay and smooth the ground to cover their tracks. In the narrow passageway, he strained to reposition the bale that sealed them in. Again and again he adjusted it, pulled on it, making certain that it fit so well as to be unnoticed from the outside. Satisfied at last, he rolled over on his back and lay still, breathing hard.

"It smells in here," came Cyvia's tired voice in the darkness.

"Shh, now, darling, you'll get used to it. See how cozy we are?" Malka soothed her. "We're all going to sleep. Come, let's snuggle and think about a nice dream to have."

"I want my doll," Cyvia whimpered. "Why couldn't I have my doll?"

"Tch, sleep, darling Cyvia. Sleep, now. You'll feel better when you wake up."

Recovered, Avrum felt his way along the straw-covered floor, bumping into one set of legs and then another. Gingerly he eased himself against the wall. He desperately wanted to flick on a flashlight but resisted the temptation, not knowing if the light would be visible from the outside. They'd have to experiment with that tomorrow night.

Manya pressed herself as close to Meyer as she could. She was trembling with cold and the effort to keep from screaming in this cramped, pitch-black, smelly enclosure. Yet, in another way, the darkness was rather nice, she thought. Here she was, in Meyer's arms, with his parents no more than a few inches from her feet. Think of it! It was quite daring! She nuzzled closer and placed her hand on Meyer's cheek. She felt him smile and stifled a giggle of delight. She leaned her head against his and felt his lips on her hair and on her cheek, settling hard on her mouth. She shivered with delight and pressed the length of her body against his.

Meyer awoke with a start. How long had he slept? It was so dark in the haystack there was no way of knowing the time. Nor did it matter: he had no place to go. Trying to get comfortable, he reached into the wall of hay behind his head to pull some loose to fashion a pillow. "That's better," he sighed as his arm gathered Manya closer.

Then he heard something. His eyes shot open and he sat up abruptly, Manya stirring but not awakening. He closed his eyes and tried to concentrate on the muffled noises from the outside, wishing everyone would stop breathing for a moment so that he could sort out the sounds he wanted to hear. He pictured the fields as he'd seen them the day before: corn furrows, wheat fields, sugarcane, Josef's house, the barn, more open fields, the fort . . . THE FORT! Soldiers, guns, horses, and trucks. Suddenly he knew what it was. He lay back against the hay, his skin prickling.

"It has begun," Avrum said quietly.

"It sounds like it, Papa," he answered, trying to match his voice to the same even tone as his father's.

"Today will be very difficult, Meyer. The little ones especially will be frightened and bored. We must fill the time with talk; it will help us pass the hours. We must try not to think about what is going on in town. Remember that, for Manya, every sound will mean possible tragedy for her family. We must help her to think of other things."

"I know, Papa, I know," Meyer replied. "It must be daylight by now. Do you think we can turn on a flashlight?"

"Soon, but not yet. Let's allow the others to sleep as long as possible. No more talking now."

Meyer let his thoughts carry him away. There were many good times to remember, and he knew the children would like hearing some of the old stories again. Although he didn't like waiting, they would all have to—for days, even weeks. It didn't seem possible that they could hide here indefinitely. Now that he thought about it, he didn't believe his father had ever considered what to do after leaving the haystack. All their energy had been devoted to getting into the hiding place; they'd never discussed a plan for leaving it.

After a time, Meyer sat up suddenly, grabbing his neck and rubbing his face and arms. It seemed as if something was creeping over his skin. Realizing it was only bits of hay, he explained to his family, who were awakening now, "I'm itchy all over. It reminds me of Russia, but not so bad as it was there."

"Why were you itchy when you were in Russia, Meyer?" asked Toba.

"The lice—don't you remember, Toba? I told you—"

"Tell it again," piped up Cyvia. "What are lice?"

"Lice are tiny bugs that get in your hair and crawl around. Then they lay eggs that are glued to each strand of your hair, and when the eggs hatch, there are more bugs crawling around. You scratch and scratch so much that your head bleeds, but still you have to scratch some more. Lice hop around and get in your clothes, and they keep laying more eggs. It's terrible, Cyvia, terrible! You think you'll go crazy!" As Meyer looked around at the people facing him, each began to scratch imaginary itches.

"But the lice didn't come first," he began. "This story started not long after Motl and Shuyl went to Russia. Things were difficult in Hrubieszow, with lots of talk about the Germans and Russians invading Poland. Many people went to Russia. Quite a few came back, telling about bad conditions, no work, no food. That was when Manya's brother Ely went too. I was almost fourteen when my brothers left, but Papa wouldn't let me go with them then."

"When *did* you go to Russia?" asked Minka.

"It was about a month after Motl and Shuyl left. The rumors of what was going on in Warsaw and Cracow had gotten worse and worse. Finally three of my friends—Wolf, Dudie, and Buzi—and I decided we couldn't wait any longer. Papa had finally agreed to let me go if I would try to find Motl and Shuyl.

"So, off we went. The border was open and we crossed into Russia. A Pole rowed us across the river in his boat. Wolf's father arranged it. I had a cloth bag with a little food—bread, apples, pears, some pressed white cheese. The Russians didn't want a lot of people near the border, so they loaded us on trains and took us to Grodno. We stayed there a few weeks but we couldn't find work, so we went wandering around from place to place. We stayed in Minsk for a long time, with no money, no ideas about what to do, and no success in finding my brothers.

"Life was very hard. We slept wherever we could find a place, sometimes in the park, often on the floor in people's houses. We could take only cold baths—icy cold. The people who tried to help us did all they could, but they hardly had enough for themselves, so we kept moving on. We got discouraged and homesick and started thinking that things in Hrubieszow looked pretty good compared to Russia.

"Soon the lice were all over us. We went to a river, soaked in the cold water and washed our hair. We combed and brushed it until our scalps were raw, trying to get the lice out. I shiver to think of it now but it worked. We got rid of those awful bugs. We sold whatever we had to get money to buy other pants, shirts, and jackets and throw our old clothes away. We continued to move around and look for work to get a little money to buy food, sometimes loading trains in exchange for a meal. But even with money we had to stand in line, and sometimes after waiting for hours we still didn't get a turn. We waited all night in line once, and I was about twenty-five people away from the window of the store when it was announced that there was no more food to buy. They just closed the window."

"But what did you do? How did you get something to eat?" asked Toba.

"We didn't. We stayed another night, waiting. We decided then that we were probably going to die in Russia so we may as well go home. It couldn't be any worse there."

"How could you get back home? Did you walk?" asked Minka.

"It wasn't easy, and we were very hungry. But we walked along the roads and hoped that a truck or wagon or cart would pass by and give us a lift. We heard that the border guards were getting more watchful and that you needed money to pay them off to get across. Some people urged us to stay in Russia, saying things like 'You might starve in Russia, but you won't get shot.' Finally, I met a man who knew where we could cross. He had a friend who would let us through for money or valuables. Buzi had a pair of nice boots and I had a pocket watch. Dudie surprised us all by pulling out a gold coin his mother had given him for emergencies."

"As it turned out, the guard, a Pole on the Ukrainian side, was very nice. He saw how much we wanted to go home, and he refused to accept anything for helping us. We stayed near the border for five nights, waiting for a good wind or snow."

"Why would you want wind or snow?" asked Toba.

"Because the river was frozen, and a strong wind would blow snow over our footprints after we walked across. On the fifth night it was safe for us to go. Wolf had decided he would stay in Russia because he thought it was safer there, so three of us sneaked over the river. We reached the German side, but didn't know what to do to get home. There was a Jewish community nearby, where people raised money to help us get to Warsaw. Buzi and Dudie decided they liked Warsaw and felt they had a better chance of getting work there than anywhere else we'd been. I just wanted to go home. I spent a few days looking around and trying to figure out how to get a ride, but when I couldn't stand being homesick any longer, I started walking. A truck driver finally gave me a lift. I got a ride on a couple of wagons after that, and then walked the rest of the way.

"I remember when I came into the house, the first thing Mama asked was about Motl and Shuyl. I had to tell her that I never found them. Papa was upset with me. He told me I shouldn't have come back home, that things were getting very bad. All the Jews had to wear armbands with the Star of David on them, we weren't allowed to walk on the sidewalk when the Germans were present, and there was a curfew."

"Did you go to see Manya?" asked Minka.

"Oh, yes, as soon as I got back. I remember Mama was crying and telling me I'd better be home by six o'clock. I didn't think I'd be later than that, but when I got to Manya's, we talked and talked, and the next thing I knew, it was after curfew." He turned to Manya. "Remember that, Manya? Remember how we sat in your little room?"

"I remember, Meyer," she said, reaching for his hand. "I also remember how you used to pretend to pay attention to the other girls before you went to Russia. In spite of that, I went to your house day after day while you were gone to see if your family had any news about you."

Meyer looked toward his three sisters and Chaim. "I'll tell you something I have only told Manya before now. When I was in Russia, I thought about Manya all the time, remembering all the wonderful times we had had together. Although things were bad in Russia, that isn't the main reason I came back. It was Manya that brought me back. I missed her so much. I didn't realize how much I loved her until I was away from her. I want you to remember always what I've told you. Whenever you're sad or things are very bad, you must make yourself think of happy thoughts and how much you love Papa and Mama and each other. This won't make the sadness go away, but it will make it easier and you'll have something to fight back with that nobody can take from you. Do you understand what I'm saying?"

For the first time, Chaim spoke. "Meyer, I've been doing that all this time." Chaim had listened to Meyer's words carefully. He had always looked up to the older boy. "Memories are painful," he said slowly, "but it does help to think of things as they used to be. I remember following you everywhere you went and being so glad when you came to our house to see Manya or play dominoes with my father." His voice cracked, and Manya quickly finished his thought.

"Ah, yes, Chaim, I know." She paused. "Meyer, the night you returned from Russia, I remember you weren't wearing an armband. I told you that people were beaten or killed for that. But you said you wouldn't wear it because it was degrading and you wouldn't abide by the Nazis' dirty rules."

"I changed my mind about that pretty quickly," Meyer admitted. "I learned what I had to do to stay alive."

"Didn't anybody fight back?" asked Cyvia.

"Yes, Cyvia, they did, but maybe not in the way you're thinking," answered Avrum. "People did many things they weren't supposed to, like holding secret religious services, smuggling food and medicine into the ghetto, listening to radios, or hiding out like we're doing. You see, if people had fought back with fists or guns, the Nazis would have punished other Jews. Do you understand?"

"I'm not sure."

"Think of it like this, Cyvia," explained Meyer. "Minka does something wrong, but when she's caught, not only does Minka get punished but so do you and Toba and Mama. Minka feels so bad that everyone else is getting punished for what she did that either she confesses to what she did or she promises herself she'll never do it again. After all, she doesn't want harm to come to others."

"People had to be very careful about what they did," added Manya. "Remember the time with your hat, Meyer?"

"Oh, yes," said Meyer with a wince. "I was feeling good that day, on my way to Manya's. About four blocks from her house, I was walking on the sidewalk and I saw two Germans coming toward me. I remember noticing that they were SS officers, but maybe I didn't see them soon enough or maybe I just wanted to show them I wasn't going to obey the rules. I should have stepped off the sidewalk and tipped my hat, but I didn't. They called me dirty names and pushed me off the walk, beating me on the face with their fists. I wanted to hit them back, but I knew they would shoot me if I did. When I finally fell on the ground, they kicked me a few times and then walked off. I was in a lot of pain, but I managed to get up and drag myself to Manya's house."

"You were lucky, Meyer," said Avrum. "I saw many people killed for less than what you did."

"I know. After that, I did as I was told—followed all the rules. All but one, that is," said Meyer, grinning.

"Which one was that?" asked Cyvia.

"The curfew," he replied. "I never observed the curfew. I wasn't stupid about it, but when I wanted to go to Manya's, I went— almost every night for three years. We all learned how to do what we wanted and still give the Germans the idea that we were obeying them. It was the only way to survive. We fought back but in small ways, smart ways—ways that gave us satisfaction, but also allowed us to live. That was the most important thing: to keep hope for tomorrow."

Manya's thoughts wandered. She could hear spurts of gunfire in the distance, and she knew what it meant because she had seen it with her own eyes.

Once she and Meyer had secretly followed a German-led march of elderly Jews to the edge of town. As they had watched from a distance, the Jews had been lined up in front of foxholes dug by the Polish Army in its early attempts to defend the city against invasion. The noise had been deafening: shrieking, praying, pleading, then gunfire and more gunfire. Manya had opened her mouth to scream, but no sound emerged. The bodies had crumpled into the gash in the ground. She had stood paralyzed while dirt was pushed into the hole over the bodies. Then the Germans had departed. The horror, however, had intensified as the mound of earth undulated with the efforts of the half-dead to claw themselves out of their grisly grave.

Manya and Meyer had crept away from the scene silently, for there had been nothing to say.

It was the end of the day following the night the Korenblits had fled Hrubieszow for their hiding place. Josef Wisniewski heaved his body out of the chair and walked to his front door. He stared into the distance at the town he had grown up in. It was quiet now, its citizens getting ready for bed although it was still early. They'll go to bed to forget what they have seen today, he thought, to forget what they have allowed to happen.

He listened to his mother and sister in the kitchen, clearing away the supper dishes. Very soon it would be time to take food to the Korenblits, but he wished there were someone else to do it. He didn't want to face them, to answer their questions. He felt somehow responsible for the horrors he'd witnessed today, and he was ashamed.

As much as he believed there were many good Poles, they hadn't been in evidence this morning. No, they sat inside their homes and let the Nazis get on with their deportation and massacre. Later, he had sat in the otherwise deserted tavern, trying to dull his raw nerves with vodka. For some reason he had thought that helping the Korenblits would assuage his guilt, make it easier for him to observe the expulsion of others. Last night he had thought his mood would be jovial. Last night he was looking forward to tricking the Germans by hiding a Jewish family. But he was wrong. Tonight he was very, very weary. He felt as guilty as if he himself had held one of the guns. How could he describe the scene?

He had seen a deportation before, with its violence and death, and he had seen hope flicker in the victims' eyes when some were chosen to stay and some to leave. But today there had been no selections. Today, everyone had been taken.

He had gone into town that morning—October 28, 1942. Why he had gone, he wasn't sure. It had taken only a short time for the well-organized Nazi brigade to storm the town. Trucks and cars appeared as if from nowhere, discharging loads of soldiers and shutting off all chance of escape. Orders were barked on the streets of the Jewish section for Jews to vacate immediately and line up in rows. Rifle butts pounded on doors, punctuating the guttural commands, as troops burst into homes and dragged out dazed mothers, fathers, children.

A few doors were opened cautiously by residents, then were roughly thrown wide by corporals and privates whose faces were twisted with loathing as they shoved families to the ground outside. As the streets filled, figures streaking here and there for the alleys were shot down by staccato bursts from machine guns. Some watched terror-stricken, holding their children close, while others ran mindlessly, abandoning their sons and daughters. Infants were tossed in the air and blown apart by rifle shots. Polish neighbors watching through shuttered windows turned away.

The screams dulled as the first group was herded together by trucks and gun-wielding soldiers, pressing the captives on top of each other. Some tripped and were shot as they fell; others stumbled and were trampled, then kicked aside. Big hands gripped little hands, half-carrying the small ones lest they fall and be lost. Other hands reached ahead to hasten those in front, pitching them off balance; some used a free hand to steady a partner.

Behind them came cries of more frenzied victims and unceasing German orders. The train depot was just ahead; a thick column of steam rose from the locomotive. There was no time to look back—the past was gone forever.

Josef shook his head and sighed. Pulling on his jacket, he strode into the kitchen for food to carry to the haystack. Without a word, he left the house and was on his way.

CHAPTER THREE

The circle tightens

*In 1939, 3.3 million Jews were living in Poland. This,
the world's largest concentration of Jews, was chiefly a
legacy of the tolerance extended to them by Polish
kings and nobles during the Middle Ages. At that time,
when Jews were oppressed elsewhere in Europe, they
were welcomed as traders in largely agricultural
Poland. By the 1880s, however, antisemitism had gathered momentum and led to violent pogroms, especially
after the death of the relatively tolerant leader Marshal
Jozef Pilsudski in May 1935.*

*With the Nazi occupation of Poland in 1939, many
Poles joined enthusiastically in discriminating against
and persecuting Jews. Other Poles, however, helped
Jews to hide and to escape, their actions sometimes
motivated as much by hatred of the Germans as by
sympathy for their victims. Giving assistance of any
kind required great courage for, on July 27, 1942, a
German proclamation warned that any Pole who tried
to hide Jews, or to assist them in hiding, would be shot
dead. This was no empty threat: in numerous well-
publicized instances, Poles accused of helping Jews
were indeed caught and killed, and the warning was
trumpeted to every corner of the country.*

For seven nights the routine had been the same for those in the hiding place. Josef came to the haystack around ten o'clock with food and other necessities. He would signal, and Avrum and Meyer would crawl out. They were always glad to see Josef, their only contact with the outside, because he passed on information about what had happened in the city that day. But it wasn't only the food and news that consoled the hiding family; it was also the knowledge that the outside world still existed, even though they were isolated from it.

He was always the same Josef, with the smell of liquor on his breath. But as each day came and went, his face grew more somber. The Germans were intensifying their search for Jews who had escaped the deportations, putting immense pressure on Poles to aid in their hunt.

Each night Josef stayed at the haystack for about ten minutes. He always said the same thing before he left: "Everything will be fine. Don't worry. Nobody has any idea that you're here. I'll see you tomorrow." Then he would turn and amble off.

After visiting their cornfield toilet, the group would file back into the haystack, eat, discuss Josef's report, tell stories, and drift off to sleep, usually at dawn. By early afternoon they were awake again. Avrum would open his prayerbook and read aloud. He would tell a story from the Torah; then someone else would tell a story or recall an incident—anything that was amusing or adventurous or interesting. Then the pattern was repeated for the next twenty-four hours, and the next.

One night, it grew later than usual and Josef had not arrived. Meyer looked around the small group. Josef had mentioned again last night that Poles were looking in every conceivable place for hidden Jews in order to claim the bounty offered by the Germans. There were eight of them in the haystack. Eight people: eight pounds of sugar. A Polish family could live well trading that virtual gold on the black market.

"Daddy, I can't wait any longer. When can I go to the bathroom?" Cyvia whined.

"Josef's later than usual," Malka said uneasily to Avrum. "Do you think something has happened?"

"You know how careful Josef has been. He probably just wants to make sure everything is safe."

"He'll be here soon," Meyer added, with assurance. "We don't have to worry about Josef. He hasn't failed us yet and he won't now."

"If need be, we have enough food to make it through tomorrow," said Avrum.

Meyer sensed the tension building. He knew they should talk to take their minds off their concern about Josef. Suddenly he thought of a story he could tell and began laughing.

"What is it, Meyer? What's so funny?" Manya asked.

"I was just thinking back," Meyer laughed. "I'll never forget the time when my friends and I figured out a way to play a joke on that farmer on the other side of town, the one who was always so grouchy. We'd sneak into his barn very early in the morning and milk his cow. I can still taste that warm, bubbling milk. Then we would hide when we heard him coming. He couldn't figure out what was wrong with the cow when it didn't give any milk. We'd listen to him cursing at it; then we'd run away. We did it several times."

The laughter became contagious as one by one the others joined in. Cyvia held her stomach with her hands as her giggle rang out.

"Wait!" Chaim recollected. "I remember something else you told me, Meyer: the Russian soldier who tied an alarm clock around his neck! I still don't believe it!"

"It's true, I swear! He'd never seen a wristwatch before and I guess he thought that a clock would be just as good. We'd see him coming down the street with that thing bouncing against his chest. It was all we could do to keep quiet until he passed by!"

Cyvia squirmed, waving her hands, warning of her loss of control.

"Meyer, please, no more," said Toba. "Poor Cyvia, she's going to wet her pants!" Her plea only sent them into another helpless outburst.

When the laughter had died down, Avrum made a decision. "Since we don't know when Josef will get here, we'd better go to the cornfield. But we'll all go together, rather than in small groups as usual. Wait here while I check to see that it's safe."

Avrum inched his way to the opening and listened for a few moments before sliding the bale of hay from its slot. After peering around the entrance, he pulled himself out and slowly walked around the haystack. Confident that there was no one there, he signaled the others to join him. "Now, stay together, be as quiet as possible, and hurry."

As the group headed for the cornfield, Avrum pulled his son aside. "Meyer, I'm worried. We must find out what has happened to Josef. If he's been caught, it might be too dangerous for us to stay here."

"Why don't I go to his house and talk to his mother?"

"That could be far more dangerous. Someone could be watching the house."

"It's all right, Papa, I can make it. We have to find out what's going on."

"All right. But you must return here immediately. You promise?"

"Yes, I'll go straight to the farmhouse and back."

"Go quickly, then. I'll tell the others where you've gone."

Meyer moved silently into the shadows. Maybe one of the animals is sick and Josef is still in the barn, he thought. He'd better check there first.

The night was chilly, but the air felt wonderful on his face. Meyer always liked this kind of night. Before the war, he and Manya had often walked in the park in the evening. He'd wrap his arm loosely around her, but as the night grew colder, he'd pull her tightly to him to combine the warmth of their bodies. Someday they'd share that closeness again.

It wasn't long before the barn loomed into view. When he couldn't see a light inside, he doubted that Josef was there but he had to make sure. Meyer pushed the door open just a crack and peeked in. It was dark, but he could see outlines of the animals. Except for an occasional snort from a horse, it was quiet. He opened the door a little farther, causing it to creak, stirring the animals from their sleep. He could see better now as a splinter of moonlight shone over his shoulder. "Josef," he called softly, "are you here?"

There was no response. He closed the door behind him. He'd have to go to the house although it was very early in the morning and he'd probably frighten Mrs. Wisniewski by knocking at her door.

The house was just across the yard from the barn. He scurried in its direction and stepped up onto the porch. All the shades were drawn, so he couldn't see in, but he could detect a dim light through a gap in one window covering. He lifted his hand and tapped gently on the door. There was no response. He tapped again and waited.

He heard some movement inside, then a woman's voice: "Who's there?"

Meyer hesitated, then summoned the courage to speak. "It's Meyer Korenblit."

The door opened and Mrs. Wisniewski stood there in her robe, a look of panic on her face. They both knew that he was putting her in tremendous danger by being there. If anyone saw him, it would mean death for them all.

"Come in quickly before someone sees you." She shut the door behind him, nervously fingering her rosary. "What is it? Why are you here?"

"I'm looking for Josef. He didn't come with the food tonight." Meyer saw her face relax and realized that she had thought he had come with bad news about Josef. "It must be one o'clock in the morning. We were afraid something had happened."

"It's way past one o'clock; that's why I'm worried too. He left the house at six-thirty this morning as usual, and I haven't seen him since. He didn't come home for dinner."

"Where do you think he could be?" asked Meyer.

"Maybe the Germans . . . no, why should they take him? He has done nothing to them," she said. Her eyes narrowed as she looked at Meyer.

"Well, if they did, maybe they just wanted to question him. Or perhaps they know he's hiding us," Meyer blurted out.

Mrs. Wisniewski crossed herself and resumed her rhythm with the beads, her eyes pleading for Meyer to deny his words.

"No, that can't be so," he said, trying to calm her, "or they would have come here for you and your daughter. They would have searched the whole area."

Meyer groped for more words of comfort, but could find none. He decided he'd better leave and not endanger the old woman further.

"I must go now. I have to get back to my family," he said, heading for the door.

Mrs. Wisniewski grabbed Meyer's arm. "Wait! Let me give you the food." She went to the kitchen and returned with a big covered pot and two loaves of crusty bread.

"Thank you, Mrs. Wisniewski. Everything will be all right," Meyer said reassuringly.

The woman shook her head, then peeked out the window and opened the door. "You mustn't come back here. It's too dangerous for all of us."

Meyer nodded, turned, and left. Juggling a loaf of bread under each arm and holding the pot with both hands, he trudged off in the direction of the haystack, disappointed. He'd have to report to his father that there was no news of Josef. If only there was a way. Suddenly he stopped. Of course! There was someone who'd know if something had happened to Josef. Although Meyer had promised his father to come right back, they were desperate to know what was going on. Meyer turned 180 degrees and started walking as fast as he could toward John Salki's house.

Meyer knew he was taking a big chance by going to see the commissioner. Salki lived on the main road outside the city, between the fort and the brick factory—both Nazi-occupied areas. There was nearly always some movement on the road: from the fort to the brick factory, from the brick factory to the city, from the city to the fort. It was a dangerous area to intrude upon. With about two miles to cover, he was already having trouble balancing the cumbersome pot, and the loaves of bread kept sliding out from under his arms.

He calculated the time quickly, knowing every second was precious. He would have to allow two hours for travel time; that would leave only an hour before daybreak and he would need at least that long at Salki's. His approach to the house would have to be gradual, for even though Salki's door was always open to people in need, his official status as commissioner of roads meant that he was also subject to unannounced visits by Germans.

Meyer was sure that Salki wouldn't be upset with him for coming at this hour. He had gone there at strange times before and, besides, Salki was a close friend. On a previous occasion, he had told them that the Germans were planning to take away a certain number of Jews, but not everyone. Although the haystack hideout had been ready then, Avrum had wanted to save it for when there would be no next time. Salki had offered to help and had hidden the Korenblits for several days under a false floor in his attic.

Commissioner Salki wasn't overly impressive at first glance. He was in his mid-thirties, about five-feet-six, a little on the heavy side, with a small bald spot on his head. He always wore his uniform and tall black boots, his pants tucked neatly into them, an ever-present cigarette burning between his fingers.

But his stern official appearance could not conceal his warm, friendly hazel eyes. The commissioner had always been nice to the Korenblit family because of a favor Avrum had done for him years ago. Salki was married and had four children, the eldest a thirteen-year-old boy, Janek. Even before the war, the Korenblits and the Salkis had been good friends. For the past three years, since the Nazi invasion, Salki had helped whenever necessary, without a moment's hesitation and asking nothing in return.

Meyer's fingers were numb now as he skirted the tree-lined

road into the city. Stumbling into the brush across from Salki's house, he gratefully set down the pot and let the bread fall. As he watched the house, the sound of his own breathing filled his ears. His eyes meticulously panned the street. Even when he was satisfied that he had a clear path to the house, he forced himself to scan it one more time. There was nothing. He half-crawled into the open, and then raced toward the house. Diving for a shadow by the door and crouching in its safety, he held his breath to listen, then reached up and knocked.

Meyer listened for footsteps from inside, but all he heard was the wind blowing softly through the trees. For the first time since he had left the haystack, he felt the cold of the November morning. Maybe he should knock again.

He raised his hand, then heard a weary voice: "Is somebody there?"

"Salki! It's me, Meyer Korenblit. I need to talk to you."

The door opened and Meyer hurried inside.

"Meyer, what are you doing here? You know how dangerous it is for you to be out. The Nazis would shoot you on sight."

"I know, I know. But something has happened to Josef."

"What?"

"I have no idea. But he didn't arrive with the food tonight and he's never failed to show up before. Do you think the Germans have him?"

"I don't know, Meyer. I haven't heard anything. I told Avrum it wasn't good to trust Wisniewski—that drunk." Salki's voice rose in anger, the words hissing through his teeth. "I warned him something like this could happen. You'd better stay here until tonight, when it will be safer to go back to the hideout. Since this last deportation, the Nazis have been sending out patrols at all hours to catch any Jews who may have escaped. They don't want to miss even one. The dark hours are no longer safe the way they used to be."

"I understand, John, but I can't stay here. My family would worry and wouldn't know what to do. I told Papa I'd be back soon."

"Then do as you must, but remember, it's risky. As for Josef,

I'll check around town later today. Gorski might know something; I'll go to see him too. Now, listen to me, Meyer: if I find out anything, I'll send Janek to the hideout. The Germans know he is my son, and they won't bother him. If you don't hear from me by nightfall, tell your father to leave the haystack and come here. We'll put you all up until I can find a safer place. Now go quickly, and be careful."

With two steps and a single bound, Meyer was off the porch and racing across the clearing to the bushes where he had left the food. As he placed the loaves back under his arms, he felt the dull ache of a cramp begin in his shoulder. He had to think of another way to carry them. He buttoned the bottom of his jacket and stuffed the bread inside, high enough for him to brace the pot on his belt buckle. He pictured Manya waiting for him in the haystack as he struck out into the fields once more.

"Shouldn't Meyer be back by now? He's been gone a long time," Manya asked the others in the haystack.

"There's nothing to worry about, Manya; he'll be all right," Avrum responded. "Knowing Meyer, he probably went to Josef's favorite taverns to find him," he joked, trying to ease their fear. But he too was worried: Meyer had been gone nearly four hours.

Avrum had spent that time encouraging the others to talk, even allowing them to switch on the flashlights for a short time. He suggested that they divide the sparse leftovers and stale bread for a snack, but no one seemed hungry. Cyvia had prevailed upon him to braid some straw into a doll, which she then wrapped in a handkerchief and serenaded in a squeaky voice. The older girls, eager to find amusement somewhere, stuck straw in their noses and ears, making faces and giggling.

Manya watched the merriment wistfully, wishing Meyer were there, then thinking of her own family. Malka saw her face and reached out to put an arm around Manya, gently and lovingly brushing the dark blond hair away from her face. With this maternal gesture, the tears that Manya had bravely held back for seven days spilled down her cheeks. Meyer's mother held her until she felt Manya's shaking stop, then whispered to her, "Meyer and Josef will be all right, Manya. They'll be all right." After Manya had quieted herself, Malka crawled to the opposite side of the haystack, quietly ministering to her sleepy daughters.

Manya watched the older woman with deepening affection. With the closeness and affection she'd shared with this group during the past week, she felt that she wasn't an outsider any longer: she had been accepted by Meyer's family. She couldn't wait to tell him, she thought sleepily. She struggled to stay awake as she heard Malka speak.

"Avrum, something must have gone wrong," Malka said softly. "First Josef disappears, and now Meyer. He's been gone too long—at least three hours. Aren't you going to do something?"

Avrum didn't want to tell his wife that it had actually been four hours. He was concerned himself. Why couldn't Meyer ever just do as he was told? He could not think that Meyer had been caught; he had too much faith in his son and his God to believe that. He had to believe that Meyer would return soon. The alternative was unthinkable.

"Now, listen," he began. "For three years we've seen the horrors of this tragedy all around us, yet somehow we've made it this far. There is a reason: God is watching over us and He will bring Meyer back here safely. Meyer is just being careful to make sure nobody will find us."

Then Avrum was silent. He thought he heard something. Yes, there it was again. Could it be Josef?

"Papa, Papa, it's me," came a voice from outside.

It was Meyer. Avrum heard a relieved sigh from Malka as Meyer entered the haystack.

"Tell us, son, what did you find out?"

Meyer explained that he had gone to the barn and to Josef's house, learning nothing in either place. "After that, I went to Salki's, figuring if anyone would know what had happened, it would be him."

"And what news did he have?" asked Avrum.

"He doesn't know anything either. But he's going to try to find out and send word with Janek. If Janek doesn't come, it will mean there is no news of Josef, and then we are to go to Salki's house to hide. We'll stay there until a safer place can be found."

Avrum looked at Malka, then around the room at the rest of the group. They were all waiting for his response.

"I don't know if that's the best thing to do," he said slowly. "I've been thinking—maybe it would be better if we went to Mislavitch. I know that our friends Achler and Tomitzki would help find a place for us to stay. Or there is the possibility of escaping through the underground. Salki and Gorski could help us with that, although the arrangements might take too long— there are so many of us. What do you think, Meyer?"

"I would rather go to Salki's and then see if he can smuggle out a few at a time through the underground. Then, when we're safe, we could help others escape too."

"I still think that Mislavitch would be the best choice," Avrum responded. "The underground seems like a long shot and would be risky for such a large group."

"Going to Mislavitch would be a long walk for the girls," said Malka.

"I know, but it's more dangerous here right now. We have to do something; we have no choice."

With Avrum's last words, the decision was made. They would leave for Mislavitch as soon as it turned dark.

Meyer leaned heavily against the hay. "Oh, I'm tired," he murmured to Manya.

"Do you want something to eat? I think there's enough for a few bites, anyway. Maybe you'd feel better—"

"My God, the food!" Meyer jumped up. "I brought food from Mrs. Wisniewski! I put it down outside. Wait." He scrambled back outside and retrieved his bounty.

"We've gone a long way together," he said to the pot as he pushed it along the tunnel floor and pitched the bread inside. "Now we'll see if it was worth it."

Meyer had eaten his fill of Mrs. Wisniewski's stew, using his bread to sop up every drop. Sleep came easily and was deep, and he awakened to the glow of a flashlight and a clatter of dishes. He thought it must be late afternoon.

Meyer watched his mother wrapping dishes and utensils in clothes to soften their rattle on the long walk ahead. As she filled the baskets, she tested the weight of each so that even Cyvia could carry her share. Then, picking up a loaf of bread, she tore chunks from it, tossing them to her family.

"Dip these in the leftover stew," she ordered, nudging the pot to the center of the group. "Come, come," she insisted when no one moved. "It may not look so good, but we need to eat. We can't take it with us, and we will not waste it. There may be a time when we'll be grateful for even the smell of such food."

Manya obediently reached into the pot, scooping a healthy portion onto her bread. One by one the rest complied, and before long, the pot was scraped clean. They settled back, feeling the heaviness of the food and the journey they were about to undertake.

Avrum figured they should wait one more hour to make sure night had fallen to cover their journey. Normally he could travel the eleven miles in three or four hours. But tonight they'd have to make their way through the fields and, with the children, there was no way they could travel that quickly.

"Now, girls," Avrum addressed his daughters, "you understand that we have a long walk, and we must go as quickly as possible if we are to arrive at the flour mill before dawn. Do you remember the flour mill, Cyvia, where Papa used to have a business?"

"Of course she doesn't remember, Avrum," Malka broke in. "She was too young. It's Minka you used to take on the wagon."

"Ah, yes, that's right, isn't it, my little Minka? You liked to watch the big stone wheels grinding the grain, didn't you? And you, Toba, I remember how you helped me with the sacks. You used to tell me the flour mill needed dusting, right?" He chuckled as his eldest daughter beamed at him.

"We'll tell stories and talk of old times when we get to Mislavitch. But first we must get there, and the journey is very dangerous. You must promise to do exactly as I say and make no noise. We don't want the soldiers to catch us, now do we? You understand: there will be no chance to talk outside."

The girls nodded their promise.

"Very good. I think we're ready. We'll wait a few moments to be sure it's good and dark."

Silence settled on the group.

Then Avrum spoke again. "Shh, what's that?" They all strained their ears to identify the sounds.

"It's a dog," Meyer announced.

"A dog, yes, but there's something else. Shh!"

A voice singing a shaky tune penetrated the walls of hay. A grin crept across Meyer's face as the sound became intelligible.

"It's Josef," he cried. "I know it is. Listen, Papa—can't you hear?"

Avrum pressed his ear to the hay as the words wafted through the haystack: "Wheat and flour, flour and wheat. My life is dry—do you hear me, dog? A little vodka makes it easy to swallow the flour and wheat. . . ."

Avrum scrambled for the tunnel and outside, with Meyer on his heels. When they shoved the bale of hay outward, they were startled at the darkness—where had the time gone? But Josef's big hand reached down to pull them out of the haystack. They pounded each other in greeting, almost dancing on the hard ground.

"Josef, for God's sake, where were you?" Avrum cried.

"Why didn't you come last night?" Meyer chimed in. "I went looking for you."

"Yes, my mother told me," said Josef sheepishly. "I went to town last night, I'm afraid," he explained. "It wasn't too late when I came home, and I remember unhitching my horse and putting him in the stall, but I can't recall anything else. I woke up this morning in the barn."

"The barn?" shouted Meyer. "That's impossible. You couldn't have been in the barn. I looked for you there!"

"Well, maybe you were looking for a Josef who was standing up, Meyer. This Josef was passed out on the ground."

The three stared at one another, then laughed.

"Then everything is all right?" asked Avrum.

Josef faced him, his look serious and dark. "I don't feel so confident, Avrum," came the heavy reply. "The situation is worse than before. The Germans haven't let up the pressure; they're like madmen, obsessed that our city be *Judenrein*. That's all you hear. There are notices posted everywhere. But there's more: they're hounding the Poles, shooting anyone who is even suspected of helping Jews. I fear for my mother and sister, Avrum. I can't ask them to sacrifice their lives. I never thought it would get so bad or last so long. You're welcome to stay here as long as you want, but I don't think I can endanger them any longer by coming to see you here."

Avrum put an arm around Josef's brawny shoulders. "It's all right, my friend. You've already done more than any man could ask of another. God grant me the time to do the same for you. We are thinking of going to Mislavitch. Also, Meyer saw Salki last night, and we can go there for a time anyway."

"Avrum, I feel I have failed you. We thought this plan would work, but I have the feeling I'm being watched. No one can be trusted."

"Enough, Josef. Put it out of your mind. Salki will take over now; then we shall see," Avrum said consolingly. "You're a good friend and a decent man, Josef. We'll always be in your debt."

"*Do milego zobaczania*," Josef said in a husky voice.

Meyer grabbed the man's outstretched hand in his own.

"Yes, Josef. Until we meet again."

Meyer saw the tears in Josef's eyes. He moved closer to Avrum, and father and son watched as Josef summoned his dog and walked ponderously toward the farmhouse. More than ever, they felt they were on their own.

CHAPTER FOUR

Friendship and

its limits

"Over the wall, through holes, and past the guard,

Through the wires, ruins, and fences,

Plucky, hungry, and determined

I sneak through, dark like a cat.

"At noon, at night, at dawn,

In snowstorm, cold or heat,

A hundred times I risk my life

And put my head on the line.

"Under my arm a gunny sack,

Tatters on my back,

On nimble young feet,

With endless fear in my heart...."

--Henryka Lazawert
"The Little Smuggler" (1941)

From a HOLOCAUST READER, edited by Lucy S. Dawidowicz.
Henryka Lazawert was a young poet killed in Treblinka concentration
camp in July, 1942. This poem celebrating child smugglers was a popular
literary recitation in the ghettos. Copyright Behrmann House, Inc.
Reprinted with permission. www.behrmannhouse.com.

Avrum shook his head wistfully as Josef disappeared into the darkness. "Our friend has lifted the burden of his family's danger from his shoulders," he said to Meyer, "but he looks as if he is bearing a bigger one: his conscience. He should think about how much he's already done to help." Avrum paused. "But we must get back inside and decide what to do."

"Do you think we'll see Josef again, Papa?"

"I hope so, son, but I'm afraid it will be a long time."

"So many people, Papa, all our friends. The kids I grew up with and went to school with. Where are they now? Do you think any of them are still alive?"

"We can only pray that some are."

"What about the Nagelsztajns? I wish we could find out if they're all right. Maybe in a few days I can sneak into town."

"No. I know Manya and Chaim are worried, but you'd be endangering us and them if you went. Besides," Avrum added, "we may not be here in a few days."

Avrum looked thoughtfully at his son. He's grown up a lot in these three years, he mused. We could never have made it this far without him. Thank God for Manya. If not for Meyer's love for her, he might still be in Russia searching for his brothers. Meyer and I have shared fear and sadness, exchanged worries and hopes, and all of it has made us closer and more trusting of one another. Had our lives been normal, we might never have achieved such a bond. That would make it all the harder to lose one another now, he thought, opening the entrance of the haystack. Then, he stopped himself. No, he resolved; such weak thoughts will betray the Jews. The Nazis may kill me with bullets, but I'll never allow my own thoughts to defeat me.

As Meyer and Avrum reentered the haystack, Cyvia saw them first and called out, "What did he say? What did Josef say?"

"Things aren't good," Avrum began. "Josef can't bring us food anymore. He says the Nazis are arresting Poles they suspect of helping Jews. He isn't scared for himself, but he doesn't want to endanger his mother and sister. Poor Josef—the man feels he has failed us. Almost the entire Jewish population of Hrubieszow has been killed or deported. Yet here we are, alive and together, because he was willing to risk his life rather than turn his back on his friends. He did say we can stay here as long as we want and that maybe later when things calm down he'll be able to help again. If there were more people like Josef, maybe more Jews would be hiding out safely."

"So last night he didn't come because he was afraid of being watched?" asked Malka. The dim glow from the flashlight gave off just enough light for everyone's face to be seen. For the first time in many days, she saw her husband break into a smile.

"No. Josef didn't come because he got drunk, fell asleep in the barn, and didn't wake up until noon today," answered Avrum.

There was total silence in the haystack, and then, as if on cue, everyone broke out laughing. It was a moment of relief they all needed.

"Now, however, we must decide what to do," said Avrum. "It's too late to leave for Mislavitch tonight. Salki said he will continue to help us, and we still have Gorski. Remember, Josef doesn't think we're in danger here. He was just afraid of being seen when visiting us. I think we should have Meyer go back to Salki and find out what he thinks is best."

"I'll go immediately, Papa," Meyer said, heading for the outside and motioning Manya to follow him.

As they crawled through the tunnel, Manya couldn't help thinking how much she didn't want Meyer to leave again. Why must it always be his job to take risks? she wondered. She decided to assure him that he didn't need to prove anything; he was already a hero in her eyes. As they emerged, she saw him scramble to the side at the opening, then felt his strong arms grip hers, drawing her the rest of the way out and pulling her to him.

Falling back against the haystack, they clung to each other, their embrace wild and hungry one moment, tender the next. Then, without a word, he was gone. Manya inched her way back into the haystack and to her place beside Chaim. She took his hand and gave it a sweet kiss and a warm pat.

"He's on his way," she told everyone.

There was no bread or pot of stew to slow Meyer down this time, and he was able to run as fast as he could to Salki's and back. He was still breathing heavily when he made his way into the haystack.

"What did Salki say?" asked Avrum.

"Let him catch his breath," urged Malka, passing Meyer a cup of water.

Meyer swallowed the water in one gulp and took a deep breath. "Salki thinks the best thing for us is to stay here. He and Gorski have been checking around town, and nobody has even a clue that we're here. The Germans have already searched this area. That doesn't mean they won't come back, but for the time being he and Gorski feel this is the safest place."

"What about food, Meyer?" asked Malka.

"For the next few nights I'll go to Salki's and get it. Then maybe they can work something else out."

That wasn't the answer Avrum wanted to hear.

"Maybe we can get by with what we have for a few days," said Avrum. "I don't like the idea of your going over there so often."

"Don't worry, Papa. I can do it. I know I can do it."

Three days passed, and one night, anger got the better of Meyer.

"A machine gun, that's what I'd like to have," he exploded, startling the others with his vehemence. "I'm tired of all this. I could set a gun up in a secret place and mow down at least some Nazis. Maybe then they would leave us alone!"

"Meyer!" cried Malka. "How can you even think such a thing! You know what's happened in other cities. Remember what we heard about Lodz? The Nazis don't wait for a reason to kill a Jew, but when they have an excuse, it gives them even more pleasure. We've seen it ourselves right here in Hrubieszow! And now you would risk—"

"Mama, don't worry," said Meyer. "I only mean that I think about it sometimes. After what we've been through, anyone would want some power over them—to make them fear for their lives every time they walk down the street or go to sleep at night, just as they've done to us. But I know it wouldn't really do any good."

"We must keep reminding ourselves that we're safe here," Avrum said calmly. "Everything is working out."

"Yes, it's working out," responded Meyer, "but for how long? We have to sit in here hour after hour, day after day—for who knows how long? Weeks? Months? I'll go crazy, you hear? I can't stand it!"

"Control yourself, son!" Avrum commanded. "We're all cooped up. We're all bored and tired of waiting. We all want to get out. But we must strive for patience and continue to believe that we'll be all right."

The musty air in the haystack crackled with tension from ten days of isolation and immobility. Even Avrum had to fight for clarity of mind to counter his son's frustration, but he knew that doubt was unacceptable—they had to believe they would win and not allow tedium to destroy them.

Suddenly, they heard sounds from outside. The silent group splintered into twos and threes, heads drawn together, arms wound protectively around each other. Voices outside shouted, sounding close one second, farther away the next, then closer still. But the words were muffled, indistinguishable to those who lay listening in the house of hay. They concentrated also on what they didn't hear. There was no gunfire and no noise from engines. No barking, therefore no dogs. No familiar chant, so no Josef. But what was it? Now it came from one side, then another. Sometimes they heard bursts of chatter, once in a while a yell, and a few times, laughter. The voices continued most of the afternoon, then faded away. It was a long time before anyone spoke.

"Do you think we can check outside now?" Meyer finally asked.

"I'm not sure we should go out tonight. Someone may be waiting outside," Avrum responded.

"I know," Meyer retorted, "but if Janek brought the food and someone else finds it, that could give us away."

"You're right, son, but let's wait a bit longer just to make sure the boys have come."

For the previous three nights, Meyer had gone to Salki's house for food, as they'd agreed. But tonight it was to be delivered, for Salki felt that changing the routine would avoid suspicion. They agreed that his son Janek and Henrik Gorski, the police chief's son, would bring the food and leave it near the haystack. There would be no signal, no communication. The quicker it was done, the better. Only in an emergency would Janek break the code of silence and speak to the hidden family.

Everyone was pleased that Meyer wouldn't be going into town for a while. Each night they had suffered through the same ordeal, wondering if he would make it or if he had been caught. It had seemed that each time he left, it took longer for him to return.

But there was one person who wasn't pleased, and that was Meyer. He was tired of being trapped in the small enclosure. He knew it worried everyone when he left, especially Malka and Manya, but it relieved his anxieties to be out and doing something useful. Why couldn't they understand? Manya of all people should realize how important it was. No, he stopped himself; she understands. It's just that she cares so much that she doesn't want anything bad to happen. Manya's only thinking of me.

"Meyer, let's go see if they've come." Avrum's voice interrupted his thoughts.

When Meyer and Avrum emerged outside, they could see the food wasn't at the entrance, so they walked around the haystack. Nothing!

"Maybe they buried it under the hay," Avrum suggested, prodding the base of the haystack and circling again. Then he felt something. He dug the hay away, and sure enough, there were the baskets.

"Very clever," murmured Meyer.

Avrum picked up the baskets. Meyer replaced the hay, then followed his father back inside.

"Listen to me, everyone," said Avrum when they finished eating. "Tonight we aren't going out in twos. We'll all go together, so it won't take as long as usual. After what we heard today, we don't want to spend any more time outside than absolutely necessary."

"What do you think that noise was, Papa?" asked Cyvia.

Avrum looked at her sharply. "I don't have any more of an idea now than when you asked me before," he snapped.

Cyvia's eyes widened and she struggled to stop the tears from coming.

"She was just asking," Malka said sternly, putting her arm protectively around her youngest daughter and hugging her.

"I know—it's just that I'm worried about those noises. They were very close." Avrum opened his arms and motioned for Cyvia to come to him. She threw her arms around his neck. Avrum squeezed back and kissed her on the cheek. "I didn't mean it, Cyvia. I'm just worried about our safety. I didn't mean to hurt your feelings, my baby," he said tenderly.

"It's all right, Papa. I love you."

"And I love you, Cyvia." Avrum hugged his daughter again, then started for the tunnel. Before removing the bale of hay from the opening, he whispered over his shoulder. "Remember, be as quick as possible, and don't make any noise."

Once outside, they broke into two groups, with Malka and the girls going to one area and Avrum, Chaim, and Meyer to another. After a few moments, when Avrum turned to walk back to the haystack, he noticed that Meyer had disappeared.

"Chaim, did you see Meyer?" asked Avrum.

"No, I didn't see him after we came out. Maybe he went back to the haystack with Manya," Chaim suggested.

Soon they were joined by Malka and the girls.

"Where's Meyer?" asked Manya, immediately noticing his absence.

"He'll be back in a few minutes," Avrum answered, trying not to sound concerned. "I asked him to check the area to see if he could pick up any clues about the voices." He hated to mislead her, but how could he say he didn't know? They would just start worrying again.

"Everyone, go inside," Avrum instructed. "I'll wait out here for Meyer."

"Can't we stay too, Papa, until Meyer gets back?" asked Minka.

"No, it's too dangerous for everyone to be standing outside."

"But it feels so good out here," she pleaded. "It's like being buried in there."

"I'll tell you what, Minka," Avrum offered. "We won't close the entrance for a while. Then the fresh air will go inside. Remember not to turn on any flashlights."

Slowly they made their way inside, reluctant to end their few minutes of freedom. Five, ten, fifteen minutes passed. Still no Meyer.

Finally, Avrum, still waiting outside, heard a rustling in the field. "Meyer, is that you?" he whispered.

"Yes, Papa," answered Meyer.

"Where have you been?"

Meyer's coat was slung over his shoulder like a satchel, and it was bulging. "I have a surprise, Papa. I'm sorry I worried you."

"Meyer, you shouldn't run off like that without telling me. Your mother and Manya get very upset. I run out of excuses for you."

"I know, Papa. I'll try to remember," Meyer promised, laying the bundle on the ground.

"What's that?" asked Avrum.

"The surprise. I'll show you inside."

When Cyvia saw the big bundle her brother dragged into the haystack, her questions started. "What's in your coat? Is it something for us to play with?"

"On my way back from Salki's last time, I took a different route across Josef's farm and found these. When we went out tonight, I decided to get some." He pulled out a round object.

"What is it?" asked Toba.

"They're sweet turnips," said Meyer. "Since we haven't had anything sweet in so long, I thought it would be nice."

Avrum just shook his head, and Manya threw him a knowing glance as she wrapped her arms around Meyer.

The pattern for the next seven days was the same. Every day the voices returned. The pressure on those inside the haystack was unbearable, as their questions and concerns mounted. How many people are out there? Are they Nazis? Are they Poles? Why do they keep coming back? Do they know we're in here? No, they must not, or they would have grabbed us when we went outside at night. They would have stopped Janek and Henrik from bringing food. Those two boys would be dead by now, along with Salki and Gorski. Maybe the Germans have set up this routine for their sadistic pleasure. No, they might play with one Jew to frighten a group, but here there was no audience for them to terrify.

In the beginning, it had been easier on the hidden family. They had talked, told stories, prayed, and at times even laughed. But there was little talking now because of the voices heard regularly outside. And when they did talk, tempers often flared.

Once in a while Meyer would even get mad at Manya. This made Avrum unhappy above all. He wished that Meyer would consider what Manya and Chaim must be going through. They had no idea about the fate of their mother, father, brother, and sisters. Were they still alive? Had they been found? Deported?

"We have to get out of here," said Meyer finally. "I don't know what those voices are, but we can't stay here much longer without finding out what's going on."

"If there was a problem, Salki would let us know, wouldn't he?" asked Malka. "Maybe he'd leave a note with the food."

"Yes, he'd get word to us, Malka, but I don't think he would dare write anything down," answered Avrum. "If the wrong person came across the note—"

"So," Meyer interrupted, "you think as long as the food is delivered, we should stay where we are?"

"That's exactly right. We have no reason to believe we're in any more danger now than when we first arrived."

"But the voices," Meyer prodded, "the voices are reason for concern."

"Perhaps, but so far they've brought us no real danger. If the SS or some unfriendly Poles knew we were here, they would have taken us already. We must be patient—as hard as that may be."

"But don't you want to know what's going on out there? It's been seven days since we've had any news."

"Of course I want to know, but there's nothing we can do," answered Avrum.

"Yes, there is. I can go talk to Salki," said Meyer.

Avrum nodded thoughtfully at this suggestion. Maybe that would help to reassure everyone. "Okay, Meyer. Go to Salki's."

Manya held Meyer tightly before his departure, not wanting him to leave again. But slowly she released her grip, knowing it was best for all of them that he go to investigate.

Meyer kissed her tenderly on the lips and whispered, "I love you."

Again, Manya held her brother's hand for comfort as Meyer slipped away.

"I was going to send for you in a day or so," Salki said, looking at the haggard boy in front of him. "The Nazis have changed their orders. They're no longer going to deport or kill Jews—at least young healthy Jews," he added. "They've put out a bulletin calling for Jews hiding in the area to come out. They need them for work."

"But is it safe? Can I bring my whole family?" asked Meyer with cautious enthusiasm.

"I don't think everyone should come. They've set up a small work camp at the old ghetto, but there are only young people in it—between the ages of fifteen and about thirty. I didn't trust what the Nazis were doing at first. I was sure it was a damn trick so the murderers could finish their filthy work. But from what I've seen, it may be true—at least for now. What will happen when the work is done, I don't know," Salki said straightforwardly. "It's up to you to decide what you want to do. I'll help all of you any way I can."

"You hate them, don't you?" asked Meyer. He could see the anger on Salki's face, the tightening of his jaw, and knew the answer before Salki spoke.

"They're murderous bastards who care nothing about life. But it's not just the Germans. There are many Poles who are helping them. They're just as bad as the Nazis, maybe worse. Someday they will all get what's coming to them," Salki answered angrily.

"Why don't you leave?" asked Meyer.

"I do what I can here to make it a little easier for some people. I'm not a heroic person, Meyer. I've done some things I'm not proud of, believe me. I only try to do what I think is right, what anybody should do. It may not be a lot, but it might help a few people a little."

"Is that why Gorski does it, too?" asked Meyer.

"Yes, he's helping because it's the right thing to do. No one will ever know how much he is doing to help people." Salki paused. "But now tell me, what have you decided to do?"

"I think the best thing would be for me to sneak into the ghetto and see if it's safe. Then I can tell the others," answered Meyer.

"If that's what you want, fine. I'll send Janek around to find you once you're in the ghetto to see if you need anything. And Meyer, you can't just walk in and start work. Find a man named Silberstein. Report to him and he'll inform the proper authorities about you. He's a good man."

Meyer started for the door, then abruptly turned around. "I almost forgot one of the things I came here to find out. Every day for the past week we've heard voices outside the haystack. Sometimes they're very close; other times they're farther away. There's yelling and screaming and even laughter. Do you have any idea who's out there?"

Salki tried to keep from smiling as he nodded apologetically. "Yes, I know. Every day I've sent Janek and Henrik to the field to keep an eye on the area around the haystack. I told them to act as if they'd just gone there to play games. They were to warn you if they saw anyone coming."

Meyer stood dumbfounded. This whole time, they had been terrified that the Nazis were closing in, when it had only been the two boys watching out for their safety.

When Meyer returned to the haystack, he found it difficult to convince his parents that he should go to see the work camp for himself. They were frightened for themselves and for him. Finally, Meyer was sure his father understood, but his mother most assuredly did not. She wanted them all to stay together. The mood lightened a bit when Meyer told them about their young guardians. Now they knew that the voices belonged to people protecting them. Besides, Meyer had assured Malka, if things weren't right in town, he'd come back. With that, she seemed more content and even promised to watch over Manya.

He made it back to town without incident, but shivered a bit when he entered the ghetto area and saw doors of houses standing open and windows smashed. He wondered if any of the houses were occupied—they all looked deserted.

Salki had said to go to a house behind the old Jewish Center. There, Mr. Silberstein admitted Meyer without comment. He assured Meyer that Jews were welcome to return and were very much needed by the Nazis. The work, he admitted, wouldn't be pleasant. Some workers would have to remove belongings from the houses of their former neighbors. Others would build roads, haul household goods, work in the brick factory. But they'd be quartered in acceptable housing and, it seemed, protected from indiscriminate slaughter. There were no guarantees, he said, but for now it could be a livable situation, definitely safer than hiding in the woods or trying to leave the country. Meyer wasn't sure that he agreed and said that he'd have to return to his hiding place and discuss it with his family before making a decision. Silberstein objected strongly to this idea, saying that Meyer would jeopardize both the ghetto and his family's safety by trying to go back. The Germans could be watching, he explained, and they could get the idea that the ghetto leadership was connected with the resistance.

Meyer finally agreed to stay in town for two or three days to observe the conditions under which they would live if they stayed. He presented himself for work the next morning and spent twelve hours carrying furniture down flights of stairs and into trucks; yanking down draperies; piling up pots and pans, dishes, utensils, linens, and lamps; dumping out drawers of shirts, socks, underwear, and baby clothes. He felt ashamed as he and the others handled, even evaluated, the personal belongings of their faceless owners, and he realized that sooner or later someone, perhaps he, would perform the same sickening task at his house or Manya's.

He wasn't able to reach the Nagelsztajns' house—it was too far toward the center of town. The small ghetto area was an isolated section near the Zamosc bridge and adjacent to the Jewish cemetery. The streets—alleys, really—were unpaved and the houses run-down, but those conditions were not of concern to Meyer. It was far more important that the Nazis were inviting the Jews to come out of hiding to work. For the last seventy-two hours, Meyer had watched and thought while he labored, attempting to examine the Nazis' motives from every angle.

Each day more Jews arrived in the work camp, so Meyer could see he wasn't alone in accepting the situation. But he made an important decision: he couldn't recommend that his parents join him. John Salki had confirmed Meyer's suspicion that "Jews to work" meant Jews deemed capable of work, and the Nazis translated that to mean young. It wasn't the kind of message he wanted to send to the haystack, but it was the only one possible. Perhaps his parents and sisters could make it to Mislavitch now instead.

He'd send for Manya and Chaim and perhaps Toba to join him, knowing they could get along quite well. In fact, he was hopeful about setting up a little home with Manya and had already informed the head of the work camp to expect three more members of his family. He even had the house picked out. They wouldn't have it all to themselves, of course, and it looked nearly ready to slide down the embankment into the creek behind it, but anything was better than being trapped again in that haystack.

The next day Meyer was standing in the trees by the creek waiting for Janek. Salki's son had been sent by his father to the Jewish section ostensibly to carry an official communiqué to the ghetto, but really to talk to Meyer. Somehow the boy always appeared when Meyer needed him—sometimes to deliver information but more often to receive a message to carry back. He never looked suspicious, sauntering along as he did with a broken branch or pitching rocks into the creek.

Janek didn't break stride when he saw Meyer, but plucked his slingshot from his back pocket and stooped to gather pebbles. Pausing to fit the stone into the sling, he moved a few more feet in Meyer's direction, then turned his back and aimed the slingshot at the ice-encrusted water.

"Janek," whispered Meyer. The boy held his position as if waiting to spot just the right target.

"Janek," Meyer repeated, "you must go to the haystack. Tell my family that I'm going to stay here and I want Manya to join me. Tell them it's all right for Chaim and Toba to come too."

Janek let the sling loose and watched the stone skip across the creek's surface. He nodded very faintly as he placed another pebble into the sling and took aim again, panning the opposite bank.

"Janek," Meyer continued, "tell my father that the rest of them wouldn't be safe here. They should go to Mislavitch. Let him know we'll be fine and that I'll get word to him somehow. Tell him"—he paused, swallowing hard—"tell them all, I love them."

Janek lowered his hands and waited to hear more. When Meyer said nothing, the boy raised the slingshot again and fired the stone skyward, following its trajectory and finally hearing the crunch of its landing on dried leaves. He tapped the slingshot against the palm of his hand, and put out a foot to test the water's icy edge. Then, he trotted away, alternating his feet between the bank and the ice.

Moments later Janek was cavorting through the bare trees, kicking leaves and swinging around tree trunks, but moving efficiently toward his destination. Soon he was in the fields running full blast, angling his outstretched arms like the wings of a plane. Once in a while he pirouetted, bending his arms to aim imaginary guns at make-believe cities; then, mission completed, he'd be off again. He playfully circled the haystack twice before collapsing against it and sliding down to sit on the ground. The entrance was to his left. He looked all around him, decided it was safe, and yanked the bale of hay outward. In seconds he had fit his small frame into the tunnel and replaced the door.

Holding their breaths, the inhabitants of the haystack strained to see the figure entering their refuge.

"Mr. Korenblit, I have news from Meyer," Janek began, and then transmitted Meyer's message. Avrum gave the boy some water and thanked him. Janek's eyes shone with excitement and pride in carrying out his mission. "So you understand, then? Manya and Chaim and Toba should sneak into town. Meyer will be waiting for them."

"I understand, Janek. They will go in a few hours. But be quick, my boy, you must be on your way. We don't want your father to be concerned."

"Do you have any message to send back?" asked Janek, crawling toward the tunnel.

"No, I think Meyer will know that they will come. There's no sense in your taking any more risks today. Thank you again, Janek. You are a very brave young man."

The boy smiled and scooted out.

"Maybe we could go right now," said Manya. "It sounds like it's safe."

"Well, yes," said Avrum, "but the rest of us can't go yet. We'll have to wait until dark. Maybe you should too."

"I really want to go now. It could be *more* dangerous to go into town after dark. There might be more guards around then. Toba, Chaim, what do you think?"

"I think Avrum is right, Manya," said Chaim. "We should wait until it's dark. And I don't think you and Toba should go yet. Let me go first. I'll make sure it's absolutely safe for you to come."

"But Meyer has already said it's safe," she protested.

"Just one more day, Manya. Please stay here until I check."

Manya reached out and gently took his face in her hands. "All right, Chaim, you go first."

The hours passed slowly for Manya, as there was no sleep for her that night. She could only think about Chaim. She was responsible for her little brother. Her parents had expected her to take care of him, to watch out for him. Why had she let him go alone? If they'd gone together, they'd all be safe in the ghetto now.

Manya looked across the haystack. Malka was cradling Toba for as long as possible, expecting that she wouldn't see her eldest daughter again for a long time.

Manya had promised Chaim she'd wait until he sent word for her and Toba to come, but she finally decided she couldn't wait any longer. Four days had passed since Meyer had left. She had to see him to make sure he was safe.

She drew a deep breath. "I think Toba and I should leave now."

Startled by Manya's announcement, everyone sat up.

"But we haven't heard from Chaim yet," responded Avrum.

"I know. But we don't have any idea what's happening. What if the Germans decide not to let anyone else into the ghetto? Then I couldn't be with Meyer or Chaim."

Avrum knew it was useless to argue with Manya if she was determined to leave. He nodded his head.

Toba hugged her mother; then the others moved to envelop her in their arms. Manya winced as she replayed her own departure from her mother in her mind.

Then, the two girls were scrambling through the tunnel. Very soon, they were out. They stood up on shaking legs and gazed toward the tree-rimmed city that was their destination. It was beautiful. They moved haltingly into the fields a few hundred yards.

Suddenly Manya saw the army jeep. It was about half a mile from them.

"My God! It's the SS! Run!" she shrieked, grabbing Toba's hand. "This way!"

They streaked across the field, not quite sure where they were going. Manya scanned the horizon for anything that could hide them—anything! Then she saw Josef's barn. She dragged Toba along in its direction.

Heaving one of the barn doors open, Manya pulled Toba

inside and yanked the door shut. After shoving Toba up the ladder to the loft, she scaled it herself, threw it to the ground, and dived to the bottom of the hay.

She tried to listen, but all she could hear was her heart and the rasp of her breathing. Oh, Meyer, she thought, I may not make it now, but always know that I love you. She could hear the engine coming closer and closer. It stopped just outside the barn.

The girls held their breath lest they set a single blade of hay in motion.

"Raus!" came the bellowing from below. "Kommt raus!"

Manya heard slamming and banging as the barn door was opened and the stalls were searched. Then the ladder struck the edge of the loft. She couldn't feel her heart beating. She heard the grunts of a heavy man climbing the ladder. Hay flew everywhere as the soldier continued to demand that they give themselves up.

Suddenly, there was a thud just beside her head. She saw the prongs of a pitchfork cut through the straw, again and again. She lay there waiting for the tool to pierce her chest and hoped she would die immediately. I love you, Meyer, she whispered, I love you forever.

Then it stopped.

She heard steps again on the ladder, but going down this time. Then a couple of laughs as the soldiers made departing sounds. The engine outside coughed to life and carried the soldiers away. Am I alive? thought Manya. I'm alive! she answered herself. Don't be too quick to come out, she thought; they might be hiding down below. It could be a trick.

She lay very still and drew a long breath, holding it to listen some more, then slowly exhaled. After a while, she felt around her under the hay. Fear struck again. Oh, God! The pitchfork! What if Toba . . . ? How could she tell Meyer?

In a moment, though, she felt something brush against her shoulder and saw Toba's hand reaching out to her.

"Toba!" Manya whispered. "Are you all right? Are you hurt?"

Meyer's sister choked back a sob and dug her fingers into Manya's shoulder. "I think I'm all right," she said. "I think so."

They gradually extricated themselves from the hay and peeked over the edge of the loft, surveying the barn. Everything looked normal. Very carefully they descended the ladder.

"What now?" whispered Toba. "Can we please go back to the haystack? I don't want to go to the ghetto. I want to be with my mother and father. I want to stay with them."

"I understand, but we can't go now, Toba. We have to wait until it's dark."

Manya was silent for a moment, then expressed her thoughts out loud. "We'll have to ask Josef to hide us. I hate to do it, but we have no choice."

The girls cracked the barn door and peered outside. It was only a few hundred feet to the door of Josef's house. Somehow they both knew to cross the yard casually. If they were seen, they hoped to be mistaken for the two Wisniewski women. At the door, they didn't knock, but quickly tripped the latch and slipped inside. Josef jumped when he saw them. Manya conveyed her apology with her eyes. Josef must have seen the Germans search the barn, for he said nothing but hurried them into a back room.

"Just until it gets dark," promised Manya as Josef returned to his mother and sister, closing the door behind him.

The girls heard a steady hum of voices coming from the kitchen, then an emphatic "We can't!"

A few minutes later Josef tapped on the door and entered. "I'm sorry, really sorry," he said in a low voice, "but you can't stay in the house. My mother thinks it's too dangerous. Those Germans could come back. I'm so sorry."

He started to leave, then seeing the stunned expressions on their faces, leaned close to them and added in a whisper, "If you want to hide in the barn, it's all right."

The girls nodded and filed silently down the hall and out the front door, then slipped across the yard and into the barn. An hour or so later, Josef opened the barn door and slid a tray of food and water to them without saying a word. After eating and drinking, they began to shiver with the cold and snuggled together for warmth.

It seemed to take forever for the sun to set and night to

descend, and they waited at least another hour before leaving the barn and entering the fields.

"I'll go with you to the haystack, Toba, just to make sure you get there all right," offered Manya.

"You don't have to, Manya. I'll be fine. You'd better go on into town. Meyer and Chaim will be waiting for you."

"But I'm responsible for you," Manya protested.

"I'll be fine. Really, it's all right. Go on," Toba insisted, turning Manya in the other direction. "Meyer's waiting."

They hugged like sisters, then separated. Toba waved, and Manya blew a kiss. I wish she would come with me, Manya thought, but I know what it's like to want your mother and father.

She took a deep breath and gazed at the silhouette of the city. Yes, Meyer was waiting, and maybe, just maybe, he'd know something about her parents. She had to go.

Like a sentry, Meyer had patrolled the edge of town closest to Josef's farm night after night, but each night he was disappointed. What was going on? Where were they? He wasn't cut out for all this waiting. Maybe tonight, he thought, or tomorrow—yes, tomorrow at the latest. Then he heard footfalls. He peered into the darkness. The skirt told him it was a female stumbling across the hard ground. He'd make his move if only he could get a glimpse of the girl's face. He cursed the absent moon. There! Wait—no, not yet—maybe—oh, yes, he was sure: it was Manya!

He stepped out of the shadows and swept her off her feet. They hugged and kissed and moaned their whispers of relief and love. Still arm in arm, Meyer guided her through the dark streets and into a small house. He led her down the hallway and into a bedroom, where they collapsed on the bed. They held each other fiercely, then Meyer drew back.

"Someday, Manya, we'll have our own home and family," he whispered. "Ani, l'dodi," he chanted softly.

"V'dodi, li," Manya cried.

With this simple Hebrew verse—I am my beloved's, and my beloved is mine—they vowed their devotion. It was the best they could do for now.

CHAPTER FIVE

"The neighborhood"

"Ghetto" is an Italian word, first used in the Middle Ages to refer to a special section of towns in Italy where Jews were confined. Within the ghetto, Jews generally exercised control over their own affairs, but outside it they were severely restricted. Ghettos were abolished in Western Europe by the nineteenth century, but were reintroduced by the Nazis in the countries they occupied. Concentrating the Jews into small confined spaces allowed their captors to control virtually every aspect of their physical existence, from food rationing to work assignments to the tedious counts, usually twice per day, of those inside.

Jews called the work camp in the old Hrubieszow ghetto by its Polish name "Dzielnica" ("the neighborhood"). In it, Jewish youth of the area, numbering 160 at its peak, were allowed to live in exchange for the harsh labor they performed. These youth, however, were not only physically strong; they were resilient— and inventive.

Manya squeezed her eyes shut against the early morning sunlight. Where was she? She rolled over on her side and bumped into someone lying next to her. Meyer. Of course. She was no longer in the haystack; she was in the ghetto work camp.

They were relatively safe here, or so Meyer had said, because the Germans needed them to work. She'd been out of the haystack for less than twenty-four hours, yet already she felt more free. She had slept in a bed and could roll over and stretch out without worrying that she would disturb someone. She hadn't slept so well in a long time.

Meyer stirred next to her. She opened her eyes to watch him, recalling their reunion the night before. Her mind had been racing as she reached the ghetto area. She hadn't known when or where or how she would rendezvous with Meyer. She could still feel the uncertainty. Which way should she go? Then a familiar voice was breathing into her ear, brawny arms were lifting her off her feet. It was Meyer; he knew what to do.

They spoke well into the night in that little bedroom. First came Meyer's queries: "Is everyone all right? Have you been getting the food okay? Where's Toba? Have my parents gone to Mislavitch? Where's Chaim?" This last made her eyes fill with tears. Seeing her reaction, Meyer had held her close again, offering reassurance that Chaim would join them soon.

"Tell me," he had pleaded, and she had done her best to fill in the days he had missed with his family. Yes, they had gotten the food. Toba had gone back to her parents. They were fine and about to leave for Mislavitch. Chaim, had insisted on leaving the haystack first to make sure the ghetto camp was safe, and she had not seen him since. Then she had described the scene in Josef's barn, her voice shaking with the memory of coming so close to being stabbed by the pitchfork.

Manya's thoughts were interrupted by the sudden aroma of something in the air that she hadn't smelled for a long time. Coffee! Meyer had explained last night that they were given rations. While they weren't going to get fat on what they received, he'd said, they wouldn't starve either. And there were ways of getting extra food.

Manya heard sounds coming from elsewhere in the house and lifted her head to listen.

"Shh," said a sleepy Meyer, pulling her closer. "It's all right. It's only Sam leaving."

"Sam?"

"He shares this house with us. Lie down, Manya, just two more minutes."

She lay back contentedly. Maybe today we'll find out something about my family and Chaim, she thought. Maybe I can get to my house somehow. Meyer had had to admit to her that he hadn't been able to go there to check on them.

She felt a warm kiss on her shoulder and a firm pat on her backside as Meyer rolled out of bed.

"Up, Manya, get up," he urged. "You have to report to the office, and I have to go to work. They'll give you a work assignment in a day or two, but after you check in this morning, you'll probably just stay in the ghetto today."

"So everyone just goes to work each day? That's it?" she asked.

"Well, no. First we all go down to be counted. Then we go to work," he explained.

"Why do they count us? Should I be counted too?"

"Not until after you've registered with the head of the camp. The Germans want to keep track of us, so they count in the morning and again when we come back at night."

"How many Jews are here? Anyone we know?" she asked.

"About forty-five or fifty, but there are a few more every day. Some we know; some we don't. Sam is from a little town—I can't remember the name—it's not far away."

"But what do we do at work?"

"Oh, different things. I dug vegetables one day, but most of the time we've helped clear out houses, move furniture—you know, empty everything out. They're shipping the furniture to Germany, every bit of it," he said sadly.

"Doesn't it make you feel terrible to take those things away? Meyer, we knew many of the people who lived in those houses, who sat on that furniture!"

"The first day, it made me sick, really sick. But a fellow working with me said I'd better get over it. I realized he was right. You can't think about it; you just do it," Meyer said soberly. He sat silently on the edge of the bed, then pulled on his boots.

"They'll be lining up soon," he announced, giving her a kiss. "I'm so glad you're here, Manya. Come, let's eat breakfast, then I must go."

All too quickly for Manya, they finished eating and were standing at the door. "Remember, wait about half an hour and then go to the office. They'll take care of you."

"Would they know something about my family?" Manya asked hesitantly.

"Ask them. Things change every day; they could have information today that they didn't have yesterday. Just promise me that you won't do anything foolish like trying to go to your house. If Silberstein has any news about them, we'll talk about it when I return tonight." Meyer could sense Manya's uneasiness. "Just be patient and take no risks. I want you here when I get back. Promise?" He was relieved when she nodded soberly.

After Meyer left, Manya went to the work camp's office. When she was not given a work order for that day, she returned to their little house and walked through the rooms straightening the beds and pulling back the window coverings. The sunlight perked up the shabby rooms but cold air blew through the window frames and she knew she'd have to replace the blanket curtains before sunset. She washed their cups from breakfast, checked over the food supplies, and decided to make noodles for the evening meal.

She looked out the window, seeing a figure here and there but no one she knew. She was surprised by how quiet it was but guessed that most of the people were out working. For hours she delighted in staring into the bright street and feeling the sun's warmth on her face. She could see a grove of trees from the back window and knew that to the right, beyond it, lay the fields and the route to the haystack. Was Meyer's family still there? And where was Chaim?

That evening, Meyer and Sam came bounding through the door together. Meyer had stopped off at central provisions for some beets and carrots. Sam had somehow come into possession of a scrawny chicken and handed it to her, saying, "Here's something special. Tonight we celebrate your arrival!"

Manya was so touched by Sam's thoughtfulness and their spirited homecoming that she was infected with their enthusiasm. She plopped the bony bird into a pot and stewed it, adding the delicate noodles toward the end. After devouring the tasty meal, they lingered over the empty plates, talking. Meyer brought out the dominoes they'd found in the house, and they laughed as they clacked the spotted tiles on the table and Manya drew one after another, unsuccessful at matching. Time stopped for them that evening; like children, they made a game of everything and giggled at each other's laughter. They were exhausted when they blew out the candles—all together, one, two, three—and started to bed.

Suddenly, there was a tapping at the door. They froze. Who could it be at this hour? No one from the ghetto was allowed out after curfew.

Meyer tiptoed to the door. "Who's there?" he whispered.

"It's Chaim," came the response.

Meyer fumbled at the door latch, unable to open it quickly enough. One second he was alone at the door, and the next instant Manya was pushing him away, reaching eagerly for her little brother.

"Oh, Chaim, you're safe. I was so worried. Where were you?"

"Take it easy, Manya. Let the poor boy breathe," said Meyer, hugging her brother himself. Even Sam joined the happy trio, relighting the candles before going to get Chaim a glass of water.

"Please. Tell me what happened to you," Manya begged.

Chaim explained that he had hidden throughout the night

he'd left and most of the next day. "I wanted to see what was going on in the ghetto, what people were doing, what the Gestapo were doing. After I was sure it was safe, I came out. I was going to report to the office like Janek told us, but on the way I ran into Damone."

"Damone!" exclaimed Manya. "He was one of the Gestapo who beat up Daddy all the time."

Chaim nodded. "I was hoping he wouldn't remember me from the times I went to work with Daddy, but he recognized me at once so I just walked up to him. He looked sharply at me and said, 'So, you are still here!' I nodded and said I heard there was work to be done. He told me there were jobs if I was willing to work hard and that I should report to the office in the ghetto. By the time I did that, everyone else had gone to work. I was assigned to a house and told to report for work the next morning. I was trying to figure out how I could get word back to you and Toba, so I asked if Meyer had registered. They told me he had and where he lived. I assumed that you were at work all day, Meyer, so I waited till now to come."

"Oh, Chaim. I'm so glad you're safe," Manya said, wiping happy tears from her eyes. "To think you were nearby all day and I didn't know it."

Chaim looked around the room. "Where's Toba?"

"She went back to the haystack to be with her parents," Manya answered. There was an awkward silence as Manya and Chaim thought of their own parents.

Manya forced herself to put sad thoughts out of her mind and focus on her brother. "Chaim, do you think you could eat something?"

"Maybe a slice of bread, if you have some."

"I've got something better than that," she said, running to the kitchen. For an hour they talked, rekindling their earlier gaiety, while Chaim ate the leftovers from their dinner. It was only when they noticed that Chaim was struggling to stay awake that they ushered him to bed and collapsed themselves.

The next day Manya was sent to the fields to dig vegetables. Unaccustomed to so much exercise, she was weary and sore when she returned to the ghetto that night. But as she walked home, the thought of both Chaim and Meyer waiting there eased her fatigue.

Manya had been in the ghetto camp for four days. At the morning count, she stood in line next to Meyer, holding his hand.

"Sixty-two, sixty-three, sixty-four. . . ."

The first day she had had to leave Meyer to go to work had been difficult. She had hoped that they would be assigned to the same work detail, but each day she had been sent to one area of town and Meyer to another. As for the people in the camp, some of the faces were familiar but most weren't. She was happy to see two former classmates, Tovah and Molly. It was comforting to know that at least a few more people from Hrubieszow had survived the deportations.

The last number was counted. Everyone was there. Manya squeezed Meyer's hand and released it as the group broke up and headed for various destinations. She said goodbye to Chaim and joined her group going into the city.

When she walked into the first house and saw clothes, furniture, and dishes all over the floor, she just stood and stared. It looked the same as her house had the first time the SS had barged in. She wanted to turn and run, but Meyer's words came back to her: "You have to get used to it. That's why we're here. If we weren't working, they'd send us off or kill us." He was right. It was essential to do as you were told in order to survive.

It was nearly lunchtime when Manya came out of the house, her arms laden with clothes. She tossed her bundle onto the pile and looked up. Her heart stopped for a moment, then started beating twice as fast. There, strutting down the sidewalk toward her, was Wagner. At times, when her father had worked at Gestapo headquarters, this man had given him extra food and told him he would take care of him. Other times, Wagner had beaten her father so badly he could hardly walk home. She had also seen him beat other Jews in the street for no reason. Yet she couldn't help but remember what Wagner had done once to save her family.

She could still feel the terror that night of being ordered out into the street with her mother, brothers, and sisters. Hundreds of people had been pushed this way and that, and finally herded to the jail and crammed into a small basement room. Manya and her mother, Mincha, clung to the little ones, pushing others out of the way in an effort to stay together.

Into this room that normally held twenty-five people, the Nazis had crammed more than a hundred. There was nowhere to move, no space even to turn around. The heat became unbearable. Manya could smell the sweat in the room and felt the moisture running down her own body. People around her were crying. Others shoved each other trying to reach a little window at the back of the cell, covered with metal bars and glass, hoping to look out for what might be the last time.

For hours, they huddled together until suddenly the door to the cell opened and the guard called out, miraculously, "Nagelsztajn! Nagelsztajn!" Numb with fear, Mincha hesitated, weighing the situation, then turned to the door, drew her children closer, and motioned for Manya to bring up the rear. They stumbled through the maze of people, at times forcing their way past and trying to ignore others' murmured protests. Reaching the door, Mincha exited past the impatient guard, followed by the younger children, but just as Manya was about to step through, the door slammed shut.

"No!" she screamed, pounding her fists against the door. "Wait! I belong with them! Mama! Mama! Help me!"

No rescue came. She slouched limply against the wall.

It was twenty-four hours before she heard the bolt slide, the door open again, and her name called. The throng surged forward, blocking her path and complaining noisily. Manya fought her way through them, waving her arms and trying to call out. When she stood before the guard at last, he shoved her out and rebolted the door. Manya followed him down the hall and up the stairs, then stood trembling before him. He pointed to the exit. "Go on," he spat, "you're free to go."

Very slowly Manya moved toward the door, expecting the guard to call her back any second. Touching the door latch, she hunched over, prepared to receive the bullet she felt certain would cut short her escape. But there was no sound, no threat from behind, and in an instant she was outside.

Her knees buckled as she stepped off the wooden sidewalk onto the street. But then her mother was at her side, hugging her and crying. Some hours later they explained that when her father had heard they'd been taken, he'd gone to Wagner and begged him to get them released. Wagner had done so, but somehow Manya had been left behind. Her father had gone to Wagner again to plead. No one could understand why this man who so easily performed countless acts of brutality could also show mercy. But he did.

Now, as Manya stared down the street at Wagner, she wondered if he would remember her. Would he know where her family was? Should she risk talking to him? His cold eyes and aloof manner frightened her, yet she felt oddly sentimental toward him. She had to speak, she decided, moving closer. She stopped in front of him. His steely eyes met hers.

"Good day, Herr Wagner," she began. Wagner ignored her greeting, his face blank.

"I don't know if you remember me, sir," Manya continued. "My father used to work for you. Shlomo Nagelsztajn is his name. I . . ." She stopped when she saw the beginning of a smile—or was it a leer?

Then he spoke, and his face became friendly, his eyes almost kind. "Of course I remember," he said. "You were the one left behind in the jail that time, yes?"

She nodded. "You were responsible for getting me out."

He nodded, showing no emotion.

Manya hesitated. Maybe she should save her questions for another time. She didn't want to make him angry.

"Herr Wagner," she went on, in spite of herself, "I haven't seen my family for a long time. Do you know where they are? If they are all right?"

His expression cooled, then softened again. "They're in a good place, young lady," he said. "We have sent them to a good place to work. Don't worry about them."

"It's just that no one has seen them or knows anything," she stammered. "Will I see them again soon?"

"I told you they're in a good place," he said, the ice returning to his eyes. "You'd better take care of yourself and not worry about them."

Manya wanted to ask where this place was, how long they'd been there, when they'd be back. But Wagner's face told her he would say no more. She forced herself to smile and nod gratefully as he turned his back and strode away.

She could hardly wait for the work day to end so she could rush home and tell Chaim and Meyer that her family were alive. That news would help Chaim; he had continued to feel guilty about leaving them. Now he would know they were all right, that he'd made the right decision. She kept reminding Chaim of the last words their mother had said the night they parted: "If we are separated, maybe one of us will survive."

After Manya's group returned to the ghetto and was counted, she ran to the house and burst through the door yelling, "Meyer! Chaim!"

"What is it?" asked Meyer, coming from the kitchen with Chaim to meet her.

"Mama and Daddy are alive! Everybody is still alive! I found out today. They were taken to a place to work. They're safe."

Chaim's body, which for so long had sagged, came to life. A glimmer came to his eyes, and he managed a small smile.

Manya grabbed him and hugged with all her might. "You see, Chaim, we're alive and the rest of the family is alive. We may even be able to see them."

"How do you know all this?" asked Meyer.

"I found out from Wagner."

"Wagner!" Meyer repeated incredulously. "Did he just come walking up to you?"

"Of course not," answered Manya. "I went up to him."

Meyer stared at her in disbelief. "Are you crazy? It's not good to draw attention to yourself that way."

"But my father used to work for him."

"Yes, and Wagner beat him!"

"But Wagner also saved our lives one time."

"I'm not forgetting that. But that man is a beast and you shouldn't trust him. Besides, he's unpredictable. Instead of talking to you, he might have . . . well, you know."

Manya nodded soberly and continued to hug Chaim. In spite of his hesitation, a small thrill of relief rushed through Meyer's body. Yesterday Janek Salki had told him that the food left outside the haystack the previous night had not been picked up. That must mean his family had escaped to Mislavitch. Now Manya had heard news about her family. Both the Korenblits and the Nagelsztajns must still be alive.

M anya had just finished cleaning the dinner dishes one night when Meyer called everyone together. "We've been here for two weeks now. I think it's time to make plans."

"What do you mean—make plans?" asked Manya.

"There's still a lot of work to be done here in Hrubieszow. But what happens when the work is finished? Do you think the Nazis are just going to leave us here in peace? No, they'll send us to work elsewhere or something worse."

Meyer looked around the small circle. The only movement came from the newest member of the household, Leon, who fidgeted in his chair. He'd been brought to the ghetto by the SS a few days earlier.

"Do you have something in mind?" asked Sam.

"Yes, I do. We've all been taking small things from the houses we've worked in to trade for extra food. What if we took a little bit more and stored it here in the house?"

"But what good would that do?" asked Leon.

"When the time comes, we can trade it for money, papers, passports, whatever we can get. We'll find someone to sell things to. Then we'll use the money and papers to get to a neutral country, like Switzerland."

"Do you really think we could make it?" asked Leon.

"It's worth a try," Sam quickly responded. "Anything is better than just waiting. Besides, Meyer is right: the Germans aren't going to leave us here when we're finished with this work. I think it's a good idea, Meyer."

"What if the Gestapo come and search the house?" asked Manya.

"They would kill us for taking as little as we have already. We'll just have to be very careful. If anyone seems suspicious, don't take anything. We have plenty of time. They aren't going to move us out tomorrow or the next day."

Meyer felt better after they'd agreed to this plan. They weren't going to sit around and wait for the day the Germans would send them away. They had a plan for the future.

For the next two weeks they brought various items back to the house. While they hadn't amassed much yet, Meyer could see a problem coming if they didn't find someone to take the goods. As he and Manya walked to the morning count, he thought about John Salki. His son Janek was still coming to the ghetto, at great risk, to check on them. Maybe Meyer could give the boy some things to take back to his father. Even if Salki couldn't get rid of the materials, perhaps he could store them temporarily.

Meyer was still thinking when he heard his name called. It was an acquaintance, Isaac Hipps, who had been assigned to dispense work orders today. Isaac called some more names, told them to stay behind, then dismissed the rest of the group to go to their designated work. Meyer watched the group break up and go in various directions. With nearly 150 people now in the ghetto camp, hardly a day went by without a new face popping up in line for the count.

"You twelve will be going to work at the fort," Isaac informed the group he'd pulled aside.

"Do you know how long we'll be there or what kind of work we'll be doing?" asked one of the young men.

"I'm not sure. All they said was to send twelve men to the fort today. You'll probably be cleaning up there. And no one will be going with you, but you all know what will happen if the same number doesn't come back. They know how many are expected."

The twelve young men started walking. Meyer had seen the

others before, but most were not from Hrubieszow. It was a long walk to the fort, and they were in no hurry to get there. The longer it took, the less time they'd have to work, since they would still have to be back for the evening count. There was very little talking as they left the ghetto and walked into the Polish section of town.

Walking through the city brought back memories to Meyer. So many times he had played in the street, with Chaim tagging along, being yelled at for making too much noise or messing up someone's flowerbed.

They came to the main street of the city. There, in the fork, sat the cannon still pointing straight down the brick avenue that led into town. This was the weapon that was to stop invaders who would harm the people of Hrubieszow.

Meyer remembered the first day of the war, when hundreds, maybe thousands, of Poles of all ages—Jews and non-Jews— had marched to the cannon, vowing to fight the Nazis to the very end. People had put aside their differences and stood there proudly, together. They had marched to the fort singing the national anthem.

Now the road was empty except for twelve Jewish workers. The once-menacing cannon looked small and tame, having never fired a shot. And some of those same Poles who pledged to kill the Nazis had helped to murder the very people with whom they had marched so short a time ago.

The group of young men was nearing the fort when they noticed a woman outside her house, sweeping the porch. Meyer recognized her immediately as Anna, an old friend of the Koren-blits. Her husband had been a colonel in the Polish Army. Anna glanced up, looked at Meyer, then waved and called out his name. She moved off her porch and enfolded him in a warm embrace. "Meyer, how are you? It's been so long! Where is the rest of your family? I think about them often."

"I'm fine," he responded, "but I don't know where my family is. We were separated during the last deportation."

"That's terrible," she said sympathetically. "When the Nazis rounded up the Jews and sent them away, I feared the worst. It's so good to see that you're alive."

"It's good to see you, too. How is your husband?"

Her expression darkened. "I haven't seen or heard from him since the Germans came in and the Polish Army left. It's been nearly three years."

"I'm sorry," Meyer said.

"Yes, I'm doing the best I can, but it's not easy," she replied. "But can I do anything for you? Do you need food—or clothing?"

"No, they're giving us enough. But thank you anyway," he answered. "I must go now. I've been assigned to work at the fort. I'll see you again." He turned and ran to catch up with the rest of the group.

As he entered the gate to the fort, his mind was racing. He had the seed of an idea, and Anna was the key. Maybe I can help her and she can help us, he thought.

Once inside, the twelve were met by a sergeant from the regular army. He said if they did what they were told, they'd be treated well. Then he made work assignments. Meyer would be cleaning out the horse stalls and helping care for the animals. Well, Meyer thought, he'd make the best of it and do a good job. If his idea was going to work, he'd have to keep this assignment as long as possible.

There was a great deal of work to do, since no workers had been sent to the fort before, but the day went very quickly for Meyer. He swept and shoveled, laid fresh hay, and repaired bridles. He curried the horses and polished the saddles. It was mid-afternoon before he unwrapped the bread and cheese he'd brought for lunch. He took only a few minutes to eat, then moved to the next stall, and the next, until time to go home.

Walking out of the fort and past Anna's house again, Meyer thought about the plan he'd been formulating all day. He knew it was risky, but if Anna would cooperate, it could help all of them. He would ask her in a few days. Meyer couldn't wait to tell the others.

That same day, Manya walked purposefully to work with her group. For weeks she had been stripping houses bare, removing everything right down to the mezuzah beside each front door. But since Meyer had presented his plan to salvage everything they could, she had faced the grim task more calmly, even hopefully. Having a goal helped to ease her feelings of guilt as she assessed the goods in each house.

Any truly precious jewelry had been confiscated years before, but she sometimes came across silverware, fine table linens, velvet bedspreads and draperies, and an occasional piece of silk. Her winter coat helped camouflage the valuables she stuffed into a pocket or wound around herself and held secure with a makeshift belt. Although the items would bring far less than their true value, every scarf or clock or piece of porcelain was treasured, for it might bring them a bit closer to freedom.

As Manya moved along the streets with the others, she wondered what she would come across today. She hardly noticed the bakery in her old neighborhood as they passed it. But then they turned right toward the marketplace, and she saw the shoemaker's and the tailor's.

Suddenly, the group stopped. She looked up. They were in front of her family's house. A sick feeling came to the pit of her stomach.

Wait! she wanted to scream. Don't you know this is *my* house? I can't do this! But they didn't care. To the guards, it was just another house.

The faces of her co-workers swam before her eyes and she felt herself spinning and then falling. Then there were arms tight around her. She saw her mother's face, but the voice that called her name didn't sound right.

"Manya, you fainted. Manya! Are you all right?" the voice continued. "What is it? Are you ill?"

Manya tried to focus on the concerned face that peered into hers. It was Esther, a friend from the work group. "You have to snap out of it, Manya. Quick," Esther went on, rubbing Manya's hands and slapping her face. "You don't want the Germans to see you like this."

Esther pulled Manya to her feet. "Here, lean on me. That's better. We'll be inside this house in a minute; you can sit down in there until you feel better."

"No-o-o," Manya howled, covering her eyes. "I can't. It's . . . I can't!"

"What is it? What's wrong?"

"Oh, don't you see, Esther? It's *my* house," she cried, burying her face in her friend's shoulder.

"Oh, Manya. I'm so sorry. I didn't know." Esther paused. "But, Manya, you *have* to go inside, you know that. If you refuse, it's over for you. Isn't that right? Manya! Answer me!" Esther insisted, shaking her. "They'll kill you or ship you off. Think of Meyer. Do you want never to see him again? You must force yourself to pretend it's just another house, another family. Get up now, before the guards get suspicious. Move!"

Meyer. Manya wondered what he would do in her place. Do what they say, he'd told her. He would go in, and so should she. In a few hours, he would share this hurt with her and comfort her. Manya allowed herself to be propelled through the door and up the steps. She kept her eyes lowered as they climbed, for she didn't have to see to know what it would look like. It would be no different from the other homes she'd been forced to pick clean, except that here they would find no silver or velvet. In this house there was glass instead of crystal, cotton instead of silk, the rough sheets laboriously and lovingly patched, the Sabbath tablecloth long ago bartered for a sack of flour.

They reached the first landing, and Manya stopped. Esther tried to push her along, but Manya shook her head. "I . . . I have to see . . . I'll come upstairs in a minute."

"Manya—you're not going to run away, are you?"

"No. I just have to see something. It won't take long, I promise."

Checking for guards behind her, Manya ducked down the hallway off the landing. She could hear noises from the workers above. When she reached the steps, her heart pounded as if it would explode. They *could* be here, she thought. It was possible, even though Wagner had said they'd been taken away.

She crouched by the top step, trying to see below, and held her breath in an effort to catch the faintest sound. Nothing. She descended on tiptoe, keeping her back to the rough brick wall that bordered the right flank of the stairwell, remembering to avoid the creaky second step from the bottom. Pausing to listen again, she turned to her right very slowly.

There in front of her should have been the haven Shlomo had so carefully crafted, the work he was so sure would save his loved ones. But bricks that had helped to seal her family's hiding place were now strewn about the room and broken, and only a fraction of the wall her father had built remained.

"Daddy?" she whispered at the edge of the wall. "Mama?" she called, bending down to peer inside.

It was empty. The window was wide open; wooden slats that had boarded it up hung at angles where they had previously been nailed. The scene showed evidence of a hasty departure. Had it also been violent? Manya couldn't be sure. The solace she had drawn from Wagner's words disappeared.

She crawled behind the wall. With trembling fingers, she picked up a dress that lay in a heap on the floor. It was hers. She clutched it to her.

By the bit of light piercing the musty darkness through the broken window, she saw a broken cup. A comb. Then, a small nightgown. A man's shirt. She felt her head spin.

"Oh, Mama," she whispered, "I pray you are all alive. I want to believe Wagner, but sitting here in this house, this room that was to keep us safe and together, makes me wonder if he told the truth." She gathered the bits of clothing, stroking her cheek with the shirt, nuzzling the nightgown, tracing the teeth of the comb with her fingers. Tears ran down her face and dropped on the dress in her lap.

"Whatever happens, wherever you are, know that I love you," she addressed her family. "I miss you, I miss you so much. God, please watch over them, wherever they may be."

Manya stuffed the old dress down the front of her coat, then raised her fists to her head. "Oh, God, I wish we weren't Jews!"

CHAPTER SIX

Best-laid plans

On January 14, 1943, British Prime Minister Winston Churchill and U.S. President Franklin Roosevelt met to plan an Allied invasion to free Europe from German domination. On the Eastern Front of the war, in Russia, the German armies were surrounded by Soviet forces and generally in disarray. For the Nazis, these military pressures made the expeditious deportation and killing of Jews even more urgent, and on January 20, SS head Heinrich Himmler made a special request for more trains to speed "the removal of Jews" from the German General Government, which included Poland.

There is no evidence that the five inhabitants of the house in the Hrubieszow ghetto knew of any of these developments which would eventually have important consequences for them. As far as they knew, their hopes for survival were dependent on their own devices—and the help of a few cherished friends.

Meyer ran down the deadend street to their house in the ghetto. Seeing Anna that morning had been a stroke of luck. He couldn't wait to tell Manya and the rest that their dream of escape could quite possibly be within reach now.

He bounded up the steps and charged through the door.

"Manya!" he called when he didn't see her. "Manya, come here. I have exciting news! Where are you?" He looked in the kitchen, then peeked out the little window toward the outhouse. Its door was standing open, so she wasn't in there. He went back into the main room. Then he saw the dress, flung over the back of a chair. He reached out and fingered the softness of the faded fabric.

This was Manya's dress. He had seen it many times, but not recently. How had it gotten here? He knew Chaim was working on a cleanup detail; perhaps he or Leon or Sam had found it. But as fast as these possibilities came to mind, they couldn't silence what he feared to be true. His previous excitement turned to rage. He touched the dress again as if his precious Manya herself were inside it, and then moved toward the bedroom.

Manya lay curled up on the bed. Her cheeks were wet and her eyes swollen. When she opened them, Meyer saw a dull glazed look. He'd seen that expression on other faces but never before on hers, and it frightened him.

Bending down, he cradled her face with his hands, then wrapped his arms around her protectively, as he felt the tremor of her sobs. He rocked her tenderly while she tried to choke out words, murmuring, "I know, I know," over and over.

"It'll be all right," he whispered, "I'll make it all right."

He stroked her hair and kept rocking. "We'll get out of here and somehow we'll find your mother and father. We'll do it, Manya; I know we will. And do you know why?" he asked. After a moment, he felt her shake her head. She was coming back to him.

"I'll tell you why, my darling," he said. "Because we are strong and we love each other. Isn't that right?"

He felt her nod.

"Yes, I thought so," he went on, then squeezed her very tight. "And I'll tell you something else, Manya Nagelsztajn. We're going to have a big wedding one day like no one ever saw before in Hrubieszow. And both of our families will be there. We're going to have a big house with electricity and faucets, even a bathroom inside. And babies, we're going to have lots of babies. You'll like that, yes?" he asked, drawing away to look at her. He nodded when he saw her tearful smile, and hugged her some more.

Suddenly, they heard an excited voice from the other room.

"Meyer, Manya, look what I have!" yelled Sam. Getting no response, he came bursting into their room. "Oh, I'm sorry," he said when he saw Meyer holding Manya in his arms. "I didn't mean to interrupt."

"No, it's all right, Sam. We were just coming out."

"Is something the matter, Meyer? Can I help?"

"Manya was upset about something she saw today," Meyer answered. "She's better now."

As Meyer and Manya emerged from their room, holding hands, the outside door opened, and Chaim and Leon walked in.

"What's the matter, Manya?" Chaim asked immediately.

Manya let go of Meyer, grabbed her little brother, and squeezed him very tightly, whispering in his ear, "I love you so much, Chaim."

He hugged her back, waiting for her words as she pulled back and looked at him intently.

"I was in our house today, Chaim."

She could feel him stiffen, but he didn't say a word. He just held on to her, not wanting to answer. Finally in a choked voice he responded. "I already know, Manya. I've been there."

She stared into his eyes. "When?"

"The first night I came here," he said softly.

"Oh, Chaim, no! Why didn't you tell me . . . !" she began, but stopped when she read the message in his eyes: he had wanted to shield her from this hurt. She hugged him again. "I love you," she whispered again.

Meyer saw Sam and Leon shift awkwardly. He placed an arm around brother and sister and tenderly drew them apart. "Let's see what Sam brought," he said encouragingly. "Then I have some news."

Sam picked up a small bundle—something he had hidden in a dirty brown rag. When he unwrapped the cloth, he was holding a fine china bowl.

"Where did you get that?" asked Leon, admiring the piece.

"Someone had hidden it under a loose floorboard in one of the houses I was in today. We should be able to get a good price for it, once we find someone to buy it."

"It's beautiful, Sam," Meyer agreed. "And that's what my news is about. I may have found someone who'll help us."

"You have? Who is it?" asked Leon.

"An old friend of my family. Her name is Anna."

"Are you sure you can trust this woman?"

"I really think so. She and her husband were good friends of my family. When I saw her today, she seemed very pleased to see me and asked about my parents."

"What are the details? When do we start taking things to her?"

"Not so fast, Leon. I haven't even asked her yet."

"But shouldn't you have asked her when you were talking with her? How can you be sure you'll see her again?"

"I'll see her, don't worry. Just leave it to me."

"I don't see why she would risk doing this. I understand she's a friend, but this is very dangerous," said Sam.

"I think she'll agree," explained Meyer, "because I'm going to make her a proposition that will help her as well. Her husband was in the army and she's alone, so I think she would welcome some extra money. I'll offer her half of what she collects from selling what we take her."

"Do you really think she'll do it, Meyer?" Manya asked.

"I believe she will. She was so happy to see me. She offered me food, clothes, whatever I needed. She wants to help. All I have to do is tell her how. I'm sure she'll agree."

The cleanup crews worked on Manya's family's street for nearly a week, until every house there was empty. Consequently, she was surprised when they were led back on Saturday to the three-story brick building that had been her home. But when she saw it this time, she gasped. The roof was gone, and half of the top floor. A rickety scaffolding hugged one side, some ladders were propped against the front, and there were piles of baskets and coils of rope all around.

Hammers and chisels were distributed to the men in the group, and they were directed to climb the ladders and scaffolding. As they ascended, each one pulled up a length of rope and secured one end, letting the other trail to the ground. The women were then called forward and handed baskets.

"You are going to tear down this house," the officer began. "The men will crack the mortar, load the loosened bricks into the baskets, and lower them to the women. Each of you women will untie a basket and fasten an empty one to the rope. Then you'll take the bricks from the basket and stack them in that truck. You will not throw them. When that truck is full, another will arrive. Get to work!"

Manya couldn't believe her eyes. This fine brick building had been here for more than a hundred years. Her mother's family had lived here all that time. Why should it be knocked down? Oh, Meyer, if you could only see what they are doing. I can't help them erase the last trace of my family's existence.

Yes, you can, she knew Meyer would say. Yes, you can. Say it, Manya: Yes, I can. Say it! his voice in her mind insisted.

"Yes, I can. Yes, I can," she stammered out loud.

She heard a man shout something from above and looked up. He shook the loose rope impatiently. Manya caught the swinging line, then fumbled with its ragged end. Her numb fingers finally tied the cord securely to the basket handles.

Up it went like an autumn leaf floating on an updraft. A moment later it descended, filled with bricks and swaying to and fro. She steadied it with her arms and guided it to the ground. Untying the knot, she fastened the line to another straw container.

There were fifteen or twenty bricks in the first basket, which she tugged and pushed toward the trucks. She had moved it only half the distance when she saw the second basketful descending from its rope. Beads of sweat trickled down her chest; needles of panic shot up her back. She'd have to work faster.

I don't understand why this must be done, she thought. But I'll do it. I'll do it to stay alive and be with Meyer.

She stooped over, picked up the basket, and staggered to the ramp at the rear of the vehicle. Pitching her body forward for leverage, she dragged the bricks onto the bed of the truck.

One by one she stacked them in a neat pile, alternating the rows as she had seen her father, the bricklayer, do so many times before.

As Meyer finished up his chores at the fort and put away his tools, he thought about his visit to Anna's house that morning. When his work group left the ghetto, he had explained to the other men that he had to make a stop on the way. They had seen Anna and Meyer talking a few days ago, so they asked if that was where he was going. Meyer told them that Anna thought he might hear news at the fort about her husband.

Meyer explained that he'd promised Anna he would find out what he could and stop at her house every other day or so to report. He hated to mislead them, but he knew he couldn't divulge the arrangements for transferring the smuggled goods. When he had approached her with the plan, she had jumped at it. "I'll do anything I can to help you," she said. "Your family was always very kind to me and my husband." She said she knew someone who would pay a good price for the items, although she didn't tell Meyer who it was and he didn't ask. The fewer people who knew the details, the safer the exchange would be.

The men in Meyer's work group agreed to take their time as

they passed Anna's house so that Meyer could run around to her back door. When they expressed surprise that he would take such a chance for her, he explained that she had been a family friend and that one day she might be able to help him. These were reasons they all could understand.

As the group approached Anna's house, they had walked very slowly and Meyer slipped away from the group. It had gone without a hitch.

Now, as Meyer aligned the brooms, shovels, and pitchforks in the stable's storage area, he was eager to get home to tell Manya and the others. On the walk back to the ghetto, his feet hardly touched the ground, but he stood patiently for the count, then ran down the street. He burst through the door yelling, "Manya, Manya!"

She came rushing from the kitchen when she heard him. She had worried all day about the delivery he was planning to make that morning.

"Is everything all right?" she asked.

"Yes, yes," he answered, "everything went perfectly." He grabbed her and spun her around, laughing.

"Wait!" she laughed. "Tell me what happened. Don't act so silly!" She giggled, giving him a hug and pulled him toward a chair. "I want to hear every word. Chaim! Sam! Leon! Come in here, quick—Meyer's home."

The three young men joined the couple in a rush, all talking at once. "So, tell us, Meyer, tell us," said Sam. "From the beginning."

"All right, all right. This morning, I explained to the other men that I had to stop at Anna's house, and they agreed to help. We got near her house, and I sneaked away to her back door. She was standing there waiting. I pulled the silverware out of my pants, handed it to her, and left. The whole thing took less than two minutes. Then, I ran around the other side of the house and caught up with the others."

"And no one saw you leave?" asked Leon.

"There was nothing to see. For all anyone knew, I ran back there to use the outhouse," Meyer exclaimed, tousling Chaim's hair.

"It's going to work!" Sam cried, dancing Leon around. "We're going to get out!"

Meyer, Manya, and Chaim latched on to the joyous pair, pounding each other on the back. It was the first occasion in a long time when they accepted the moment for what it was. No one injected words of caution; no one worried about how long it might take. They had the will to find freedom, and now they had the means.

With hope restored, the five housemates settled into a routine. They spent twelve hours each day laboring for the SS, digging, dragging, and hauling—whatever they were told to do. They resisted passively, stretching out each process to increase the likelihood they'd be needed tomorrow and the day after that. They tramped home each night, stooped with fatigue.

The next twelve hours belonged to them, and they used it as much to try to create a sense of normalcy in their lives as they did to renew their energies for the next day. In the evening they talked, reminisced, worried, made plans, exchanged rumors, or quoted news overheard from a talkative German soldier. They analyzed and examined it all, searching, picking over the often garbled bits of information, looking for truth and meaning and the effect it would have on them.

Then they played cards or dominoes and sipped glasses of tea. At some point most evenings they would select the items Meyer would carry to Anna the next day. Many times this process proved to be entertaining, although Meyer didn't always share their amusement. "This is serious," he'd remind them, and they knew it was, knew that none of them would have wanted to make the dangerous exchange in his place. But they couldn't stifle their giggles—not when he had that bowl under his shirt or when the silverware jingled in his boots.

During the past month they had had a few rather pleasant evenings. But there had been some chilling ones too, like the evening Meyer came home with a gun. He had found out that some men in the ghetto had weapons. "We're at a disadvantage by not having a gun," he had told Manya. "If something should happen to challenge us in the ghetto, we should be prepared."

She had begged him to think of the consequences if the weapon were discovered. "They'll kill us if they find it!" she had cried. "It's too dangerous." But Meyer hadn't listened and, one evening after work, produced a pistol and forty rounds of ammunition. Manya was furious and frightened, but Meyer assured her he would be extremely careful with it. "We have it just in case," he told her, "and no one outside of this house is to be told we have it. I don't plan to use it unless I have to," he promised.

"Where did you get it?" Manya finally asked.

"It's best that you don't know," Meyer replied.

And so, several times a week, Meyer would bring out the pistol from its hiding place in an old boot and instruct the others in its use. "What is the first thing you do?" he quizzed Manya.

"Undo the safety catch," she answered.

He'd nod approvingly, remove the ammunition, and go on with the lesson, making each of them practice at aiming and pulling the trigger.

The gun made Chaim feel safer, but he wouldn't touch it. He sat patiently and listened, but as the pistol was passed to him, he always motioned for Manya to take it. He couldn't seem to shake the thought of what it could do.

It was a great relief to Manya finally to be reassigned. She had gradually become accustomed to cleaning out uninhabited Jewish houses, convincing herself that the previous occupants were alive and had simply been sent away to work, like her parents. When all this was over, these people, like her family, would return safely to Hrubieszow.

But today she'd be working in the ghetto, and she was pleased. There was more independence and peace here. No one would watch every minute to make certain she was working. No one would kick her if she forgot for a moment and drifted off into her own thoughts.

Not being part of a cleanup brigade would eliminate any possibility of picking up items Meyer could take to Anna. But that was all right for a day, for they still had goods hidden under their bed awaiting delivery. Soon after Meyer had made the arrangements, some three months ago now, they had decided that going there every other day was too risky and may supply too much material for Anna to handle. They wanted to be careful not to pressure her, so they settled on a frequency of twice a week.

Meyer knew that Anna didn't sell everything he brought her. Once he went inside her house and saw, draped over her bed, a beautiful plush bedspread he had given her some days before. He couldn't help but smile to himself when he thought about the trouble he had had in getting it to her. Manya must have wound it around him four or five times, so that his coat had barely fit. And to make matters worse, it had been a warm day. Well, there wouldn't be any money coming from that ordeal. But he didn't mind; he considered it partial payment of the debt he owed Anna for helping them.

They had no idea who was buying the goods or for how much. Meyer told Anna to get what she could and hold the money for him. As weeks rolled by, Anna repeatedly offered encouragement. She told Meyer not to worry, that everything was going well, and that he was due quite a sum of money already and soon — very soon — there would be a large payment. Feeling grateful, Meyer insisted that she keep a generous share for herself.

When Meyer told his housemates at dinner one night that their goal must be almost within reach, they talked all night about how they would escape. Soon Meyer will ask Anna for the money, Manya thought that morning, as she set aside her chores and headed to her house for the lunch break. Aside from waking up each day and knowing that she was with Meyer and Chaim, escape was her only pleasant thought.

She was in the kitchen warming leftover vegetables when someone knocked at the door. It couldn't be the Gestapo; they didn't bother to knock. Then she heard a voice call out her name. "Manya! Manya Nagelsztajn! Are you in there?" The voice sounded urgent.

She rushed to open the door. "Mr. Silberstein, what is it? Why are you here?"

The older man checked over his shoulder before he stepped in and closed the door behind him. Manya stared at him. His lips were tight and his jaw set. He swallowed hard before speaking. "The Gestapo just left the office, Manya. They want to see Meyer when he comes back from work," he said solemnly.

She couldn't believe she'd heard right. There must be some mistake.

"Oh, my God," she cried, her hands clasped tightly at her mouth. "Are you sure? Why do they want him? What will they do to him?"

"I'm sorry, Manya, but I don't know. It can't be good though. They asked for Meyer by name. I wish I could tell you more, but they didn't say anything else. Their instructions were to have Meyer Korenblit report to Gestapo headquarters when he returns."

"What should I do?" Manya whispered.

"That's for you to decide. All I can do is pass on the information I have. What happens now is up to you."

It was just as well, Manya thought, for she knew what the Nazis would do if they discovered Mr. Silberstein had told anyone they were looking for Meyer. She had to think of a way to handle this by herself. She thanked Mr. Silberstein as he left.

The next thing Manya knew she was standing outside the house, alone. She knew something had to be done quickly. The Gestapo might not wait for Meyer to return from work; they might go directly to the fort and pick him up. She had to get to him before they did. She would change clothes and walk to the ghetto entrance. Then she would tie a scarf around her head and cross into the Polish area. Dressed this way, she'd look like a Polish woman and could make it across town to the fort. She'd have to remember to take off her armband.

She turned to go inside and get ready, then heard her name. "Manya, what is it? Why are you upset?"

It was their friend Isaac Hipps. "Oh, Isaac, I don't know what to do," she cried. "I have to go and warn Meyer that the Gestapo are looking for him. Something terrible is going to happen!"

"How do you know this, Manya?"

"Someone just told me. They want him to report when he gets

back from work. I'm going to sneak over to the fort and tell Meyer not to come back."

"That will be very dangerous, Manya. You could get caught. And you know they don't let people near the fort without permission."

"I don't care. If he comes back here, they'll take him away for sure. I have to go," she insisted.

"Listen to me, Manya. I'll go instead. I have a pass, so I can get through without any trouble, and I can run faster than you can. Doesn't that make sense?"

"Yes," she responded, "but why should you take such a risk? I should go—it's my responsibility."

"Nonsense, Manya, we have to help each other. Trust me— it's much safer for me to go. Do you know exactly where Meyer is working?"

"In the stable with the horses."

"All right," he said. "I'm on my way. Stay calm, Manya, whatever you do. Stay calm and don't do anything foolish."

As Manya watched Isaac run down the street, she knew he was right. His long stride would carry him faster then she could have managed. Meyer's life was now in Isaac's hands—and legs.

It seemed a miracle that she'd run into Isaac. He was a trustworthy friend who wouldn't tell anyone what was happening. Isaac was also one of the few Jews who had a pass that enabled him to walk around the city without being stopped. He got the pass because he was an amateur electrician and was often called upon to perform skilled labor for the Germans.

Now Manya didn't know what to do or where to go. What if Isaac didn't get there in time? Or couldn't find Meyer? Or was ordered to work by a passing SS officer? Oh, God, please help Meyer and Isaac. Manya stood in her doorway long after Isaac was out of sight, whispering, "Hurry, Isaac, hurry!"

Isaac showed his pass to the guard on duty and walked into the fort as nonchalantly as possible. He made his way across the grounds toward the stables as if he had an official job to do.

Meyer was hard at work when he heard someone call his name. "Meyer," the voice said, "are you here?"

He walked out of a stall and came face to face with Isaac. "What are you doing here?" Meyer greeted his friend with a smile. There was no return smile, and Meyer could see that something was wrong.

"Speak Polish, Meyer, so the Germans can't understand us. I've come here to warn you. The Gestapo are looking for you. They asked for you by name. You must not come back to the ghetto."

Meyer was stunned. "Why do they want me? How did you find out?"

"Manya found out and told me. She was going to come herself, but I talked her out of it," Isaac answered. "Now if you can think of somewhere to go, you should take off as soon as possible. Don't wait until the work day is over. If the Gestapo check to see where you're working, they may come here to get you."

Isaac's eyes were sympathetic, but there was nothing more he could do. He wished Meyer good luck, turned, and walked out of the stable.

Meyer stood there, frozen with indecision for a moment. He had to make up his mind; why couldn't he think? He had to get out of the fort, but which side of the fence was the safest? Finally, an idea emerged from the jumble in his mind. He'd try to make his way to Salki's or maybe Gorski's. Yes, that was it. Those old friends could help him decide what to do next.

Slipping out of the stables, he headed to one side of the fort grounds. Behind one of the outer buildings, he could get close to the barbed wire fence. His instincts were firing instructions. With each step, his heart pounded five times. This danger wasn't some general roundup of Jews. This was personal. The Nazis wanted him, Meyer Korenblit.

He was at the fence. The building shielded him from view. Outside the fence, open fields. Danger. Then a grove of trees. Refuge.

He dived to the ground, and lying on his stomach, reached under the lowest wire. His outstretched fingers clawed at the hard ground, the toes of his boots dug the turf for traction, and everything in between flattened to avoid the barbed wire. It seemed to take forever to slide under. Like in a nightmare, he imagined guards just behind him, inching closer and closer, gaining on him as he fell.

Then he was out. He jumped up and headed straight for the trees. He leaned gratefully against one, knees like jelly, looking back. Nobody had seen him; no one was coming.

That evening after work, a worried Manya took her place in line for the count. Seeing Chaim approach, she motioned him to stand beside her and linked her arm through his. As the count proceeded, she scanned the faces—desperate to see Meyer, but knowing that whether he had escaped or been arrested, he wouldn't be there either way. When she saw Isaac, she avoided his eyes, afraid to look, more afraid not to, wanting information but dreading to hear it.

Damn! Why couldn't they hurry up with this stupid counting—if it went on much longer, she would scream! Then she heard the SS officer shouting angrily. She hadn't noticed the group of workers who had just returned from the fort.

"There are only eleven," she heard him say. "There were twelve this morning."

Manya watched another officer stride menacingly toward the group of men. "Who is missing?" he bellowed.

No one spoke.

"I asked a question. You will answer. Who is missing?" he repeated, then accosted the silent group one by one. "Do you know? You? You?" Eleven shakes of the head.

Manya stole another look at Isaac. Not a muscle moved in his face, but now she could see it in his eyes: he had gotten the message to Meyer in time. She was sure of it. She turned to look straight ahead and found herself staring directly into Mr. Silberstein's face. He had his customary blank expression, but Manya caught an almost imperceptible nod. She looked away.

The officer spun around to face the entire group. "You know it's useless to keep quiet—more useless to try to escape. No one will help a Jew escape. We'll find out who is missing—someone will tell us. Perhaps one of you, eh?" he said with a smirk. "We'll

bring him back and make an example of him so you can be reminded again of what happens to anyone who doesn't cooperate."

He spoke the next words very slowly and distinctly. "And I
promise you one more thing: if any of you have helped him, you
too will be punished, do you hear?" Then he whirled around and
spat a command for dismissal over his shoulder.

Their arms still linked, Manya steered Chaim toward their
house. She imagined that everyone was looking at her, knowing
that she was responsible for this tirade. She expected to hear the
officer threaten to shoot fifty people if no one came forward to
confess. Perhaps they would think of that tomorrow, she thought
with a shudder.

Chaim tightened his hold on Manya's arm. "I didn't see M—,"
he began in a whisper, but was cut short by an elbow in his ribs
and an abrupt shake of Manya's head.

She would explain later that Meyer was gone. Where, she didn't
know.

CHAPTER SEVEN

Separation

A man consists of three elements: a body, a soul, and a passport.

—An old Russian saying

APRIL 1943

Meyer was sitting in John Salki's attic hideout. He had taken the long way around the brick factory and through the back fields to get to Salki's house, and he didn't think anyone had seen him. Salki's wife was there alone when he burst through the back door. After he explained that he'd run away because the Gestapo were looking for him, she immediately sent him up to the hidden room in the attic, telling him to be absolutely quiet, that John would be home in a few hours.

There was no one for Meyer to talk to. No one to tell him everything would be all right. Even the seeming sanctuary of the attic hideout did not curb his fear. He was trapped again, knowing the Gestapo could come bursting in at any second and drag him off.

Finally, Meyer heard a door open downstairs. Voices rose through the wooden boards. Then silence. He held his breath. There were footsteps on the ladder leading to the attic. He peeked through the slats of the hidden room and saw the trapdoor to the attic open. As he waited, scarcely breathing, to see who it was, a familiar voice called softly, "Meyer, it's me, John."

Relief rushed through Meyer's body, and he quickly removed the planks from the hiding place and stepped out to greet his friend. "John, they're looking for me. I didn't know what else to do."

"I know, Meyer. My wife told me. You made the right decision by coming here. Do you have any idea why they want you?"

"No, I don't. The only thing I can think of is that they found the gun I had hidden—" He stopped short when he saw the look on Salki's face. Meyer had never told him about getting a gun. In fact, Salki had warned him not to.

"I told you what the Nazis will do if they catch a Jew with a gun. They don't even allow Poles to have weapons without special permission," Salki said sternly, shaking his head. "This is serious, Meyer, very serious."

Meyer nodded sheepishly. He wished he had listened to Salki.

"Did you hear anything about this today? I'm worried about Manya and Chaim. Should we warn them?"

"Manya was the one who sent word to you," John reminded him. "She would surely have known if they were looking for her too, and she and Chaim would have come here. I'm sure of it."

Meyer knew his friend was right. "Maybe Manya went back to the haystack."

"I can send Janek there to find out, but it's far too dangerous for him to check at the ghetto today. The Nazis will be watching the house for you to return. Tomorrow or the next day will be safer. I'll check with Gorski; perhaps he can find out what's going on."

"What am I going to do, John?"

"I don't know. We'll gather as much information as possible; then we'll decide. Patience must be our ally, Meyer. That's a quality you would do well to develop. I'll send something up for you to eat, and then you must try to get some rest."

It was hours before Salki returned to tell Meyer that Janek had found no one at the haystack. Salki had gone to Gorski as well, but the chief of police didn't know why the Gestapo were looking for Meyer. Gorski hadn't even known that Meyer was wanted, although the Nazis usually kept him informed of such things. Gorski assured Salki he'd get what news he could tomorrow. The only other information Salki had was that there had been no killings in the ghetto that day.

Meyer sighed in relief. Manya must still be all right. He would just have to wait until Gorski and Salki could get more information. Sometimes he thought if the Germans didn't destroy him, the waiting would.

It was morning at last. Manya sat straight up in bed, looked around, and realized she must have fallen asleep after all. How long she'd lain there the night before—how many times she'd gotten up, how she'd won the struggle against racing out into the darkness to look for Meyer—she didn't know. But she had finally convinced herself that waiting was her only alternative. The Germans might be watching their house, and she had no intention of leading them to Meyer. Not that she knew for certain where he was.

But today she was determined to try to find him. She had been sensible for the last two nights but tonight, after work, she would go to Salki's. That was the most likely place for Meyer to be. Even if he wasn't there, Salki might have some news of him.

She would have to remove her armband, put on her Polish garb, and sneak through the ghetto after curfew. Once in the Polish section, she'd be all right. Now all she had to do was to get through the day. She'd work very hard so that the time would pass quickly. She could almost feel Meyer's arms around her already.

She leaped out of bed, straightened the sheets and blankets, drew a comb through her hair, and dipped some water to clean up. She decided not to change from the clothes she'd slept in.

Then she thought of Chaim. Already quiet-natured, he had withdrawn even further when she told him that Meyer was wanted by the Gestapo. Although Chaim would be upset to hear her plans, somehow Manya would have to make him understand that she wasn't abandoning him by going to Meyer and that she would be back. Perhaps if she asked Chaim to help her, he would feel less excluded. She didn't want to frighten him, but—

What was that? Tiptoeing into the next room to investigate, she heard the noise again. It was outside the front door. Cautiously she opened the door a crack and peeked out. There was no one there. Puzzled, she looked around again, then started to close the door.

"Here!" came a voice. "Over here!"

Manya pulled the door open wide.

"Where?" she whispered. "Who's there?"

"It's me, Janek Salki. My father sent me with a message."

Finally Manya could see the boy crouched between some bushes.

"It's Meyer. He's at our house," whispered the boy.

"Is he all right?" Manya whispered back.

Ignoring her question, he continued. "Meyer wants you to come there tonight. Can you do it?"

"Yes, yes. I was just planning . . . tell him . . . I still don't know why he's wanted," she stammered.

"Will you come?" Janek asked again.

"Yes, of course. It may be quite late, but I will come."

"I'll tell him. He asked me to come back right away."

"God bless you, Janek. I was so worried. Thank you. Thank you for coming."

The boy made no reply as he edged away from the house and disappeared. It was all arranged: tonight she'd see Meyer, and together they'd figure out what to do.

A few hours later, the others in Manya's work crew cleared shelves and drawers while she ran a dustrag around the empty surfaces. Reaching to a high ledge, she flicked the cloth along its length. When something skittered at the back of the shelf, she reached up to investigate. It was a small carved box inlaid with mother-of-pearl. Would have been a nice treasure to deposit with Anna, she thought wryly, starting to toss it on a nearby pile. But wait, her thought continued; perhaps there was a use for it even without Meyer to connect with Anna. If she could work out a way to continue smuggling goods, it might help raise money for Meyer to escape. Manya would pick up the plan where Meyer had left off, only taking items to Salki instead of Anna. She slipped the little box deep into her coat pocket and took up the dusting again.

Later that day, her cleaning completed, Manya stooped over, picked up a pile of clothing, and headed outside. As she stepped from the doorway, she glimpsed the familiar face of Wagner, the Gestapo officer who'd known her family, coming down the street, gesturing with his riding crop to another group of workers and barking an order. Oh, God, she thought, please let him pass on by. She quickly dumped her bundle onto a larger pile and turned to rush back inside.

"You there, Nagelsztajn!" Wagner shouted. "Just a minute. I want to talk to you."

Manya stopped and with great effort turned around.

"It *is* you. Yes, I thought so," he said, coming closer.

"Good day, Herr Wagner," Manya stammered, as he stopped in front of her. He stared at her without speaking, casually slapping the palm of his gloved left hand with the riding crop. The strokes of leather on leather and his piercing eyes achieved their intended effect, and Manya's knees began to tremble. She made herself speak. "You wanted to talk to me, Herr Wagner?"

He gave her another long, purposeful look. "Yes, I want to talk to you, Miss Nagelsztajn," he said, accentuating the "Miss" in a mocking simulation of respect. "Your boyfriend—Meyer, isn't it?" he began, pausing to examine her reaction. "I thought you might be able to tell me where he is. My superiors want to talk to him."

"Meyer?" she repeated, stalling for time to think.

"Well?" he added impatiently.

"No, Herr Wagner," she answered. "I don't know where he is. He went to work a few days ago and never came back. He didn't say anything to me—not even goodbye—and I thought we were very close."

His eyes searched her face for a sign of deception. But Manya returned his stare directly and innocently.

"It figures he just ran off without telling you. You Jews are all alike, thinking only of yourselves. So, you aren't able to help me? You have no information?"

Manya shook her head.

"You'd tell me if you knew something, wouldn't you?"

Manya nodded, but didn't speak.

Wagner studied her intently. "You're perspiring a lot for such a cold day," he said slowly.

"It's the work, Herr Wagner," Manya answered. "I was working very hard."

"Ach! Working hard! You people don't even know what hard work is," he said in a disgusted tone. "Well, I can see you'll be no help to me—you'd better get busy." He turned to go, then spoke again. "If you hear from your young man, tell him to give himself up. He'll be better off—and so will you."

Manya glared at Wagner's back as he moved off down the street.

Returning to the house after work that evening, Manya dashed into the bedroom and pulled off her clothes. She bathed quickly and dressed again, pulling on her Jewish armband and stuffing a scarf into the pocket of her dark dress. As she started for the next room, Chaim appeared in the doorway. "What are you doing?" he asked quietly.

"I just got cleaned up a little bit, that's all," she said casually. "Are you hungry?"

"Manya, what are you going to do?"

"We're going to eat something as soon as I—"

"I didn't say 'we.' I said 'you.' You're getting ready for something. Tell me what it is."

Manya wrapped her arms around Chaim. He was close to tears.

"I'm so afraid, Manya," he pleaded. "Since Meyer left, every time I see a German, I think he's after me. Every time I hear a sound at night, I think they're coming to get us. Now I see you preparing for something, and you're keeping it a secret. Are you going to run away too and leave me behind?"

"No," she said, squeezing him tighter. "I'd never leave you like that. You have to believe me. Come," she said, leading him toward the bed, "sit down with me."

Manya explained that Meyer was hiding at Salki's house and that tonight she was going to sneak over there to see him. She asked her brother if he would go with her to the gate of the ghetto. When he shook his head, she didn't know if he was disagreeing with her decision to go or refusing to accompany her. No, Manya told herself; he's trying to shake off the urge to cry. She realized how very young he was—how brave, how lonely he'd been. She had Meyer, but Chaim had only a small part of her. She imagined him lying alone in bed each night, and winced to think how he must have envied the closeness she shared with Meyer. It was only natural that Chaim might think she'd leave him behind.

She hugged and kissed him and told him she loved him, swearing that he was as important to her as Meyer. She promised that she'd always take care of him and pleaded with him to understand that she had to go to Salki's. She assured him over and over that she'd be all right and would be back.

Then Sam called to them from the other room, wanting to know where everyone was and if they were going to have dinner.

"Chaim and I are talking, Sam. We'll be out in a little while. Just fix yourself something to eat. I don't feel like cooking tonight." She heard Sam grumbling to Leon, but brushed it aside and turned back to her brother. They sat in the darkness for a while, holding each other.

"You know, Chaim," she began, "Sam knows that Meyer got away, but he doesn't know where he is. You can't tell anyone what I've told you. It isn't that we don't trust Sam or Leon; we just can't put Meyer or Salki in danger. We have to be strong enough to keep this secret. Do you think you can do it?"

Chaim looked very tired as he nodded.

Manya tried to rub some energy into his hunched form, then stood and drew him upright. "You must be hungry by now—maybe just a little bit?" she chided, pinching his cheek and smiling. "Come on, let's see if Sam and Leon left anything for us!"

Chaim pulled back and looked at her solemnly. "I'll go with you to the gate tonight, Manya," he said shyly.

"You don't have to. It's all right—"

"No, I want to help. I love Meyer too, and if I help you, I'll be helping him."

"Just knowing you're with me is a help, Chaim," she said, stroking his curly hair. "I'm not as brave as I sound. But Meyer needs me, and I have to see him."

They stumbled into the dark kitchen and lit a candle. Manya found some leftover noodles and potatoes and placed them in a soup plate for Chaim. She poured milk over it all and tore off a piece of ry. read.

"Milk soup," he grinned. It was his favorite.

She sat down with him and nibbled some bread while he ate,

talking easily now and enjoying the special attention. Sam and Leon soon yawned their good nights and headed for bed.

An hour or so later the conversation trailed off and Chaim saw a look come over his sister as if she were a thousand miles away. He was silent for a time, then spoke. "Do you want to go?"

She looked at Chaim's thin face, then nodded.

He managed a nervous smile and stood up. "Let's go, then," he said, snuffing the candle flame with his fingers.

They tripped the door latch and crouched very low. As their eyes adjusted to the darkness, they listened to the night. There was no sound or sign of activity in the ghetto streets. Hand in hand, they slipped through the doorway and outside.

Cautiously they inched their way three blocks to the ghetto entrance. It didn't matter that guards were on duty there, for Manya wouldn't leave the ghetto at that point. Not far away, there was a slim passageway between two buildings, with just enough room to slither through if they turned sideways. The opening emptied into an alley on the Polish side.

Manya could feel Chaim's trembling — or was it her own? She saw the ghetto office just ahead. They had made it. She took his arm and they knelt down. Yanking off her armband, she stuffed it down the front of her dress, then tied the scarf around her head. Taking his face in her hands, Manya kissed her brother. "I'll be back," she promised.

He settled in to wait, as Manya walked purposefully but not too fast through the deserted streets. She grew a bit dizzy from looking ahead, then behind her, then forward again, but she had to make sure no one was watching or following.

Manya's teeth were chattering from the cold when she got to Salki's house. She tiptoed up the front steps and placed an ear to the door. The house was silent. She knocked softly. In a moment the door cracked open and John Salki peered out. Behind him she could see the dim flickering of a single candle. His cautious eyes surveyed the street behind her before he motioned her inside and closed the door.

Silently she followed him up the stairs to the second floor and into one of the bedrooms. Placing a hand on her shoulder, he held her still for a moment so that she would know to wait. He disappeared into the upper hallway and returned with a ladder, which he maneuvered soundlessly through the doorway and into position against the bedroom wall.

He climbed up and, arms outstretched, pushed hard against the ceiling. A two-by-three foot section slid heavily away with a scrape and a thud. Then he descended the ladder and reached for Manya's hand, pointing up. When she looked again, he was gone.

She stepped on the first rung and felt the old ladder bend with her weight. It seemed to tremble more with each step she took. Then her groping hands felt the floor of the attic. Her feet advanced another rung, her shoulders cleared the opening, and she flopped forward.

Something touched her arm. Before she could raise her head, she was lifted and pulled away from the trapdoor opening. Familiar arms locked around her; a beloved voice whispered in her ear. When she stopped shaking, Meyer led her into his hiding place and repositioned the planks to seal the entrance.

They were unable to speak at first. Manya just kept saying, "Oh, Meyer, why?" They held each other tightly, trying to make up for the days apart.

It was two hours before Manya crawled back to the trapdoor exit, climbing down slowly backwards as Salki steadied the ladder. In silence, Manya continued downstairs alone as John removed the ladder and Meyer replaced the trapdoor above.

In seconds she was on her way back to the ghetto. Poor Chaim, she thought. He must be freezing. She quickened her pace, knowing she wouldn't appear suspicious because anyone out on a cold night like this would hurry.

She passed the cannon in its mantle of ice. Not too much farther, and she would reach the passageway to the ghetto. Then only a few blocks to the house—and bed. She would sleep tonight, she was sure of it. Perhaps Chaim would climb in with her and they could snuggle together like in the old days. He would like that, and so would she.

Five days had passed since Meyer's escape from the fort. Five grueling days of sitting, wondering what was going on, worrying what might happen any minute. He was also desperate for news of his parents and sisters. Finally, he decided that he had to go to Mislavitch to look for them.

It had been most difficult to explain to Manya that he was going away for a few days. She had been worried about him while he was hiding at Salki's, but she was also uneasy about him leaving.

Meyer and Manya weren't the only ones worried. Salki knew that when the Gestapo were looking for someone, they put pressure on everyone. That was why he had reluctantly agreed to Meyer's plan to go to Mislavitch. Neither he nor Gorski had been able to find out why the Gestapo wanted the young man, and they didn't want to push for information for fear it would arouse suspicion. With Meyer gone, they could more aggressively pursue the answer. If the Nazis became suspicious and watched or even searched their houses, Meyer wouldn't be there.

It was a cold, clear evening when Meyer stepped from the back door of Salki's house. The moonlight cast silhouettes of the two men against the building. It was nine o'clock, plenty of time for Meyer to reach his destination before morning.

"Be careful, Meyer. Remember, be cautious even with old friends. Times have changed," Salki warned.

"I know. Don't worry, I'll be careful."

They shook hands, and Meyer turned and walked toward the fields. Hours later, the moon had reached its peak and was making its descent when he reached the outlying farms of Mislavitch. There were few sounds in the predawn air, but each one was intensified by the quiet that surrounded him as he crouched in the underbrush near his father's old flour mill. Did Isaac Achler still live there? Could he be trusted? Would he help? Meyer felt he must trust these old friends; there was no one else to turn to.

Finally at the Achler house, he knocked on the back door.

"Isaac? It's Meyer Korenblit."

Seconds later the door flew open. Isaac's arms opened for a big hug to greet the young man he hadn't seen in a few years.

"Come inside quickly. You must be hungry." He called to his wife to bring food. "How are you, Meyer? Why are you here?"

"I'm fine, Isaac, just fine. Tell me, did my parents come here? Are they safe?"

"Yes, yes," Isaac answered, smiling at the immediate relief in Meyer's eyes. "Avrum came with the family and they're safe. They are being watched over."

"Where are they?" Meyer demanded impatiently. "Are they close by?"

"They aren't far away, but I don't think you should go to them. Not everyone here is still your family's friend. Many people work with the Germans, both for material gain and because they dislike Jews. If the wrong person saw you, it would be very dangerous."

Meyer struggled to think clearly. He'd been so sure he'd be with his family very soon.

"I could go at night," he offered.

"But, Meyer, you can't even depend on the darkness to protect you. The Nazis and their collaborators are always watching. I think it's better that you stay here, and I'll get word to Avrum that you're here and safe."

Isaac's logic was unassailable but, in accepting it, Meyer had to fight to conceal his disappointment. Of course Isaac was right. Especially since the Gestapo were looking for him, any move he made was dangerous. The last thing in the world he wanted was to lead the Nazis to his family. Taking a deep breath, he finally agreed.

Seeing the boy's struggle, Isaac asked, "Meyer, is everything all right in the ghetto? What's the matter?"

Trying to hold back tears, Meyer answered, "They're looking for me."

"I know, Meyer, the Nazis are looking for all Jews."

"No, Isaac. They are hunting *me*, Meyer Korenblit!"

Meyer explained to his friend what had happened. Achler didn't know how to respond; he just sat there shaking his head.

"I'm sorry, Isaac. I don't want to cause you any trouble."

"Don't be ridiculous. I want to help you. Let's get you some

food; then you can hide in the barn while I go to Tomitzki to discuss what we can do."

"Thank you, Isaac, you're still the same old friend. Please do
me one favor. When you talk to my parents, don't tell them that
I'm being hunted. I don't want them to worry."

As Meyer sat in the barn later, frustration with waiting again
rose in him. He couldn't stand it anymore. He had to think of a
way out. Maybe now would be the time to join the underground.
But what about Manya? He couldn't leave her, and she wouldn't
leave Chaim.

Opening the barn doors ever so slightly, he peeked at the flour
mill down the road. Was it still the same, or had it been changed?
Avrum had devoted a great deal of time and work to make it successful. Meyer had loved being there beside his father, watching
the stones grind the grain, then shoveling the fine flour into the
sacks. He had to make sure there was just the right amount in
each bag, for Avrum would scold him as much for not having
enough in the sack as he would for having too much.

Then the struggle would ensue: Meyer against the flour. The
first few years, he wasn't strong enough to pick up the bundle,
throw it over his shoulder, and carry it to the chute as his older
brothers could. He would yank and pull, dragging it across the
floor. Wanting to keep up with his brothers, he would try to
move too quickly, often tripping over some object left in the middle of the room or getting his feet tangled up under the sack.
Later he was big enough to get the sack on his shoulder. With
knees about to buckle, he staggered to the chute and heaved the
burden off his shoulder. But his weight carried him forward into
the chute along with the bag of flour, and it was a race to see if
he or the bag would hit the bottom first. Lying on his back looking up, he could see the others laughing and pointing. Even
Avrum chuckled as he looked down at his youngest son sprawled
out on the floor with the sack stretched across his body and his
face covered with flour.

Soon after the war had started, Avrum had turned the flour
mill over to Achler and Tomitzki with the understanding that
after the war Avrum would take it back. Avrum had continued to

work there, hoping that if the Nazis thought the mill belonged to these two Poles, it wouldn't be confiscated or torn down. Many times during the previous years Meyer had been able to sneak back and get flour to sell on the black market. He'd even been able to give some to the Nagelsztajns after food rationing went into effect and to sell some to buy Manya her first pair of boots.

Memories helped Meyer stay calm as the morning passed into the afternoon. Isaac's wife brought Meyer lunch but stayed only a few minutes to talk.

Finally, after what seemed an eternity, Meyer saw Achler and Tomitzki walking down the road toward the barn. When they entered, he greeted the two older men happily.

"I saw your family, Meyer, and they're fine," Achler said. "Avrum wanted to come and see you, but I talked him out of it."

"You didn't tell them about my being hunted, did you?"

"Oh, no," the Pole responded. "But they wondered why you had come. I told them you wanted to check on them because you hadn't had any word in so long. I think they accepted that," he said, rather proud of himself for coming up with that story. "They send you their love. Your mother continues to pray for the day you'll all be back together."

"Now, we must get down to business, Meyer," interrupted Tomitzki. "We have a plan. It will be very dangerous, but if you're willing to try it, we'll help you."

"I'll try anything," Meyer answered eagerly. "Tell me what it is."

"You know," Tomitzki continued, "my boy Antonio and you are about the same age and build. He and I will go to the magistrate's office today and explain that Antonio has lost his identification papers. Hopefully, they'll give us another set of papers — for a price, of course. Then we'll substitute your picture for his."

"But how will you get my picture? And what about the stamp?" Meyer asked.

"You let us worry about that," Achler responded. "Just remember, you won't be able to use the papers around here. Too many people know both Antonio and you."

"You're taking a big risk by doing this," Meyer said. "I hardly know what to say. How can I ever thank you?"

"Avrum and your family have been our friends for many years, Meyer. Your father has always been good to us, and we want to repay him," Tomitzki responded.

Meyer stayed in Achler's house that night. His wife prepared a meal that seemed like a feast, even making the brown noodles he loved so much. They talked late into the night, exchanging stories of the past and the present. Meyer told them what had been going on in the ghetto. Then Isaac explained that the Korenblits had been set up in a good place and were well taken care of.

"The girls are fine although a little restless, especially Minka. She always talks about you, Meyer. How soon the two of you will play together," Achler said with a smile. "Malka is grateful that she, Avrum, and the girls are safe. But the hurt grows every day inside her, not having her sons there and not knowing if they're safe."

Meyer cringed at those words, wanting to demand that Isaac take him to his mother. But he knew he must wait and do nothing foolish. His parents and sisters were alive, together, and as safe as could be expected. That was the most important thing. And they now knew that he was alive too.

The next day Tomitzki managed to get a camera and took Meyer's picture. Then, they decided that Meyer should return to his hiding place in Hrubieszow and wait until the papers were ready. Achler and Tomitzki didn't know exactly how long it would take, so they agreed that Meyer should return in two weeks. Then he'd be on his own.

Achler had gone to the Korenblits earlier in the day to explain that Meyer was going back to the ghetto now that he was sure they were safe. Meyer told Isaac to tell his family that they were not to worry about him and that he'd be in touch with them every two weeks or so, depending on when he could get away. He also sent word that Manya and Chaim were well and sent their love and that they had learned the rest of the Nagelsztajns were safe.

That night, Meyer looked out the window until he was sure it was dark, then began his journey back to Salki's by the same route he had taken to Mislavitch.

Meyer was confident that this new scheme would work because of an experience he'd had early in the occupation. He had been returning home with Avrum and the other Jews who worked at the brick factory when they were ordered to line up upon their arrival at the plaza. The Germans walked up and down the lines, yelling and screaming at some, beating others. One of them finally made his way to Meyer's line, stopping directly in front of him. Looking right into Meyer's eyes, he said, "What are you doing in this line? Don't you know this work is only for the filthy Jews?"

Shocked, Meyer had not known what to say.

"Well?" the officer repeated.

"I *am* Jewish," Meyer finally responded.

"You are? Are you sure?" the officer demanded.

"Yes, sir," Meyer told him. "This is my father," he'd said, pointing to Avrum.

The officer stared at Meyer for a few seconds, then stormed away.

It seemed that Meyer didn't look Jewish. If I could pass as a Pole then, he thought, I can surely pass as one now.

Upon Meyer's return to Hrubieszow, John Salki had disturbing news.

"I tell you, I don't believe it." Meyer shook his head angrily.

"It's true," Salki repeated. "Gorski found out yesterday."

"But Anna's my friend. She offered to help. Why would she report me to the Gestapo?"

Salki sighed wearily. "Meyer," he began, "you know that Anna's husband has been gone a long time—"

"Of course. She used to talk to me about it. But what's that got to do with this?"

"Please, let me finish. Did she ever mention Damone?"

"Never."

"No, I suppose not," Salki said, shaking his head. "But she knew him. She knew him very well. Think about it, Meyer; where is Anna's house?"

"Across the street from the fort, but—"

"Yes, across the street from the fort. In other words, across the street from one of Damone's offices. Meyer, you must face the fact. Your friend Anna is Damone's lover."

The words echoed in Meyer's head. How could he have been so stupid? Why didn't he guess? But there had never been a clue. Meyer had never seen the Gestapo officer at Anna's house. Had Anna been planning to betray him all along, ever since he'd first approached her with his plan to smuggle goods for her to sell? "No!" he said out loud in rejection of both his poor judgment and her betrayal.

"I swear it's true, Meyer. Gorski found out that those two have been carrying on for months."

Meyer looked directly into Salki's eyes.

"There's something else to consider, my friend," Salki went on. "We know that Manya and Chaim are still in the ghetto. If Anna is responsible for reporting *you*, then they're probably not in danger and can stay where they are. We should be thankful for that."

"Thankful?" Meyer said sarcastically. "How thankful will they be when I tell them how stupid I was? How will they feel when they find out I let that woman cheat us out of our freedom? I've failed them."

"That's enough!" Salki stopped him. "I'll hear no more of this self-pity. Do you think that being free is all Manya thinks about? Or is it to be free with you?"

"With me," Meyer responded reluctantly.

"Does she sneak over here to be free? Or to help keep you safe?"

Meyer shifted uncomfortably and looked away, then nodded.

"Does she seem to care why you are wanted by the Germans?"

"No—"

"All right, then, that's what you must think about. Manya still believes in you. You have to show her that even when you make a mistake, you can recover and go on."

Two days had passed since Meyer had returned to Mislavitch to pick up the identity papers. Tomitzki and Achler had done their job well. They'd also gotten Meyer another gun. At first he was hesitant about taking the weapon, but he finally gave in.

Mrs. Salki came into the room. "It's all clear outside, Meyer," she said softly.

Meyer rose from the table and headed for the back door, checking to make sure he had the precious papers in his pocket. The woman turned out the light in the kitchen and quietly opened the door. As he moved past her and out the door, she whispered, "Be careful."

John Salki had left the house a half-hour ago. Meyer was to wait until the commissioner had time to get to Gorski's and then he was to join them to go over the plan one final time.

Meyer went to Gorski's back door, remembering the many times he'd gone there as a boy to take meat to his friend from Avrum. Now he didn't bother to knock. He turned the doorknob and pushed.

"Gorski! Salki!"

"Come in, Meyer. We're in here," came the response.

Meyer followed the voices to the living room. The two men looked up with grim smiles as he walked into the room.

"Any problems, Meyer?" asked Salki.

"No, it was very quiet," he answered.

"Good," responded Gorski. "Do you have the papers with you?"

Meyer pulled the documents from his pocket and handed them to the police chief. Gorski scrutinized them, word by word, line by line. He walked to the lamp on the table. Holding the papers to the light, he nodded his head every once in a while.

Finally, he announced his verdict: "Perfect! These are excellent. They'll do fine."

The three men smiled happily.

"If people lose their papers, they usually have to go in person to get new ones. How did they manage to get your picture stamped?"

"They stole the stamp."

Gorski snickered, "Well, we can't let all that trouble

go for nothing. We must prepare you for your trip. From now on
you are Antonio Tomitzki, not Meyer Korenblit. You must think
'Antonio' at all times. You must think and act like a Pole. You
are no longer a Jew."

The words stung. Meyer was being told to forget who and
what he was. No matter how much it might hurt, he had to do it.

"My name is Antonio Tomitzki. I'm from Mislavitch," he
repeated.

For the next hour, while Meyer studied the papers, Gorski and
Salki gave him information, grilled him with questions, and
drilled the proper responses into him.

"You must always stay calm, no matter what is happening. Be
sure of yourself at all times and be respectful of anyone who
stops you. Don't give anybody any reason to get mad or suspicious," Gorski instructed.

They then began the interrogation.

"What is your name? Where are you from? How old are you?
When were you born? What is your father's name? Your mother's?
How many people live in Mislavitch?"

Meyer's answers were automatic.

"Where are you going?"

"To Lublin."

"Why?"

"To visit a sick uncle."

"Why aren't your parents with you?"

"They couldn't leave work."

Then they'd start over.

"What is your name? How tall are you? How many brothers
and sisters do you have? Where is Mislavitch?"

And more. "Why are you so far from home?"

"I'm on my way to Warsaw. I have a job there."

"What kind of job?"

"I work in a factory making steel ball bearings."

"That's a good job. If Jews still owned the factories, you
wouldn't have work. You're happy with what we're doing to the
filthy swine?"

Meyer blanched, hesitating.

"No! You can't do that," yelled Gorski.

Lowering his voice, he put his arm around Meyer. "I know it's hard. But you must answer quickly and correctly. Answer like a Pole would, whether he means what he's saying or not. You are Antonio Tomitzki. You have to respond as he would. You can't let them shake you up. Now, can you do it?"

"Yes," came the reluctant response.

"Good, let's start over."

For two more hours, Salki and Gorski questioned, and the new Antonio Tomitzki answered, until they were satisfied they could do no more. The training session was over.

Salki left first, through the front door, Meyer waiting to give him enough time to get home.

"How are Avrum and the family?" Gorski asked.

"They're fine. I wasn't able to see them, but we've sent messages to each other," answered Meyer sadly.

"Good. I'm glad to hear that. Maybe next year we'll again be able to celebrate Passover together. You know I love your mother's cooking."

"I hope we can too."

They got up and moved to the back door. Before opening it, the chief of police turned and faced Meyer. "Tonight was just practice, a game. The day after tomorrow it will be for real. Remember what we told you. Remember it well." He put his arm around Meyer's shoulders. "Good luck, my friend."

"Manya, you know it's the only thing I can do. If there were any other way, I'd try. Do you think I want to leave you, not to be close by, not to know for myself that you and Chaim are safe? But the longer I stay here, the more danger I put everyone in. You see, we can trust very few people."

She must be strong, Manya told herself, and not show fear. Meyer was leaving, but she would show him she had the fortitude to go on. There was a lot she could do to help Meyer while he was away although she didn't tell him about the plans she had made with Chaim and Salki for how to get the money and clothes he would need when he returned.

"I know, Meyer," she finally responded. "I'll be strong and take care of Chaim. We'll be here when you return. We'll do what we must to survive, just as you will." She paused. "Do you remember, Meyer, the first time you told me you loved me?"

Meyer nodded his head shyly, his face turning pink.

Manya was using the same strategy with Meyer that he used with her when things were very bad: thinking back to the past to help get through the present. It didn't always work, but when it did, that memory gave them strength to get through one more day.

"You cried like a little baby at my bedside. You were so afraid of how sick I was," Manya reminded him. "You said you loved me so much and if I got well you'd never again look at another girl. That made me so happy. Remember?" Manya poked his shoulder playfully until his embarrassed nod admitted it.

They shared a smile, then sat quietly. Meyer gently stroked her arm while Manya held him tight.

"Manya. It's time for me to leave."

They stood and walked to the back door, where Salki was waiting.

"It's clear," the commissioner said, then held out his hand to Meyer. "Good luck, and be careful. I'll see you in a few weeks." Then he turned and left the room.

Meyer pulled Manya close. "I'll be fine. You must take care of yourself and Chaim. He needs you," Meyer whispered in her ear. "I'll be back, Manya. I love you more than anything."

Meyer pulled away and opened the door. He turned to look at her one more time.

Manya mouthed the words "I love you."

Then he was gone. Manya peered through the curtains to catch one last glimpse before the darkness swallowed him. "I love you, Meyer. I'll be strong."

Meyer made his way to Mislavitch, where Isaac Achler was waiting. He watched as Achler hitched the horse to the cart; then Meyer climbed in and lay down. Isaac threw a tarpaulin over the young man and piled vegetables on top of him.

Meyer felt the cart jerk forward. "Are you all right?" came the voice from the front of the wagon.

"Yes," was the muffled reply.

"You won't have to stay there long. Just until we get a few miles outside of town."

Meyer had traveled this road many times with his father, but he had never realized how many bumps there were. The cart shimmied across the cobblestones, bouncing him up and down and sideways. There was no room to lie flat, so he braced his feet against one side of the cart and pressed his shoulders to the other. The steady clip-clop of the horse's hooves added a rhythmic beat to the swaying wagon. It seemed like hours before the cart stopped.

"Okay, Meyer. I think it's safe now."

A grateful Meyer scrambled out from under the tarpaulin and joined Achler in the front of the cart. They lurched forward once again, at a snail's pace.

When Meyer saw the sign—Dubienka 4—he placed his hand on Isaac's arm. "I think this is far enough," he said.

When the Pole stopped the cart, Meyer jumped down. He'd walk the rest of the way so the two wouldn't be seen together.

"Thank you, my friend. I'll see you when I return. Please tell my parents everything is fine."

"I will, Meyer, and good luck. May God go with you."

Meyer threw his bundle over his shoulder and began walking slowly toward Dubienka, where he would catch the train to Chelm. Mrs. Salki had given him food for a couple of days, and he had two extra shirts and a change of underwear in the cloth bag. In his pocket along with the precious papers was money Salki had given him for lodging and more food.

Before long, Meyer was standing at the train stop on the other side of town, dawn just beginning to edge the sky. It was too early for the train, and there was no one else around yet.

He sat down to wait, still scared and wondering what he would do once he got to Chelm. It would take only one person to recognize him, only one mistake on his part, and it would be all over.

"Antonio Tomitzki," he whispered under his breath. "I'm going to visit a sick uncle in Lublin."

CHAPTER EIGHT

Caprice and choice

A primary characteristic of life for Jews under the Nazis was unpredictability. Especially unsettling was the fact that they often did not know what people around them—whether family, friends, strangers, or enemies—were thinking and to what those thoughts could lead. In such a situation, the unexpected became the norm.

"Where are you going?"
"To Chelm," Meyer quickly answered.
"That will be two zlotys."

Meyer thrust his hand into his pocket and counted out the correct change while the conductor tore off a ticket and punched it. After taking the money, he turned and walked down the aisle to the next passenger. Meyer couldn't help but glance over his shoulder to see if the conductor was looking at him. He wasn't.

Only four people had gotten on the train in Dubienka, and the car wasn't full. Meyer was glad: the fewer people, the less likely someone would recognize him. So far, everything had gone well, but next time it could be different. There had been no ticket counter in Dubienka; he had just boarded the train. But in Chelm and the larger cities, he'd have to buy his ticket ahead of time, and more people would be at the station.

The whistle blew: the train was pulling into another town. As a few more people got on, Meyer assessed his situation. How many stops were there between Dubienka and Chelm? How long between each one? How big was each town? At what times and where did the most people get on? He considered the options. Was it better to get on with a lot of people or not many? Should he sit down beside someone or try to find an empty bench?

He reached into his bundle and pulled out some bread and cheese. He was careful not to eat too much because he didn't know how easy it would be to get more. Where he was going, food was rationed and he didn't have coupons.

Meyer looked out the window. The peaceful countryside had begun its spring ritual. The grass beside the tracks was turning green. The open fields were coming to life. Cattle grazed lazily, turning their heads as the train sped past. Birds soared in a pattern in the clear blue sky; occasionally one swooped down to fly alongside the moving train. Poland was beautiful this time of year, but this spring was not one Meyer could enjoy.

"Next stop, Chelm," the conductor announced.

Meyer held tightly to his bundle, checking his pocket to make sure his papers were there. The train slowed, then came to a jerky stop. Taking a deep breath, Meyer rose and headed toward the exit, careful not to look anyone directly in the face as Gorski had instructed him. Pulling his hat down low on his forehead, he stepped out onto the platform, hoping no one could hear his heart pounding against his chest. Now what? First he must find a place to stay. He walked through the station and out into the city.

Many times he'd come to Chelm with his father on business. There was so much to see and do—the excitement of being in the city, walking down the streets, looking in store windows, watching the people. But now Avrum wasn't with him; Meyer was on his own.

Trying to appear confident, he strode up to two men standing on the corner.

"Excuse me, could you tell me where there might be an inexpensive place to stay not far from here?"

The two men looked at Meyer, then at each other. One of them recommended one hotel, but the other didn't agree. Then the second man mentioned another place. Meyer saw the other man give a half-smile.

"Is it a good place?" Meyer asked.

"Oh, yes indeed. It's a very nice place," the man responded.

"If I were from out of town, I would stay there," the first man added.

"And it isn't expensive? I don't have much money."

"For what you get, it is very cheap."

Meyer got the address and directions, thanked the two men, and left. He glanced around as he walked, making sure he would remember how to get back to the station.

Suddenly, he saw two SS men walking toward him. Meyer

immediately started to move off the sidewalk into the street to let them pass, as he reached to tip his hat. But he caught himself. He wasn't wearing a yellow Star of David. He wasn't Jewish. He wasn't even Meyer Korenblit. He was Antonio Tomitzki, a Pole, on his way to Lublin to visit a sick uncle. As the men passed, neither they nor Meyer seemed to take notice of the other.

"Thank you, Gorski," Meyer said to himself.

He found the address the men had given him with no trouble. The neighborhood was a bit shoddy, but he figured that was why the rooms were cheap. Inside the three-story brick building was a small lobby with a few chairs, a couch, and a table. In the far corner were two women whispering to each other. Meyer thought briefly that it seemed strange that the women were in a public place yet seemed only half-dressed. To the left was a counter. Meyer walked over and saw an older man reading a paper behind it. Behind him on the wall hung two rows of keys, each on its own nail.

"I'd like a room, please," Meyer said, trying to sound as if he had done this many times before.

The man got up slowly, looking Meyer over. "Aren't you rather young?"

Meyer was taken aback. "I just want a room to stay in for the night," he insisted.

"That's all anyone comes in here for," the man responded with a leer.

Meyer was still puzzled. He nervously looked around the room again and stared at the two women. Then it hit him.

"Oh, no, sir! I just wanted a room," he stammered. "To sleep in, nothing more. I'm from out of town. I didn't know where to go, so I asked two men on a corner and they told me to come here. Maybe I should leave."

"No, no, it's all right. But next time make sure what kind of place you're going to."

As Meyer lay in bed that night, he couldn't help but think of what Manya and his mother would say if they knew he was sleeping in a brothel!

That first day in Chelm now seemed like a month ago, but only two weeks had passed. It was a tormented and lonely time for Meyer: everywhere he went, every step he took, he was sure he was being watched. Yet each day as the plan worked, his confidence grew.

Meyer had stayed in Chelm for three days. Chelm was a familiar town close to Hrubieszow and if Meyer could find work there, he could visit Manya frequently and perhaps even find a way for his parents to join him. But then he reminded himself that if he settled in a particular area, he would have to go through dangerous channels to get work and a ration card for food. He shouldn't draw attention to himself that way, and he didn't want to be tied down without Manya. He had to keep moving.

He left for Lublin, and after four days went on to Radom. Then Ostrowiec and finally Zamosc. He decided to get off the train at a small village a few miles outside Mislavitch, in order to check on his family and assure Isaac Achler that all had gone well.

Isaac told him the Korenblits were still safe but growing anxious. Meyer asked Isaac to urge his father not to move because it was too dangerous. Achler said he'd do his best to convince Avrum to stay where he was. Mrs. Achler served Meyer a delicious hot meal, the first decent food he'd had in two weeks.

Then he headed for Hrubieszow.

John Salki welcomed Meyer back as if he were his own lost son. He fired rapid questions at Meyer, who matched them with his own about Manya and Chaim. Janek left the house, returning shortly with Gorski, and the three stayed up most of the night talking.

Meyer was surprised to learn what time it was when he got up the next day. He knew he had been tired, but he hadn't intended to sleep around the clock. Mrs. Salki woke him with a hearty stew and told him that Janek had been to the ghetto to tell Manya that he was back. She would be coming tonight—little more than two hours from now.

Meyer didn't wait in the attic for Manya's arrival. He was

downstairs when she walked through the door. He grabbed her, and they hugged and kissed.

"Oh, Meyer! Is it really you?"

"Yes, Manya, I'm here. I missed you so much."

"I was so worried. All I could think about was when you'd be back."

He hugged her again, and they both cried and laughed as Manya filled Meyer in on the lost days and he told her of being frightened and of how much he missed and loved her. They laughed together when he told her about his night in the brothel.

Then, all too quickly it was over. It had been three nights, and tonight Meyer would leave again.

Salki walked into the room carrying a bundle. "Here's some food, Meyer. I'm afraid it isn't the same as you've had here for the last days, but it'll keep you going," he said smiling.

"It'll be fine. Thank you." Meyer tucked the package into his knapsack.

"And here, take this. It should be enough for the next few weeks."

"I can't keep taking your money, John. You need it," Meyer protested, looking sadly at the crumpled bills.

"It isn't my money, Meyer. It's yours."

"What do you mean, *my* money?"

Salki looked at Manya, then back to Meyer. "Manya has continued your smuggling operation, Meyer, and she's doing quite well," he answered with a grin on his face. "You should be very proud of her and Chaim."

"Really, John, it's you and Janek we should thank," Manya added. "Janek often comes into the ghetto to retrieve the goods, and you're the one who sells them."

"Manya, you must stop this. It's too risky." Meyer shook his head sternly. "And, John, you're doing enough just by letting me stay here."

"Meyer, you have only one thing to worry about, and that's staying alive," John responded. "We'll be fine. I'll take care of Manya and Chaim. If I think it's becoming too dangerous, I'll make them stop."

Meyer knew there was nothing he could say to change their minds. "Someday, John, someday."

"I know, Meyer," he said, smiling as he took Meyer's outstretched hand.

Manya and Meyer moved to the back door. They stepped outside into the cool night air, embracing. Slowly Meyer pulled away. Manya held on to his hand, then his fingertips, then he was gone.

"I had a crush on him a long time ago," Manya's girlfriend Tovah admitted to Manya late one night after Meyer's departure. "But he loved you, Manya. I would see him watching you."

"He used to watch *you*," Manya retorted, "and it made me so mad I wouldn't speak to him. I felt sorry for myself and moped around the house. It was so silly." She giggled.

"Oh, I don't know, Manya. I think he paid attention to me only to make you jealous. But you better watch out," she teased, "if you don't treat him right, I might catch him yet!"

"Well," said Manya, playing along, "I could have another young man if I wanted."

"Who?" Tovah cried. "What are you talking about?"

"Oh, maybe Sam—he's sort of good-looking."

"Sam! Do you like Sam?"

"It's not me—it's him. I think he hopes I'll forget about Meyer now that he's gone. Sam does little things: touches my hand, brushes against me; you know what I mean. He talks about taking me away."

"Would you go?"

Manya's laughing face grew serious and the corners of her mouth quivered as she spoke. "Oh, Tovah, I miss Meyer so much. I think about him all the time. I would never leave him."

The room fell silent. Tovah and Manya had become very close during the weeks since Meyer had left. During the day, Tovah worked in the office at the Jewish Center, performing clerical duties. After work, she often visited Manya in their little house.

Sam and Leon always perked up when Tovah appeared. Chaim, too, seemed to come out of himself when she was around, although his deepening depression worried Manya. She shared her concern with Tovah, who made an extra effort to draw Chaim out of his shell. Sam and Leon tried also, but their attempts, though well intentioned, were clumsy, and Manya could see that Sam especially was having a difficult time coping with his own fears.

In the four weeks since his departure, Meyer had come back to Hrubieszow only once—about two weeks ago now. Manya knew that if all went well, he was due to return in a few days.

She hadn't thought very much about the rest of her family recently, devoting all of her energy instead to the needs of Chaim and Meyer. Helping them somehow helped to make her stronger. When she had doubts, she whispered them in Tovah's sympathetic ear, while at other times Tovah came to Manya for reassurance. Together they quelled the darkest of thoughts by admitting them, then casting them away.

As the weeks passed, Sam's attitude became more and more worrisome to Manya. Not only did he pressure her about becoming his girlfriend, but hour after hour he would sit in the room with them, ears deaf to their attempts at conversation, vacant eyes signaling a mind engaged elsewhere. When he did speak, it was always about escape. He was obsessed with it. They tried to distract him by offering wine or food, but their attempts often only seemed to make him more frustrated. Sometimes he would relent after a while, assuring them that he didn't mean to upset them. But with increasing frequency, he undermined the hopeful attitude that Manya and Tovah tried hard to maintain among their circle of friends.

One morning, the day dawned clear, and the sun seemed to beam a promise of warmer temperatures.

"The air feels good," Manya commented to Chaim as they walked along to the count.

"Mmm," he answered, inhaling through his nose.

"Do you have your lunch?" she asked maternally, then smiled as he patted a bulge in his pocket.

They turned a familiar corner. The routine morning lineup didn't look as it had the day before. The faces of the Jewish

workers showed panic and confusion. Too many commands
were being shouted by twice as many gun-wielding soldiers as
usual. And there was something else that gripped the pit of
Manya's stomach: there were trucks.

She looked around again. Guns. Soldiers. Fear. Trucks. It
could only mean one thing: deportation. She put her arm around
Chaim and they joined a partially formed line.

A large group of people was standing within the cordon of
military personnel. Manya heard crying, saw previously proud
shoulders heave with sobs, was startled by a tormented wail
from a female voice. She watched all heads turn, ever so slightly,
to monitor Damone's taunting appraisal of his laborers. The sun
reflected off the brass of his insignia as he paced the columns;
then Manya caught her breath when he stopped at the head of
her row. He raised an arm and flicked his wrist as if to create a
line of separation, while Wagner leaned forward to listen. Wagner clicked his heels, about-faced, and sharply repeated the command to his staff, who surged forward to carry it out.

Which group would go? Which would stay? About fifty people were herded away and prodded up the tonguelike ramps that
protruded from the gaping trucks. Manya and Chaim stood
absolutely still, holding hands in what was now the front line of
the remaining group.

The Jews left standing in the street had succeeded in control-
ling their emotions. The only movement came from the special-
detail soldiers as they assumed their guard positions on the truck.
The last sound of the deportation came as the trucks groaned
into gear.

The rest of the day was normal.

Clickety-clack, clickety-clack. Like a metronome, the monotonous sound and the regularly swaying motion of the train
lulled Meyer to sleep, though only briefly, for it was not long
between stops. The squealing of the train's approach to the next
depot brought his bobbing head to attention, and he had to
struggle to remember where he was, where he had been, and the
destination he had chosen this time.

Then it would start all over again. Clickety-clack, clickety-clack. North and south, east and west were scrambled in his mind, but he had to keep it straight. What if he were questioned, gave his practiced sick-uncle-in-Lublin response, and then discovered he was not going north, but west, toward Cracow? The thought made him shiver. He stared out the window to note landmarks—a burned-out barn here, a high water tower there—then repeated the itinerary of towns and villages connected by the ribbon of track he rode.

Time passed at its own rate, with no help or hindrance from Meyer. Rarely did he initiate a conversation with other passengers, knowing it was better to keep his mouth shut. But at times it was almost impossible to remain silent, like when he overheard conversations on the train.

"It's because of the Jews that there's a war," an old man was telling his grandson. The small boy looked respectfully at his grandfather and waited to hear more.

"You weren't born yet when Marshal Pilsudski was alive. He was too easy with them. They got away with murder while he was in power. What the Germans are doing now should have been done years before. This will teach them a lesson once and for all. The Jews, they're like ticks, sucking up everything around them, caring only for themselves. But you won't have to worry, the Germans are finally taking care of them. They're doing us a favor. Once they've completed their work, our problems will be over," the man finished, smiling.

The boy nodded his head.

Meyer wanted to scream at the top of his lungs: Are you mad? Do you know what they're doing to us? What have I ever done to you? Do you know my father? Or my little sister, who is younger than your grandson? What did she do to you or anyone? But he held his tongue.

Occasionally, he would hear someone speak up for the Jews. "It's wrong what they're doing to those poor people," a voice might say. At other times it was more of a whisper: "I don't like them, but they are human beings."

Meyer wanted desperately to believe that there were more

Salkis, Gorskis, Achlers, Tomitzkis, and Wisniewskis sitting on the train with him, behind the ticket counters, in the stores, and on the farms he passed. There had to be more, but where were they?

At this point, Meyer had been on the run for more than a month. His head throbbed with tension, and his body ached with fatigue and loneliness. He had gotten so sick once that he had to stay in Radom longer than planned because he kept vomiting.

No more, though; he was fed up with running. He had decided that he was going to ask Salki to help him join the underground of Jews who were hiding in the woods around Hrubieszow. He just couldn't keep on like this.

That night Manya could tell something was wrong the minute she saw Meyer. Although there was the happiness of being together, Meyer was far too quiet. "What's bothering you?" she finally asked.

"I've made a decision, Manya, and you aren't going to be pleased," he answered. "But I can't go on like this. I just can't. I'm going to ask John to help me get to the underground."

"No, Meyer, no!" she wailed. "It'll be all right. I'll stay here with you. Salki will let us stay."

"I have to, Manya, don't you see?"

"No, I don't see," she protested. "You'll be killed. That's what I see. What about your family?"

He didn't know what to say or do. He had to help her understand, but he couldn't seem to find the words to describe what he'd been going through. "Shh, Manya. Let's talk about it." He pulled her close, knowing how much his decision was hurting her.

Their raised voices brought Salki to see what was going on. "Meyer, Manya, what's the matter with you two?" he demanded.

"Meyer wants to join the underground," Manya said angrily, pointing an accusing finger in Meyer's face. "He's tired of running," she added a little more sympathetically.

"John, it's not just being tired of running. I'm disgusted with everything I have to do. The deceptions. Moving to a different place each night so people won't be suspicious."

"And you think it's so different in the underground, that you have the luxury of staying in one place, moving only when it's convenient for you?"

"I'm sick of listening to people talk about Jews, about me, about my family, as though we were some sort of subhumans."

"Oh, I see," the commissioner said, turning to address Manya. "I guess our friendly Gestapo and SS are now treating you with respect in the ghetto, addressing you as 'Miss' Nagelsztajn. Right, Manya?"

Meyer could hardly have missed his point. He knew what Manya, Chaim, and the rest of the Jews in the ghetto went through. They heard the same words day in and day out as he did. Only they couldn't turn their backs and walk away as he usually could.

"I'm scared, John—scared of being caught. And worrying if I'm caught what it could mean for you and your family. I'm scared for the people in Mislavitch who are helping my family, and scared for Manya and Chaim."

"I'm scared, too, Meyer," Manya said gently, taking Meyer's hand lightly in hers. "Every time I pick up something in a house and hide it in my dress, I'm terrified. But I know it will help you, so I do it."

"Meyer, you're barely seventeen years old," John added. "Of course, you're scared. I know what you're doing is difficult, but you've got to keep trying."

"John, you know how much we appreciate—" Meyer began.

"I'm not asking for your thanks," Salki interrupted with a sweep of his hand. "I only want you to understand that everything is more complicated and involves more people than it might appear. Going to the underground is out of the question; it's just not a good time. Please trust me. You're still safe with our current plan. We can talk more about this in the morning, after you've had some rest."

"John, can I stay with Meyer tonight?" asked Manya, trying to change the subject.

"No, Manya," Meyer responded quickly instead. "You must go back. Chaim will be waiting for you."

"He'll be all right," Manya assured him. "If I don't come back, he'll just think that I'm staying with you."

"You know it's fine with me, Manya. Just be sure to leave before anyone might see you," John cautioned as he left the room.

Manya curled up beside Meyer on the small bed. "Hold me, Meyer, and don't let go," she whispered sleepily.

Each time Manya went to Salki's, Chaim accompanied her as far as the passageway, helping to carry the smuggled goods and waiting patiently for her return. And each time, she had come back. But tonight she was already long overdue, and Chaim was starting to worry.

She had told him over and over it would be all right for him to return to the house without her, but he had always resisted before. Keeping the vigil was a matter of pride: if she could take risks, so could he, and he had waited faithfully in the freezing, junk-filled alley, half-dozing, time after time, until he heard her scuffling feet approach. Tonight, though, he was tired—tired of everything—and he knew she would understand if he wasn't there when she returned.

Chaim couldn't help but feel that he didn't belong here anymore. Manya spent most of her free time helping Meyer, and although Sam and Leon tried to include him in their conversations, the effort was obvious.

His uneasiness grew as he made his way to the house, realizing he had not sneaked through these streets alone since the first night after he'd left the haystack, six months ago. Now Manya was always with him. He wished he didn't have to rely on her to such an extent. He was old enough, nearly fifteen now, to be more self-sufficient. He should accept more responsibility for himself and take on more for others.

Casting aside his usual caution, he approached the steps of the house and made more noise than necessary opening and entering the door. He moved toward the bedroom, then stopped. He wasn't really sleepy—tired yes, but not sleepy. He turned around. What should he do? His eye caught a bottle of vodka on the table. He had never liked it much, but still. . . . Manya should be home by now; what was keeping her? Maybe he should go back to the alley. He didn't want to worry her, but she was certainly worrying him.

He popped the cork on the bottle and smelled the contents. Hmm. Not so bad. Why not? he thought, reaching for a glass. He poured some in. That seemed about right; that's how much Sam and Meyer poured. He held up the glass and peered at it, shrugged, and filled it up. What did he care how much Sam and Meyer drank?

He took a sip, then downed the rest. He felt fine. Of course he felt fine; what had he expected to do—faint? He was grown up now; he could drink. He could do a lot of things like an adult. He could even deliver goods to Salki once in a while. Manya and Janek didn't have to take all the chances. He would ask her about it. He refilled the glass and walked over to the overstuffed chair. No, he would *tell* her, he corrected himself. When you were an adult, you didn't ask.

He gulped the liquid and plopped into the chair. He hadn't meant to sit down so abruptly. He felt very warm, a little clammy even. Only a few minutes ago he had been freezing. Must be the liquor; he had heard it was a good thing to have when you were cold. He tipped the bottle toward the glass again. Meyer would let him help if it were up to him. He would say that to Manya. He toasted the thought and drained the glass.

When Sam found Chaim still in the chair the next morning, no amount of shaking and yelling could penetrate his stupor or break his hold on the empty bottle clutched protectively in his arms. Had Chaim been awake, he would have heard a very angry Sam threaten to tell Manya. He would have heard a very disgusted Sam exclaim at the smell of Chaim's liquor-soaked clothes. He would have seen a very amused Sam shake his head in recognition of the typical manifestations of growing manhood. And he would have felt a very sympathetic Sam hold him while he retched, then wipe his face with wet cloths.

It was only after work that day that Manya came home. After staying the night with Meyer, she had gone directly to the site to join her work mates. So the evening count would be one higher, she thought; what could it matter? What mattered most to her was that Meyer was gone and she didn't know when she would see him again.

That night, when the Germans realized they had one more than they had that morning, she almost laughed out loud. The soldier flipped through his chart and delayed the usually matter-of-fact dismissal while he struggled with the realization that he had caught a mistake. But wait, maybe it was his own error— the numbers seemed to change from day to day and were hard to keep up with. With an uncertain look on his face, he released them.

Manya was so lost in her thoughts that she didn't notice Chaim's absence from the lineup. The she heard Sam calling to her. "Guess what your brother did," Sam began.

"Chaim?" Manya repeated, glancing around. "Where is he? I don't see him."

"No, it's all right," Sam assured her quickly. "He's at home. But he was a bad boy last night."

"What are you talking about?" Manya said, stopping in the street.

"He got drunk! Oh, boy, he got drunk—guzzled my whole bottle of vodka. I came out this morning and found him passed out in a chair. I shook him and shook him, and the more I did, the more he threw up! He didn't even know where he was."

Manya was not amused. She strode past Sam toward the house.

"Wait, Manya," he called to her back. "Wait for me!"

She ignored him. These men! she thought, shaking her head. You'd think they would learn to grow up another way.

It was a warm spring day, and Wagner was half a step away before Manya and her friend Esther, deep in conversation, noticed him. They quickly scrambled to get off the wooden side-walk and out of his way, praying that he would just pass on by. The two young women stood in the gutter with their heads bowed, not only to convey a sense of servility but also in an effort to achieve anonymity. Manya thought fleetingly that she hadn't seen Wagner since that day he'd asked her what she knew about Meyer's absence.

Wagner's boots thundered a step or two past Manya and Esther, then stopped.

"Jews!" he bellowed, advancing toward them in slow, threatening strides. Manya looked up. Remembering how Esther had helped her the day when she'd faltered at her family's house, Manya was determined to help her friend now.

Wagner's black-gloved hands rested haughtily on his hips. Manya looked back at the ground without answering.

"You Jews!" Wagner screamed again, bending closer.

The young women raised their eyes. Wagner's face was contorted with rage and loathing. "Is this your private sidewalk?" he goaded.

"No, Herr Wagner," said Manya.

"Do you belong on the same sidewalk as a German officer?"

"No, Herr Wagner," Manya answered again. "I'm very sorry. We meant no disrespect. Please excuse us, we didn't see you—"

"'Please excuse us, we didn't see you,'" he mocked, staring wildly at them. "There is no excuse for you!" he screamed. "You never learn! You grovel and crawl to my face, but when my back is turned, you think I don't know how your attitudes change? You make me sick with your sniveling. I'm sick to death of every last one of you!"

Frantic to calm him, Manya tried to catch his eyes with her own, but he stared right through her. She saw a gloved hand move to stroke his chin as he pondered their fate.

Didn't he recognize her? Surely he wouldn't harm her if he did. Had he forgotten who she was?

No, she reminded herself: Wagner had never spoken a civil word to Manya when there were other people around. Perhaps if she could just play for time, he would come to his senses and think of a way to let them go without losing face. How could she steer him to that course?

"Please, sir—" she began.

"Silence!" he hissed. The voice was cold. He seemed to want

to make them suffer while he determined their punishment. There was nothing they could do but stand there. Manya grabbed Esther's hand.

The motion caught Wagner's attention. Something happened behind his face. "Oh, such good friends, I see," he scoffed. "Such good friends that you ignore your responsibility to a German. I must teach you better manners. Up!" he commanded. "Up on the sidewalk, both of you!"

Manya pleaded with her eyes.

"Move!" he yelled. The two girls jumped to comply, standing tightly together in front of him.

"You want to walk on the sidewalk? So! You *shall* walk on the sidewalk. Perhaps we'll walk together. It seems you feel worthy of such an honor. Very well, we shall walk. But that way," he said, pointing behind them. "Turn around."

Esther hesitated too long for Wagner. He shoved her with one hand, releasing the flap of his holster with the other. Stumbling to get her feet under her, she turned around very slowly.

Manya stirred.

"You stay!" Wagner ordered Manya, then turned back to Esther. "Walk!" he shouted. "Now!"

Manya saw Esther put one shaking leg in front of the other.

Then there was a terrific explosion, and Esther fell onto the wooden boards a few feet away.

Manya stood frozen. She had been sprayed with blood and bone fragments. Worst of all, she couldn't shut her eyes against the sight of Esther's oozing skull.

Manya waited for Wagner's next bullet directed at her. Get it over with! She felt frozen in time.

But no second shot was fired. Instead she heard Wagner's boots, then saw them next to Esther's crumpled form. As if he were touching a spoiled piece of meat, Wagner slipped a foot under her shoulder and rolled her off the sidewalk and into the gutter. Esther moaned.

At the sound, Manya glanced up, then stared down again.

"Bury her!" Wagner snapped, his face drained of color.

"But she's not—"

"I said bury her!"

"I . . . a shovel—I'll get—"

"No shovel. Use your hands. Then clean up this mess. I want to see no trace of it the next time I walk by here." He brandished his pistol.

Manya bent over and gingerly touched Esther's face. "Herr Wagner," she pleaded in a hoarse whisper, "couldn't I take her to the cemetery—"

"No! This is a lesson for you swine! You'll bury the bitch here . . . unless"—he leaned over to thrust the gun in Manya's face— "unless you want to die here too!"

Wagner watched the resignation pass over her face as she began digging.

A few minutes later, Esther stopped breathing.

Days passed, and the trucks were coming again. This time Manya had decided that she wasn't going to line up with the others. She'd take Chaim and they'd hide until the deportation was over. She knew exactly what to do and how. But why had Chaim left the house so early this morning? She knew something had been bothering him during the last week. He had become depressed again, thinking more and more about their missing family and about their own situation.

Now she had to find him among all these people in the street. She had only a few minutes before the Germans would be organized, and she needed every second to make her plan work.

Then she saw him just ahead. Thank God! She approached him from the rear and placed a hand on each of his bony shoulders. He stiffened as she steered him to the side of a building.

"We're going to run—to hide," she whispered in his ear. "I know a perfect place. Then, after they've left, we'll go to Salki's. They're going to deport some more today, Chaim, and we can't take a chance that we'll be among them. Come on," she urged, grabbing his hand. "Follow me."

But he pulled back.

Manya turned around and looked into her brother's face.

"No," he said, shaking his head.

"No?" she echoed. "What do you mean? Chaim, we have to hide—we have to run!" She almost had to scream to be heard over the growing noise in the street.

"No," he repeated. "I'm tired of running. I don't want to run anymore."

Manya glanced behind him and saw the Germans getting into their positions.

"Chaim, we have to go. Don't do this, please!" she begged.

"No, Manya," he answered. "I'm not running." He couldn't meet her eyes. His determination was clear.

Manya took a few steps away from him and looked toward the Zamosc bridge. There were more soldiers coming across it. There was so little time.

Gunshots ran out. The soldiers were firing warning shots in the air.

"Chaim!" she called again, but he didn't turn around. If I go, she thought, maybe he'll follow me. It was all she could think of to do. She began to run, glancing over her shoulder to see if he was behind her. He wasn't. But she had to keep going. She ducked down a side street, then another, and came back out onto the same street a block away, right by the bridge. No guards. She dropped into the high grass that flanked the river, working her way backward, feet first, under the low bridge. She couldn't turn her eyes away from the action a block away: the moving crowd, people frantically choosing this line or that one.

Then she saw Chaim in the fourth row. Manya fixed burning eyes on his face. It's all right, she kept telling herself, it's all right. They won't take him. They'll take someone else.

There was a rumbling over her head that made her jump. Then the trucks lurched into view and stopped, their brakes screeching.

She sought Chaim's face again, finally locating his curly hair. He gazed straight ahead. With the trucks in the way, she couldn't see Damone or Wagner. She wouldn't be able to catch the first sign of who would be chosen. What was happening?

Save him, she prayed. Oh, God, save him. See how pale he is. He's only fourteen! She heard Wagner's voice but couldn't make out the words. Then a section of the lines broke off, melding together so fast she couldn't be sure how many rows it represented.

Her frantic eyes skipped over the taller figures. She was looking for a shorter person, hazel eyes, brown hair, thin. There! No, that was someone else. She looked for a brown jacket, sleeves too long, and knickers belted in folds around a slender waist—maybe him! Then the boy turned; wrong again.

The fifty selected mounted the truck ramps one by one. Manya's eyes darted from one ramp to the other.

Then she saw him. They were taking him. Chaim paused only a second before he disappeared into the belly of the truck. But he didn't look around; perhaps he was only waiting for the path to clear in front of him.

As he stepped from her view, Manya collapsed into the grass. She lay there and heard truck doors slamming and ramps scraping against metal truck beds as they were shoved from the ground to the inside. She heard the engines accelerate, but the trucks didn't cross over her head. They rattled off in the opposite direction.

An order for dismissal echoed through the street. Then it grew very quiet.

Ely Nagelsztajn, summer/fall 1938.

Three of the Nagelsztajn children in 1938:
Chaim, Gittel, and Joshua.

Nagelsztajn children, early 1930s: (back row) *Letty, Ely, Gittel;* (front row) *Joshua, Baby Pola, and Chaim.*

The Korenblit family in 1938: (standing) *Toba, Aunt Rivka, Motl, Aunt Tovah, Minka, Meyer;* (seated) *Malka, Cyvia, and Avrum.*

Manya and Meyer in 1946, Eggenfelden, Germany, shortly after their marriage.

Manya and Meyer with baby Sammy in Eggenfelden, July 1947.

Police Chief Franiek Gorski with Mrs. Gorski and their daughter. (Photo courtesy of Henrik Gorski)

Meyer Korenblit and Henrik Gorski (Franiek's son), in Henrik's home in Hrubieszow, August 1981. (Photo by Michael Korenblit)

Entrance to the ghetto where the last Jews of Hrubieszow lived. Building on left was the Jewish Center. These are the original buildings. (Photo taken in 1981 by Michael Korenblit)

In the center is the house where Manya, Meyer, Chaim, Sam, and Leon lived in the ghetto. (Photo taken in 1981 by Michael Korenblit)

Meyer in 1981 at the Korenblit flour mill in Mislavitch with Isaac Achler (far right). (Photo by Michael Korenblit)

Entrance to underground airplane factory in Flossenburg, where Meyer drove the tram. (Photo taken in 1981 by Michael Korenblit)

Manya and Chaim in Newcastle, January 1982. (Photo courtesy Newcastle Chronicle & Journal, Ltd.)

Manya, Chaim, and Meyer, reunited at last. (Photo courtesy
Newcastle Chronicle & Journal, Ltd.)

A celebration at Chaim's home in Newcastle: (standing, left to
right) *Kathie Janger, Joan Korenblit, Michael Korenblit, Cecilia
Nagelsztajn, Meyer Korenblit, Judith Nagelsztajn, Michael
Nagelsztajn;* (seated in center) *Manya Korenblit and Chaim
Nagelsztajn. (Photo by Allan Glenwright, Newcastle)*

CHAPTER NINE

Loss

"To every thing there is a season, and a time to every purpose under the heaven: a time to be born, and a time to die; a time to plant, and a time to pluck up that which is planted; a time to kill, and a time to heal; a time to break down, and a time to build up; a time to weep, and a time to laugh; a time to mourn, and a time to dance; a time to cast away stones, and a time to gather stones together; a time to embrace, and a time to refrain from embracing; a time to get, and a time to lose; a time to keep, and a time to cast away; a time to rend, and a time to sew; a time to keep silence, and a time to speak; a time to love, and a time to hate; a time of war, and a time of peace."

—ECCLESIASTES 3: 1–8

Avrum Korenblit lay in a ward of chipped-paint hospital beds in the town of Sokul. His head was swathed in bandages spotted crimson from the wound they covered.

Hat in hand, Meyer approached the bed and looked at his father's face. Several days' beard peppered Avrum's chin, and angry bruises covered one side of his forehead. Meyer had to look away when his father's half-closed eyelids flickered open to reveal eyes rolled inward. Then Avrum moaned and muttered words garbled by the injury to his head.

He had been hit with a metal bar and left to bleed in the street. That's what some men in Sokul had told Meyer. They had waited for the Nazis to march away and then carried Avrum to the ghetto hospital. He had been alone, they said. No woman was with him—and no children. They told Meyer the injury had occurred three days ago. Three days ago, Meyer thought, he had been in Zamosc, only thirty miles away.

Avrum groaned again, and Meyer leaned closer to his father's ear. "Papa?" he whispered. Struggling between his desire to rouse his father and a child's instinct not to disturb a sleeping parent, Meyer called to Avrum again. "Papa? It's me, Meyer. Can you hear me?"

He gave no response.

Meyer continued. "Papa, can you tell me where Mama is? Is she coming here?"

Nothing.

Meyer sat at his father's bedside for three more days. He watched as the doctor periodically listened to Avrum's heart and peered under his eyelids. When Meyer asked if his father would get better, the doctor turned kind eyes on the son, explaining that the injury was grave and there was nothing he could do to reverse Avrum's condition. He told Meyer to keep trying to reach his father, to talk to him, to mention other members of the family. He said that Avrum might respond if Meyer called him by name, but that he must shout it. Yes, the doctor admitted, it's hard for a son to yell at his sick father—harder still to make noise in a hospital ward. But whispering was unlikely to break through his unconsciousness.

Meyer followed the doctor's recommendations faithfully. He also moistened his father's dry lips with water, swabbed his face and chest with a wet cloth, held his hand, and smoothed away the stubble on his face with a razor. And Meyer kept up a constant stream of talk, hoping something might get through.

"You can't leave now, Papa. Mama and the girls need you. I need you. Don't die, Papa, please don't die. Why did you ever leave Mislavitch? You were safe there, protected." Whenever Meyer's tone threatened to change from pleading to anger, he reminded himself that he was directing it at the wrong person. Maybe he himself was to blame for not going to Avrum the first time Achler told him the Korenblits were nervous about staying in Mislavitch. Or perhaps Isaac had become frightened and hadn't really talked Avrum out of leaving. Meyer caught himself. It was not the fault of any of them. They were all just doing the best they could under intolerable conditions.

In spite of Meyer's attempts to wake him, Avrum remained locked in the coma, moving only in spasms, speaking nothing but garbled words. Hour after hour, Meyer sat there, moving away only when the dressing on the wound was changed or when he was pushed aside by nurses hurrying to minister to his father's intensifying convulsions.

More than once, Meyer buried his head in the sheets of Avrum's bed and cried. Sometimes he fell asleep sitting by the bed, cradling his father's hand to his cheek. At night Meyer stumbled to the home of one of the men who had helped Avrum, where he slept fitfully until it was time to take up his vigil again.

When Meyer arrived the fourth morning, a nurse blocked his way into the ward. "I'm sorry—" she began, but Meyer pushed past her and looked down the row of beds. His father's was empty. He looked back at the nurse. The answer was in her eyes before he asked.

"Early this morning," she said. "It was very peaceful. We want you to know how sorry we are," she said, putting a hand on his shoulder.

He bowed his head and nodded, covering her hand with his own in gratitude for her concern. His voice was husky when he asked where they had taken his father's body.

"Downstairs," she said softly, turning Meyer away from the ward and pointing down the hall.

"Can I leave him there for an hour—would that be all right? Or half an hour, if that's too long?"

"Whenever you're ready," she said. "I'm sure you want to make arrangements."

"Arrangements . . ." he repeated. "Yes, I'll need to get a—"

"Whenever you're ready," she repeated. "We're all so sorry. You hadn't seen him for a long time, had you?" she asked.

"No," Meyer answered. "Not for quite a while."

And he still didn't know where his mother was. If only his father had been able to explain.

Meyer talked with a number of people about the burial. He was relieved to find out that he could arrange a service and that it was still legal for his father to be buried in the Jewish cemetery. If his father had to die now, Meyer reasoned, better here than in Hrubieszow, for at least here he could give him a proper funeral.

Meyer bought a coffin from a Jewish cabinetmaker who had turned his craft to more practical pursuits. Because Meyer paid in cash instead of bartering with goods, the man gave him a good price and offered to accompany Meyer to the hospital.

Setting the box down at the hospital entrance, Meyer inquired at the front desk, then the two men carried the coffin to the morgue, where they claimed his father's body. There would be no ritual washing of and praying over Avrum's remains, and Meyer had no packet of soil from the Holy Land—the ancient land of Israel—to sprinkle on top of the casket. If these were normal times, he would sit *shiva* for eight days and greet the horde of family and friends who would visit to pay their respects to his father, and each night he would light the memorial candle and recite the prayer in memory of a father:

"O heavenly Father, remember the soul of my dear father whom I recall in this solemn hour. I remember with esteem the affection and kindness with which he counselled and guided me. May I ever uphold the noble heritage he transmitted unto me so that through me, his aspirations shall be fulfilled. May his soul be bound up in the bonds of eternal life and his memory ever be for a blessing. Amen."

But his family was scattered, his friends too vulnerable to call together. Meyer was alone, coping quietly by himself with events that begged for companionship.

Later that afternoon at the stark cemetery, Meyer stood silently beside the grave site he had prepared with his own hands. His face and shirt were wet with perspiration, and his chest hurt with the effort to breathe. There may be a lot he couldn't do, he thought, but at least he could spare his father the indignity and anonymity of a mass grave, and he could bury him within the twenty-four hours prescribed by Jewish law.

The sun was low in the sky as ten men, including Meyer, circled the coffin. Nine men chorused the soft chant, for Meyer did not want to lend his approval to God by joining in. They were fools, he thought. Couldn't they see that God had turned His back on them?

Suddenly, a long-ago memory of Avrum's voice spoke to his son: "You have to trust in Him. Have faith."

No, Meyer thought, God has abandoned us. He shook his head and squeezed his eyes shut. Almost imperceptibly, he began to rock back and forth. Then, as if his body were being occupied by a force that wouldn't be denied, Meyer ripped the sleeve of his shirt. The traditional gesture of grief brought him back into the fold. He cried through the next two recitations.

As the last repetition of the Mourner's *Kaddish* began, he joined in, repeating the familiar words grudgingly at first and then with increasing conviction:

"Magnified and sanctified be the name of God throughout the

world which He hath created according to His will. May He establish His kingdom during the days of your life and during the life of all the house of Israel, speedily, yea, soon; and say ye, Amen."

He knew it would have pleased his father.

I t was as if the train's lonesome whistle echoed the mourning of the young man it carried home. Meyer sat tensely in his seat, leaning forward to speed the locomotive on its way.

"Hrubieszow," came the conductor's call at last.

The train was still easing into the station when Meyer jumped off, then picked his way up an embankment and ran quickly through a field into town.

John Salki's family was just finishing dinner when Meyer knocked and entered in one motion.

"Meyer!" Salki exclaimed, standing up. "You look terrible. Here—sit down. Was it a hard trip?"

Meyer coughed away the lump in his throat. Accepting the chair, he leaned forward, propping his forearms on his knees and staring at the floor. With breaths that came and went more like sighs, he tried to compose himself.

Mrs. Salki moved to her feet, stacking dishes and offering Meyer food. Then, from the kitchen, she called to her children, reminding them of their chores. Checking his pocket watch, Salki spoke quietly with Janek, and Meyer saw the boy nod.

"I've sent Janek to get Manya," the commissioner explained.

Meyer nodded gratefully. He still couldn't risk his voice.

Salki looked uncomfortable. Nicotine-stained fingers dug into his shirt pocket and drew out a pouch and a flat, banded sheaf of papers. Licking his thumb to coax a single sheet from the sheaf, he pried open the gathered end of the pouch. He shook out a measure onto the paper, then caught the strings of the bag in his mouth and pulled. He moved slowly and methodically, spreading, rolling, and sealing the cigarette. A match brought it to life.

"Can you tell me about it?" he finally asked, trying to convey with his tone that he was prepared to hear anything Meyer might say.

Meyer told his friend what had happened to Avrum: the

injury, the coma, the death, the funeral. When he had finished, Meyer saw the impact of his words in Salki's glistening, dark-circled eyes and in the long ash on his untended cigarette.

Then Salki covered his face with his hands, finally parting them to massage his temples. "You found no clue about your mother?" he asked, without looking at Meyer.

"Nothing," Meyer answered in a low voice. "Nothing," he repeated. "I'll have to go to Mislavitch. She's probably waiting for my father to send for her."

He followed Salki's circling fingers around and around his temples, then focused on the man's taut lips and clenched jaw. A battle was being fought behind Salki's eyes. Then his eyes fell limply to his lap as he made a decision. He took a deep breath and used it to force out the words.

"Meyer," he began haltingly, "I have something I must tell you, my friend. I'm afraid it's not good." He paused to summon his courage.

Meyer pulled upright and braced himself.

"I had a report," Salki continued. "It's not confirmed — Gorski is still checking — but it's something you have to know." The commissioner raised himself from his chair and paced the room slowly. He turned to face Meyer.

"There was a shooting. The report came to Gorski that a woman traveling by train was accused of being Jewish. She was removed from the train, questioned, and shot." He paused. "There were children with her, Meyer — three girls."

"Shot?" Meyer whispered.

"All of them," Salki replied.

Meyer let heavy lids fall over his eyes. He bent double and buried his head in his arms, rocking himself as his mother had done when he was a boy.

Then abruptly he sprang to his feet. "Are you sure it was my mother and sisters?" he demanded.

"Maybe not," Salki conceded. "As I said, the report is uncon-firmed, and we have no names. It *could* have been someone else."

"I have to go to Mislavitch to find out if they're there," said Meyer, moving to the door.

"No, wait, Meyer. Take time to think."

"I have to know, John," Meyer cried.

"But Manya will be here any minute. She's desperate to see you. She has come here nearly every night praying you'll be here. For God's sake, at least wait until you've seen her."

Holding the door wide, Meyer hesitated for a moment, then another. If he found his mother, she'd have to be told immediately about Avrum. He had to do it. If his mother was dead, he wanted to know now. He couldn't wait for anything.

"Explain," he pleaded to Salki. "My father . . . Mislavitch . . . sorry . . . few days." He crossed the threshold, then turned back. He had thought of something else. "Love," he added, and was gone.

There was no moon to light Meyer's way — just darkness. No stars to guide him — just blackness. No sounds to warn him of impending danger — just stillness.

Salki's words couldn't be true. He must have misunderstood Gorski. Yes, that was it. Or Gorski was mistaken. He had heard it secondhand, after all. His mother wouldn't have left, not until Avrum sent for her. It was too dangerous. Isaac would not have allowed her to go. She would have listened to him.

He ran and ran. Pushing himself to go faster, faster, and still faster. Move, feet! Quicker, legs! You're not tired. We have to get to Mama before she leaves. Yes, before she leaves. They would be there when he arrived. He would comfort his mother and sisters. He would stay with them, take care of them.

This must be a dream. It wasn't really happening. Meyer stumbled, tried to balance himself, but he was falling. Down, down, down. He crashed on the hard ground. Get up! It hurts. No, it doesn't!

Finally, there was Isaac Achler's house. No lights. Meyer didn't care; he'd wake them up. Thud! Thud! Thud! His fist beat his demand on the wooden door.

"Isaac! Isaac! It's me, Meyer. Get up!"

Thud! Thud! Thud!

Finally, a sleepy, bewildered Achler unlatched the door.

"You've got to take me to my mother. Right now," Meyer pleaded.

"But, Meyer—"

"Please, Isaac, you've got to. My father is dead."

The older man went limp, steadying himself against the wall. His head and shoulders sagged. He drew in deep breaths of air through his nose, trying to gain control of himself.

"Please take me to them," Meyer repeated.

"I can't, Meyer," Isaac choked, attempting to speak. "They—"

"They what, Isaac, what? You must tell me!"

"They left a few days ago," he finally got out.

Meyer felt his knees buckle, his hands began to shake, his head pounded. "No!" he pleaded. "They haven't left. I'll go to them."

Isaac grabbed him and shook him. "I'm sorry, Meyer. It's true. They're gone."

"But why? They were safe here," Meyer cried.

"I tried to talk them out of it, believe me, but Avrum wouldn't listen. He felt he was putting us in too much danger, and he was worried the family would be discovered. He wanted to find a safer place where nobody knew him. We heard there was a large ghetto in Sokul, so he went there by himself to see if it would be better. Then he was going to come back for Malka and the girls.

"When he didn't show up or send a message after three days, your mother was sure something must have happened. So she took the girls and left for Sokul. I tried to make them stay. I even said I'd go and try to find Avrum. But—I'm sorry, Meyer. There was nothing more I could say to change her mind."

Meyer tried to tell Isaac that it wasn't his fault, that there was nothing more he could have done.

But what had gone wrong? Just one week ago everyone was as safe as possible under the circumstances. Now it was all falling apart. He had to look for his mother and bring her back.

"I've got to find them."

"Meyer, you don't know where they are!"

"You said they went to Sokul. When?"

"Two days ago, but—"

"I'll find them there. Yes, they'll be there. I'm sure of it."

Isaac could only wish Meyer well as he watched the desperate young man set off.

There was no train to speed Meyer's journey in those late-night hours. But he was not going to wait, even if it meant running the whole way to Sokul. He would go as far as possible on foot and hope he'd be near enough to a town to catch a ride or a train when the sun came up.

Bypassing Hrubieszow, each step became heavier, and Meyer felt he had to rest, to lie down for a few minutes. But no, he told himself; he might fall asleep and not wake up. He kept assuring himself that Salki might be wrong. If so, Malka, Toba, Minka, and little Cyvia would be waiting for him in Sokul.

When he reached the town, he carefully sneaked into the ghetto, as he had the previous time, and found the man who had helped with his father's burial.

"I don't know if you remember me," Meyer began. "You helped me bury my father."

"Yes, of course," the man replied. "What is it? Why have you returned?"

"I'm looking for my mother and sisters. Do you know if they're here? I'm sure they came here."

"I don't think so. Not yet anyway," the man responded, trying to match Meyer's hopeful tone. "But we'll find out. Just like you, other people have sneaked into the ghetto."

"If they aren't here now, may I wait with you a few days? I know they'll come."

"Of course you can. Come, let's begin looking," the man answered, ushering Meyer out the door.

The rest of the day was spent searching, going from house to house, but with no luck. For three days Meyer waited, fighting the reality of Salki's words. At the end of the third day, he knew it was useless to wait any longer. They weren't here and they weren't coming. He returned to the cemetery. No one was there, so he could talk to his father in private. He closed his eyes and brought his father's image to his mind.

"Papa, I can't find them. What should I do?" Meyer paused in the silence.

"I'm sorry, Papa, for everything I ever did that hurt you. I'll try to believe—for your sake. But it's very hard. You did good all your life. I'll try to do just as you taught me. Someday this will be over and I'll tell my children about you, what a wonderful man you were. I'll be strong. It's just that I can't find Mama and the girls and I don't know where to look. If they're with you, Papa, tell them I tried. Tell them I tried."

Looking to the sky, he whispered. "Please take care of him. He did everything you asked of him. Don't turn away from him now." He turned slowly and left.

It was a long way back to Hrubieszow and Manya.

Reunited at last at Salki's house, Meyer and Manya talked all night. They lay on the floor, Meyer on his back with one arm bent across his face, Manya on her side, pressed against him.

"I feel like I'm dead," he sighed at last.

"I know," she answered in a hollow tone. Chaim was gone, but she could still hold on to the hope of being reunited with her family. Meyer had no such hope. His father, his mother, his sisters—all were gone.

This time it was with different eyes that Meyer observed the towns and villages from the trains. Now he wasn't so intent on remembering landmarks; he was thinking hard, working on his plan. For Meyer had decided that nothing would stop him this time from joining the underground.

He'd had many close calls on the trains. In Warsaw once, there were so many Germans on the first train that came by, he had passed it up. When the next train arrived, it too was filled with Nazis, and Meyer decided not to board it. The policeman standing in the station seemed to become suspicious of Meyer's hesitation. Twice he had seen the young man start to board, then change his mind. Meyer knew there was no choice but to take the third train that pulled in, no matter who was on it or where it was headed. That in itself was part of the problem. He had been on a journey without destination. The direction he chose to travel on any given morning might be turned around by 90 or 180 degrees by midday, all the result of his scrambled judgment.

Meyer shook his head and sighed. The conductor made a noisy entrance from an adjoining car and gave Meyer a friendly smile as he made his way down the aisle. Meyer couldn't help but think of another conductor, one he'd encountered on the train from Lublin to Chelm. There'd been no smile that time. The conductor had walked up to Meyer, taken his ticket, punched it, and started to return it. But as Meyer had reached for the ticket, the conductor had held on. "You've traveled with me many times, haven't you?"

Meyer had quickly responded, "I don't think so. I rarely ride the train."

But the conductor hadn't been convinced. Every time he had walked down the aisle, he looked over the young man. It had been all Meyer could do to stay seated and appear calm. The next time the conductor had come through the car, he had stopped beside a German soldier to talk. Meyer had known he couldn't ride any farther on that train. At the next stop, while the conductor was occupied, he had slipped out the other end of the car.

Well, no more, Meyer thought now. He was sick to death of the routine, trapped by its monotony, scared of the consequences. In all these weeks, he couldn't remember having had even one night of soothing rest. While no one had come after him or questioned his identity, he was unwilling to chance it anymore. Hearing the rumor of the death of his mother and sisters had pushed him to the brink. Gorski's confirmation of it had sent him over the edge.

As chief of police in Hrubieszow during the German occupation, Gorski had a dual role which at times caused him to walk a very thin line. He was held accountable for the actions of the citizens of the town, but he also had a responsibility to protect them. The Nazis were concerned only with his first duty, but would allow him to pursue the second as long as they were not inconvenienced.

When Gorski had received word about the deaths of four people from Hrubieszow, he had gone to the Gestapo to investigate. Since he was certainly within the bounds of his responsibility, the

Nazis had not been suspicious and had humored his inquiry. They had believed that Gorski was cooperating with them and viewed him as a loyal and trusted ally.

With some annoyance, the Germans had provided Gorski with information about the people who had been shot: one woman, they said, and three young girls. Gorski stood before them and listened as they continued, hoping he wouldn't recognize the descriptions of the people—but he did. He had wanted to be sure, so he had pushed them for the names of the victims. Their response had set his insides on fire: "What does it matter? They were only Jews. It's of no concern to you." But he had managed to control his expression as they finally gave him the names he hadn't wanted to hear.

Meyer winced when he thought of how difficult it must have been for Gorski to tell him about his mother and sisters. John Salki, Gorski, Manya, and himself had been sitting in Salki's living room. There was silence after Gorski had related his information about Malka and the girls. Meyer had been holding Manya's hand.

Finally, Meyer had spoken. "Manya, I'm going to the underground. Nothing you or they can say will stop me." He had expected her to object and was prepared to understand when she did. But she had not. She had brought his hand to her lips and kissed it, then stared out into the room.

"I don't want you to go, but I understand," she had said finally. "You've lost your father, your mother, your sisters. You have no idea if your brothers who went to Russia are alive. You want to fight back, to lash out. Do you think I don't understand? Don't you think I feel the same way? I was fighting back by helping you and Chaim. Now, they've taken Chaim, and I don't know where the rest of my family is. Now I only have you. If you leave, what have I got to fight for?" She paused. "You say you've made up your mind. So have I: where you go, I go. You must understand that."

And so it had been decided that Salki and Gorski would make contact with the underground and start making arrangements for both Meyer and Manya to escape. But it would take time, they warned, as long as two weeks, especially because only three days ago six partisans were caught and executed right outside of town. Salki and Gorski themselves no longer knew whom they could trust. For now, there was no alternative but for Meyer to get back on the train. Hopefully, by the time he returned, they'd have everything set up for him. Then, after establishing himself with the partisans, Meyer would send for Manya. Meanwhile, Gorski would see what he could do about getting forged papers for Manya, for they still believed that it was better that no one know the couple was Jewish.

Meyer felt relieved, but not triumphant. He had stuck with his decision, and in the end his friends had supported him.

Two weeks, Salki had said, and two weeks it had been, Meyer thought as the train sped along. The whistle blew.

"Next stop, Hrubieszow!"

He was through running.

"How long has Janek been gone?" Meyer asked.

Salki looked at his watch. "Not long. I sent him to Gorski's first and then to Manya's."

"But that means it will take longer for her to arrive," Meyer objected. "Manya and I need to spend as much time as possible together. Who knows when we'll be able to again?"

"I know, but it's important that we talk to you first without her. She's already frightened enough about your leaving. There's no reason for her to sit and listen to us discuss it."

"How is she, John? You've seen her often during the past two weeks. Will she be all right?"

"She cried like a child the first time she came here after you left. But she has accepted your decision. And she's come over many times since then, just wanting to talk and be with someone who knows you and cares what happens to you; I think it gives her strength. We've talked about her family, how much she misses them, and what an agonizing decision it was for her to leave them. She thinks about it constantly."

"Is she sorry she came with me?"

"Sad, yes. Regretful, no. She's been with the man she loves.

But she won't give up hope about her family. She continues to believe they are alive and that she will be reunited with them someday. And she believes in you more than anything. You may not see it all the time, but she is strong, Meyer, very strong."

"I know. I love her so much. My parents loved her also. I think they saw, even before I did, how much she cares for me. I won't let her down. Promise me, John, that after I leave you'll do everything you can to watch over her."

"Of course we will. You don't have to worry about that."

When Gorski arrived, he described what they'd been able to accomplish during the past two weeks. "I haven't been able to get papers for Manya yet," the police chief said, "but we're still working on it." He paused.

"As for the underground," Gorski continued, "I'm afraid our concerns were well founded. The partisans in the area are very fearful of letting anyone they don't know into the group. As we told you before you left, there is strong suspicion it was someone from Hrubieszow who betrayed the others before."

"But don't they trust the two of you? You've helped them in the past."

"Of course we've helped, but these days few people are willing to trust anyone completely. Too often, their confidence in someone has crumbled before them."

"Do they know the Gestapo are looking for me?"

"Yes, they do—which makes them even more cautious. They may think the reason you're still alive is that you made a deal, or that you're being watched and might lead the Nazis right to them."

"What if I told them I was not a Pole, as my papers say, but that I'm really Jewish?"

The two men looked at each other, contemplating that idea. "No, I don't think so, Meyer. It might even make it more difficult," Salki finally answered.

"Then what do I do?"

"You're to go to the wooded area two miles north of here tomorrow evening. There, two people will question you and look you over. Then they'll decide. But you must listen to them and abide by their decision. If they decide yes, you go with them. If they say no, you come back here. Do you agree?" Gorski asked him.

"Yes, but what will we do if they say no?" Meyer asked.

"We'll try again later," Salki answered.

Meyer was sure both men hoped that he would be sent back. He was glad now that Manya had not been present to hear this discussion.

"I've got to get home. It seems as if some SS men like my neighborhood," Gorski said ruefully. "They've moved in next door. It wouldn't be good for them to see me come in late at night. I won't say goodbye, my friend; only good luck. We'll see one another again. May God go with you and watch over you."

Manya arrived shortly after Gorski departed, and she and Meyer cuddled together for some time. There was so much to talk about, but words were hard to find.

"Manya, it's getting late," Meyer finally told her. "You must get back to the ghetto."

"No. I'm going to stay with you all night."

"You'll be missed at the count."

"I don't care, Meyer, I want to be with you."

"But if you stay, how will you get into the ghetto when it's light out?"

"I won't go to the ghetto," she answered. "I've been assigned to work on the farms, and they aren't far from here. I'll hide in the underbrush by the road until the rest of the girls come past and then join them."

"Aren't there any guards with them?"

"There were the first couple of days, but not since. The Polish farmer would notify the Gestapo immediately if one of us was missing, so the Nazis figure they needn't waste one of their men on that duty."

"I'm still worried about you. I don't want anything to—"

"Shh. Let's not think those thoughts. Let's just be together."

Throughout the night, neither Meyer nor Manya slept much, knowing it might be months before he could return or send for her—and maybe even longer.

All too quickly the night turned to morning, and it was time for Manya to leave.

"Manya, I love you more than you'll ever know," Meyer whispered, holding her tightly in his arms. "It's because of you that I'll be able to go on. Now you are my family, and I believe we will make it through this."

"Oh yes, Meyer, yes we will. God will watch over us," Manya whispered back. "I love you so much, and I'll be waiting for you, I promise. And my family—we'll find them once we're together again."

Meyer watched until Manya was almost out of sight and she turned to give him a final little wave.

Crouching in the bushes near the farms, Manya didn't have to wait long for her work group to pass. Then, checking to make sure there was no guard, she quickly joined them. A few of the girls asked where she'd been, but they willingly accepted her story. They all knew it was sometimes better not to know too much.

There was something different in their mood, though, that Manya sensed right away. It wasn't that they were happy, just different—more spirited.

"Why is everyone in such a good mood?" Manya finally asked.

"Haven't you heard the news?" one girl responded.

Just then the farmer came out and began giving instructions. Manya could barely contain herself. As soon as he was out of earshot, Manya grabbed the girl. "What news? I haven't heard anything."

"Those butchers are gone," she answered.

Manya didn't understand. "What are you talking about? Who?"

"The Gestapo. Damone, Wagner, and the others. They've all been transferred," she responded with a smile. "They're gone from Hrubieszow."

"Gone?" Manya repeated. "Damone—gone? Wagner—gone?" Manya could not ask it enough. "They're gone?" Then it became, "They're gone! They're gone!"

She was crying and laughing at the same time. This news

meant Meyer wouldn't have to leave. He could stay, and they could be together! She had to tell him before he left, but she couldn't leave now because the farmer might come back, She'd have to wait until lunchtime and sneak away at the break.

Time passed ever so slowly. What if Meyer left before she arrived, Manya worried. No, he just couldn't. She picked vegetables as fast as she could, convincing herself that the more quickly she worked, the more rapidly time would pass.

"Manya, don't work so hard. We have all day," one of the girls chided her.

Finally, lunchtime arrived. Manya walked casually away at first, but when she was out of sight of the others, she took off like a shot, her tired legs carrying her as fast as they could.

Throwing caution to the wind, she didn't even pretend to sneak into Salki's house. Instead she rushed in through the back door, scaring Mrs. Salki half to death. "Manya! What are you doing here?" she asked, her face white as a sheet.

"Where's John?" Manya gasped.

"He hasn't come home yet."

"Has Meyer left?"

"No. He's still in the attic."

"Tell him . . . not to . . . leave." She was panting, putting her hand on her chest, trying to catch her breath. "They've been . . . transferred! He can stay!"

"Manya, slow down. What are you talking about?"

"I can't explain now. I have to rush back to work before I'm missed. Just tell Meyer not to leave. The men who were hunting him have gone!"

When Meyer returned to the ghetto after three months of running, it was to a different house than before. Because previously full houses had been emptied by deportations, the Nazis had rearranged the housing to consolidate the dwindling number of ghetto residents, and Manya, Sam, and Leon had been moved from the first house they'd been in to another. Lying in bed in the early morning hours, Manya shut out the room and guided her dream into a fantasy of being Meyer's wife, of a

morning spent shopping in the old market, of planning a big
family dinner that would include the best food his profits from
the flour mill could provide. She let the dream dissipate, sighed,
and opened her eyes. At least Meyer was real, lying there next to
her. She snuggled closer.

He mumbled in his sleep and turned over. She glanced at the
blanket they had strung across the room for privacy, and heard
noisy yawns from Sam and Leon on the other side. In a way, she
wished those two had been lodged elsewhere this time, for their
presence seemed to magnify Chaim's absence.

The young ghetto inhabitants were nearing completion of the
available work in Hrubieszow and could make it last only a few
more months. They continued to hope that the Nazis would
come up with more projects before the present ones were
exhausted. The food was now less satisfactory, so more and more
of the items the four of them found had to be traded to Poles for
basic necessities. Attitudes across the ghetto were worsening. Circles of friends tightened, people turning inward to insulate themselves from each other. And most chilling of all, as the need for
workers diminished, they were becoming expendable, and the
old pattern of beatings and killings had begun again. It was
harder and harder to go on.

After work one day Sam seized an opportunity to speak to
Meyer alone. "I'm leaving," he announced nervously. "I want to
go back to my hometown."

"Alone?" Meyer asked.

"No, another fellow is going with me."

"Leon?"

"No, someone else. But that's not important." Sam looked at
Meyer intently. "What I need to tell you, Meyer, is that I need
information. You spent a long time running; you even had a set
of papers. I know that you must know someone who can help. I
was hoping you could tell me who."

The moment Meyer had dreaded for so long was here. His
friend needed help. Should he hand over his own means of
escape? Sam might as well have asked for his passport. Meyer
was sweating, his thoughts racing to think of another way. There

was none. Salki was the key. He had helped others besides Meyer; why not Sam too? Sam *and* his friend. But Meyer didn't know whom Sam was planning to take along. Meyer thought he could rely on Sam's judgment, but what about this other person? Meyer realized that he was thinking as Salki had said the leaders of the underground would think. No wonder the commissioner had been so cautious.

"Will you tell me, Meyer?" Sam prodded. "If you won't, just say so. I'll understand and I'll find another way."

Meyer raised a hand to quiet his friend. "I'll tell you," he said very slowly. "But you must promise to tell no one—including your friend—where you are going. Do you understand? Just get your friend and lead the way. I'll tell you how to go. Do you swear?"

Sam gave Meyer a sober look. "I swear," he repeated. Meyer stared at him a long time before he was satisfied.

"I can't promise you anything," he began, "but he might be willing to help. I haven't seen him for a while, but you can tell him I sent you. He may not be able to get papers for you, but he might find a way to put you in touch with the underground."

"What is his name?"

"Salki—John Salki," Meyer answered.

"Yes," Sam replied with the look of someone who has just confirmed a long-held suspicion. "I thought so. I heard rumors."

Meyer mapped out a safe route to Salki's house. The precious information electrified the air between the two. Sam seemed about to offer awkward thanks when Meyer spoke again.

"There's something else I must ask you, Sam, something very difficult." He cleared his throat. "You can ask Salki to help you, but you must abide by his decision. If he says he can't help, you must accept it and look for another means of escape. Can you do that?"

Sam's look grew wiser as Meyer's words sank in. "I will, Meyer—I swear," Sam assured him.

"When are you leaving?" Meyer asked.

"Tonight. So I guess I'd better get my things together." Sam rose to leave the room, changed his mind, and came close to

Meyer. He awkwardly hooked an arm around Meyer's neck and shoulders. "I want you to know I tried to think of another way. I didn't want to ask you," he said sadly. "I know you're worried." He fidgeted. "There's no way to thank you—"

"Just keep quiet and take care of yourself," Meyer answered.

"I promise," Sam pledged as he left the room.

A few days later, word came down in chilling bits of hearsay. The night after he'd heard the rumors, Meyer forced himself to go to the Jewish Center after the evening count. The conversation inside stopped when he opened the door; then, as the people there saw he was one of them, it hummed anew.

"Did you hear?" one asked.

"A tragedy," someone answered.

"You say he was hiding Jews?" a third inquired.

"Two," came the reply.

"And he was shot?"

"In front of his wife and children."

"God help them!" the chorus grieved. "Such a brave man. Such a savior."

"And the Jews?"

"Shot too."

Meyer was still trying to stay calm and make sense of the fragments of conversation as the voices continued.

"An official?" one asked.

Garbled words. Then, "roads."

"Nazis," someone supplied.

"Commissioner . . ." one person began.

"John Salki," another finished.

The pieces fell into place: Commissioner of Roads John Salki had been shot dead outside his house. His wife and children were watching. Two Jews were shot trying to escape.

Meyer and Manya grew closer still in the weeks after Salki's death, whispering to each other until all hours of the night, fingering the meager collection of valuables that might finance an escape. They assured each other that nothing would deter them and no one would stop their plan. Over and over Meyer repeated the steps they would take to reach the underground together. Time after time, they laid it out and looked at it, worrying over the weak spots, selecting rest stops and hideouts along the way.

More than one conversation trailed off because of an accidental reference to Salki, as they tiptoed around the pain of his death. The memory of Salki's disapproval echoed in Meyer's mind each time he handled the gun he would tuck in his belt when they left for good.

Salki's words echoed in Meyer's mind: "Do you think I'm not scared every time I let a Jew into my house, knowing what would happen if we were caught? Someday my luck may run out, Meyer. But it's the right thing to do . . . the right thing to do . . . the right thing to do. . . ."

Meyer had had no contact with Gorski during the last month. He wondered if Salki's death would stop the police chief from continuing his own resistance against the Nazis. It might make him more cautious, Meyer thought, but he doubted that Gorski would ever give up.

Meyer had pledged to himself that he would not approach Gorski for any more help. He had asked enough of him already. Besides, the plan he and Manya worked out looked promising, based as it was on the machinery Salki and Gorski had put in place weeks ago. All Meyer had to do was follow the steps they had outlined. Manya still had no papers, but Meyer was relying on his to vouch for both of them.

Meyer and Manya's thoughts were on their plans when they presented themselves for the dreary morning lineup. But what was this? Shrieking voices, sputtering engines, and the cadence of quickly moving soldiers filled their ears.

They scanned the scene before them. Manya's practiced eyes swept the crowd to choose a line that wouldn't lead to the waiting trucks. But there *were* no lines this time, no organized formations. People swarmed before her, swaying one way, then the other, as soldiers holding rifles sideways prodded them into groups, then propelled them into trucks.

Manya felt herself swept from Meyer's side in a sudden surge, then saw him reaching toward her, straining over shoulders, between linked arms, around another desperate hand. His fingers finally closed around her arm, and she thought it would be wrenched from its socket. Then he was behind her, his other arm around her waist.

Still they were shoved on, the pool of humanity creating its own waves as some pressed ahead to avoid the blows and others pulled back in hopes of staying behind.

Then they were climbing the ramp, Meyer nearly carrying her. It was dark inside the truck as they collapsed on wooden seats that ran the length of both sides. The ramp crashed to their feet.

The vehicle lurched roughly ahead, jostling the riders against each other. As it negotiated a sharp right turn, they were pressed still more tightly together. Then a swerve to the left sent them sliding the other way.

After a few minutes, they came to a noisy halt. Guards holding jauntily to the rearview mirrors at the front and to the spine of the canvas support at the rear jumped to the ground and hustled into position. There were no ramps this time. The soldiers ordered the Jews to jump from the trucks by themselves.

When their turn came, Meyer went first, then reached up to steady Manya's descent. He caught her to him again and moved out of the way to await the next command.

Manya squeezed Meyer's arm as she realized they had been brought to the train station. Her father had spent months there doing brick work under the Nazis' instructions. There was hardly any structure in her view that hadn't been touched by his hands. The thought was not comforting. Had this too been Chaim's last glimpse of Hrubieszow?

More shouts and echoing cries as the crowd was moved toward the track. Soldiers used their fists to knock loose the steel pinions that fastened the doors of railroad cars, then hauled them open along rusty grooves. Brandishing weapons, they forced reluctant figures into the cavernous cars.

Meyer and Manya tumbled to the floor of the cattle car. Again metal groaned on metal as the sliding door swallowed up the daylight. They heard a loud clang as the iron arm slammed into its locked position. When their eyes adjusted to the darkness, they saw in the corner at the top a small window. Some formed a human ladder to look out. Meyer and Manya did not join them.

Manya, trying not to hear the whimpering that enveloped the enclosure, buried her face in Meyer's chest to muffle her own.

So this was what all those thousands of her neighbors and friends had gone through the previous times Jews had been driven from the city.

This was what her own family must have experienced ten months ago, and Chaim only three months ago.

This was what it was to be deported.

CHAPTER TEN

Deportation and

a promise

"In this tempestuous, havoc-ridden world of ours, all real communication comes from the heart. Outwardly we are being torn apart and the paths to each other lie buried under so much debris that we often fail to find the person we seek. We can only continue to live together in our hearts, and hope that one day we may walk hand in hand again."

The young people from the Hrubieszow ghetto had been divided into two railroad cars. In one, Manya was sitting between Tovah and Meyer. The crying around them had been replaced by low whispers: "where . . . ?" "how long . . . ?" "is this . . . ?" "why . . . ?"

Manya didn't need to hear the complete questions to know what was being asked. She could finish them herself. Was this the end of everything she and Meyer had planned?

Minutes turned into hours, and still the train didn't move. The men and women inside heard occasional banging or someone yelling an order outside, but other than that, it grew quiet. Even the inside of the car was silent. Movement and whispering seemed to halt at the same time; people huddled together waiting for what would come next.

Suddenly the engine started, spitting out its message: they were leaving. The car lurched forward, then gradually accelerated. They were on their way. No one knew if that was good or bad.

Meyer pulled Manya closer. Neither spoke, but others began to talk. Meyer's attention drifted in and out of the various conversations. Then he nudged Manya. "If that works, we'll try it."

"If what works?" she asked.

He pointed to the corner of the car where the small window was. A number of people had gathered and were helping a young man climb up.

"What's he doing?" Manya asked.

"He's going to crawl through the window and jump off the train."

"But it looks too small for him to get through. And even if he does, the jump will probably kill him. It feels like the train is going pretty fast."

"Maybe. But it's worth a try."

All eyes were riveted to the tiny opening that teased them with the notion of escape. Each move the man made was felt by each individual watching. When he slipped, they all slipped. As he pulled himself up with straining arms, their bodies tightened as if to transfer their strength to him. Would he fit through the small opening? Their eyes measured him, then the window. It looked doubtful. First his arms went out, then his head. Only his wiggling torso and legs were left; then they too disappeared. He was out. Someone quickly climbed up and looked through the window to try to see what had happened. He reported that the young man had made it to the top of the car. The train wasn't going at full speed, but it would still be a very dangerous jump. Nothing more could be seen.

Only a moment passed before a shot rang out. The train slowed, then came to a full halt. No one said a word. Suddenly the door was pulled open.

Bright sunshine flooded the car, causing the people inside to shade their eyes with hands and arms. Outside, soldiers were lined up, guns pointed. One of them began to yell. "Stupid Jews! If anyone tries that again, we'll kill you all on the spot!"

The closing door again plunged them into darkness; then they heard the clang of the lock falling back into position and the train picked up speed. Once again, those inside reminded themselves that they had to be responsible for each other: no action would be taken by one that might jeopardize another.

"Manya, did you notice?" Meyer whispered. "Two things that may be good."

She had no idea what he was talking about. "What do you mean?"

"First of all, they didn't mention if they had killed him. And second, they must have orders to deliver us someplace. Otherwise, they would have killed us then for helping him escape." The first part didn't sound as convincing when he said it out loud, but

Meyer wanted to picture the escaped prisoner running briskly through the fields toward freedom.

Most of the people had something with them to eat, having taken their lunches to the morning count in anticipation of going to work that day. Those who did shared with the few who didn't. The worst part was having no water, and it was increasingly hot and stuffy inside the car.

The train sped on. Some went to sleep, others talked, but most just sat quietly with their own thoughts. It wasn't long, however, before the train was making stops. No one came to their car. They could hear no talking or yelling outside. The only sound was a big crash at the end of their car, with a simultaneous jerk that caused them to fall roughly against one another. The train sat for a while before and after the crash, then lurched again as the journey continued. The balance of the trip was full of stops and starts.

It seemed like days since they were rounded up and put on the train in Hrubieszow, but only one had passed. Through the small window they had seen the sun set, the moon come and go, and the sun rise again. Manya was asleep on Meyer's arm when the train braked for the sixth time—or was it the eighth? They had lost track.

After a moment of quiet, Meyer heard noise and commotion. People outside were yelling. He shook Manya awake. She opened her eyes and looked up. "What is it?"

"I don't know, but something's happening."

Now everyone was awake, staring at the door. They heard the familiar clank of the metal lock as it was disengaged. The door yawned open. "Raus! Raus!"

At first no one followed the order to get out.

"Raus! Raus!" the command was barked again.

Slowly they got up and moved toward the door. There was no ramp to walk down, so they had to jump.

Many more cars had been coupled to the train, and each of them now spurted people. By the time the train was empty, there were over a thousand standing beside the track, maybe twice that many.

"That's why we kept stopping," Meyer whispered to Manya. "To pick up more people."

In front of them, in rows with guns ready, were the SS. Some were holding snarling dogs on leashes. Occasionally a soldier would approach one of the prisoners and pretend he was going to release the strap and let his vicious animal attack. But then he yanked back the leash, after getting the fearful response he wanted.

They were ordered into rows of five. Meyer held Manya's hand and pulled her toward a line. She grabbed Tovah's hand. Another command was shouted: "March!"

Meyer gripped Manya's hand tighter. Where were they going? There was only open land to the right and left. In the distance in front of them, he could see buildings, lots of buildings. On they walked, getting closer and closer. Then he spotted a fence, stretching as far as he could see.

"Look, Manya, there are people there."

The closer they got, the more people they saw crowding against the fence. Meyer stared at them in horror. They were standing, but he didn't know how, for they were like sticks. He could see the outlines of bones through their striped clothes. Their skin was almost white—no, not white, gray. He had never seen a human being that color before.

"My God, what have they done to these people?" Meyer mumbled to himself. He saw them shove each other aside to get a closer look at the incoming group.

Then the people inside started yelling. A word or phrase begun by one seemed to be finished by another: "Co-" and "-berg"; "Gott-" and "-wald"; "do you know . . . is there a . . . where are you from. . . ." The fragments that reached the ears of the arriving contingent collided crazily with one another.

"They're calling out names," Manya exclaimed.

The guards shot their guns into the air and yelled at the people inside to shut up and move away from the fence.

Meyer, Manya, and the rest of their group stood in front of the entrance. It had been a bright day when they emerged from the train, but as the towering gates swung slowly open, a sudden darkness came over the camp. Perhaps it was his imagination or maybe just a cloud hiding the sun. Meyer considered it a sign.

"Where are we?" Manya pleaded for an explanation.

"In hell," he mumbled. "In hell."

"Men line up to the right and women on the left. I don't want to say it again," the SS officer yelled, pulling his gun from his holster.

No! Manya wanted to go with Meyer. But very quickly the black uniforms on either side of the group jumped among them and began shoving men to one side and women to the other. Some of the guards dragged women away and threw them to the ground. Manya's screams joined those of other women and men torn from loved ones. Outstretched hands strained to touch other outstretched hands. The gunfire in the air neither drowned out nor quieted the desperate cries. If Manya was to die, she wanted it to be with Meyer; but her protests, like the others', were useless.

With the separation accomplished, the guards marched the newcomers into camp. The eyes of the prisoners watching inside the fence showed sympathy and fear.

When the last of the new arrivals was inside, the gates were closed behind them. The two lines were led in different directions. Manya's eyes scoured the departing group of men, looking for Meyer, silently pleading for another glimpse of him. But within seconds, neither group was visible to the other.

When the men finally stopped, they stood in front of a large building. They were ordered inside and told to remove all their clothes. Meyer quickly ripped the lining of his jacket and removed a Russian gold piece that he had been hiding there. He couldn't risk putting it in his mouth, so he pushed it up his rear end. The impulse, he knew, was ridiculous. If he was to be killed, he'd have no use for gold, but at least his captors wouldn't get it.

He stood there naked, his clothes at his feet, thinking this was the end. His life was to be taken away in this godforsaken place with hundreds of other men, all standing nude, with only the Nazi soldiers to witness his last breath on earth.

"You will go into the showers and clean your filthy Jew bodies," one of the guards yelled. "You will be quick. We have no
time for slow people."

They were pushed into the shower stalls. No one's shower
lasted over a minute, if that. Even if the guards had allowed them
to stay longer, Meyer soon learned why no one would linger: the
water was ice cold. He jumped out as quickly as he could and
joined the others who were drip-drying.

After the last one was finished, the men, still shivering and
damp, were ordered into another room. There, each was handed
a set of clothes: striped shirt and pants and pair of wooden shoes.
The paper-thin garments the men rushed to put on absorbed the
water and stuck to their skin, prolonging their discomfort instead
of ending it. They also discovered that the clothing was mismatched. On some the shirt was too big and the pants too short;
on others, the reverse was true. The wooden clogs were narrower
or shorter than the feet that poked into them.

Next, they were led into still another room, with chairs
aligned in a row. The first to enter were ordered to sit, while the
rest watched their hair being cut. No, Meyer thought, "cut" was
the wrong word: the bewildered Jews' heads were being shaved.
The falling hair began to pile up on the floor.

The men were then taken out of the building and marched to
their living quarters. Each was assigned to a barracks and
ordered in. Even though it was daytime, there was very little light
inside. The floor of the barracks was dirt, and rows of wooden
bunks, three tiers high, crowded the walls from one end to the
other. Loose straw sprinkled unevenly across wooden slats served
as mattresses. As more and more people entered the barracks, it
became evident to Meyer that he wouldn't have a bed to himself,
although he couldn't see how two people were supposed to fit in
one bunk. He quickly claimed a middle berth away from the
door and extracted the gold coin from its hiding place, thankful
it was still in his possession.

Soon he was joined by an unfamiliar face. "Can I share this
bunk with you?"

"Yes, of course. My name is Meyer Korenblit."

"I'm Adam Herling. Where are you from?"

For the next hour, the two young men exchanged stories about what had happened to them during the past four years. The whispers that swept through the barracks suggested that similar conversations were going on all around them.

"Why do you think they brought us here?" Meyer asked the older boy.

"I'm not sure, but I don't think they're going to kill us. Otherwise they would have done it when we first arrived."

"Do you think the same is true of the women? My girlfriend came in with me, and I'm worried about her."

"She must be all right. We haven't heard any shooting."

"Yes, that's true. If only I could see her for just a minute."

Meyer's thoughts of Manya quickly vanished when the door to the barracks was flung open and everyone was ordered to line up outside.

"You will be issued a cup and spoon for your food," the guard announced. "You had better take care of them. You will not be given another if you lose them."

They were allowed to stay outside as a kitchen crew took food from barracks to barracks. Some of the new arrivals began to mingle with those who'd been there for a while.

Meyer grabbed Adam's arm and pulled him toward a small group standing nearby. "My name is Meyer and this is Adam," he announced.

"I'm Sol and this is Felix," a man said, then introduced the rest.

"Where are we?" was the first thing Meyer wanted to know.

"A place called Budzyn," Sol answered.

"I've never heard of it. Is it in Poland?"

"Yes. There's a city not far from here called Krasnik."

"Why are we here?" continued Meyer. "And why does every-one look so sick?"

"You were brought here to work—either in the factories or on the roads. We have to work twelve or thirteen hours a day, sometimes more. They give us very little to eat and not much sleep. The place is filthy and overrun with lice. You're only able to clean yourself, if you can call it that, maybe once a week," Sol answered him.

"But if they want us to work, why treat us so bad?"

"They really don't care whether you live or die. There are many more to take your place," someone else responded.

"How long have you been here?" Adam asked.

"Most of us have been here close to a year. No one knows for sure; you lose track of the days," Felix said.

"Will we go to work tomorrow?" Meyer wondered.

"Probably not. They'll put you through hell first. You came in looking fresh and healthy. They don't like that."

Conversation stopped as the food buckets arrived.

"A word of advice," Felix said as they hurried toward the kitchen crew. "Don't eat your bread now; save it for the morning. I promise you, you'll need it more tomorrow than you do now. In the morning you'll get only coffee."

While Meyer hadn't expected to get much food, he wasn't prepared for what he did receive. He'd eaten only once in the last twenty-four hours, and he was ravenous. He held out his cup and watched as it was submerged in the bucket and handed back to him. He spooned through the watery broth for something solid to satisfy the ache in his stomach, but the spoon came up empty. He dipped it in again. Nothing. On the third try he scraped the spoon along the bottom and was finally rewarded with a couple of small pieces of vegetable. Although Meyer was tempted to eat the thin slice of bread, he heeded Felix's words. He hoped Manya had received the same advice. Immediately after dinner, they were ordered to their bunks for the night.

After what seemed like only moments of fitful sleep, the shrill wake-up siren cut into Meyer's dreams, and for a moment he didn't know where he was. The others in his barracks were similarly unsure of what to expect as they pulled themselves from bunks and made their way outside. It was still dark as they lined up to be counted and get their instructions. They'd have 30 minutes to wash and queue up for the morning ration.

There was a rush for the latrine. Meyer quickly saw that it would be difficult to get clean, for all were going to the same place to wash and use the toilet—not just the new arrivals, but everyone, thousands of people. It didn't take long to realize he'd have to cast off his manners if he was to be one of the few who got access to the bath house.

They were given coffee for breakfast. Meyer carefully removed his bread from his pocket, and within seconds, both were gone.

Soon he was standing with the others to be counted. It was a painstakingly slow process because of the number of people. They stood there, and stood, and stood.

At last it was over, and all but the new arrivals were released to their work. Felix's prediction about a day of hell came true.

The guards ignored the new prisoners at first, leaving them standing in line for hours. Then they paced up and down the rows, staring the prisoners down and cuffing them about the head until the desired servility was established. For variety the prisoners were ordered to do situps—10, 20, 30, 40, 50, 100. The guards kicked them as their torsos rose and fell. Another command was barked, and they rolled over for pushups—10, 20, 30, 40, 50, 100, while the guards stepped on their backs.

But there was more than physical abuse. For hours, nothing but obscenities and filthy names were directed at them. And so it continued through most of the day: standing at attention, situps, pushups, standing again, and so on. When it finally came to an end, the prisoners lined up yet another time and were given their work assignments for the following day. They returned to their barracks, only to be called out a few minutes later to join the others just returning from work, all to be counted again.

After their watery soup for dinner, they were given a little free time. Someone told Meyer that if he had a wife or girlfriend, now was the time to find her. "They don't give us this opportunity every day," the man said.

It took Meyer most of the interval to find Manya. At last he spotted her in a crowd of women. Thank God they didn't cut *her* hair, he whispered to himself.

"Manya! Manya!"

For half a second, she didn't recognize the figure moving toward her. Then she went running into his arms. "Oh, Meyer, what have they done to you?"

"I'm all right. How are you?"

"It's all so horrible, Meyer. Hold me, please," she begged.

They exchanged stories of what had happened since their separation. Meyer told her he'd be working outside the camp on road construction. Manya also had a job outside the camp — in the fields picking vegetables. But Tovah, who was in the same barracks as Manya, had been assigned to the kitchen. Like him, they had met some new people.

All too quickly their time was up, and they returned to their barracks for the night.

It couldn't be much more than seven-thirty in the evening, Meyer thought as he lay on the loose straw that covered his bunk, using his arm for a pillow. He'd have to wait quite a while before it was dark enough for him to sneak to Manya's barracks. He'd gone the night before and ordinarily wouldn't risk it two nights in a row, but today he had decided they should put their escape plan into action soon.

He poked his fingers under the thin layer of straw to check for his morning slice of bread. It was still there, growing hard and dry, but he would dunk it in the tepid brew that served as coffee in the morning. Next to the thin slice were his wooden shoes. He rolled over on his back and tucked them under his head, trying not to notice the sharp edges that pressed against his bristly scalp.

Meyer had been surprised by the size of Budzyn. More practically, he had been sickened by the lice and their insidious onslaught against the thousands and thousands of identically garbed men. Just the thought of the lice sent him into a frenzy of scratching and brought a sleepy complaint from his bunkmate. Meyer willed the itching to stop and Adam to go back to sleep, for he didn't want his friend to know he planned to visit Manya again so soon. Adam and two other men had agreed to cover for Meyer last night, but they wouldn't approve of this second trip and there was no way Meyer would try to convince them by divulging his plan to escape. No, tonight Meyer was on his own. When the wake-up siren sounded at four-thirty the next morning, he would be back in his own bunk. He'd file out with the others to the latrine, then queue for coffee. It hadn't taken long for Meyer to adopt the eating style of the hungry prisoners: he learned to hold his bread in one hand and cup the other underneath, ready to catch the smallest crumb that might fall.

Before they were led away to work, they were counted, then marched out the gates—the women to farms and the men to road and factory work. The Ukrainian guards insisted that they sing as they marched. When work was far from camp, they brought their cups and spoons along. Forgetting them meant no lunch. During the midday break, they were lined up again, counted, and given the same thin soup. Meyer had noticed exchanges being made between some of the prisoners and the Poles they encountered on their way to and from their work sites. Others had confirmed that, for a price, it was possible to get food and other extras in this way. It amazed Meyer that the Poles always kept their part of the bargain; they could just as easily have stolen the valuables that the Jews gave them.

A few even helped without asking something in return. Manya had come across one of them. Although she had nothing to trade, she convinced a Polish farmer to give her some paper and a pencil. When Manya told Meyer that she intended to use the materials to keep a diary, he felt he would rather she direct her energies toward a more practical goal; but he reminded himself that was her affair. He *did* worry that the diary might be discovered. Manya assured him she had torn the paper into small squares and rolled them around the pencil, sometimes hiding the diary in the straw of her bunk and other times knotting her hair around it.

Meyer's gold coin was still hidden in his bunk. He had soon discovered that he wasn't alone in having a gold piece. Once he saw another prisoner cut such a coin into four pieces to stretch its purchasing power, for it was just as valuable to the Poles in quarters as it was whole.

In the ensuing weeks he fingered the coin often, knowing it was the only thing he had left to trade and determined that it would not be bartered too cheaply or quickly. Although his hungry stomach growled constantly, he was determined that the camp diet would sustain him, supplemented as it was by an occasional chunk of bread or a potato peeling Manya got from Tovah.

Finally, Meyer decided that he would trade not for food but for implements to escape—a far more important commodity; and one day, with trembling fingers, he handed his gold piece to a Polish man in exchange for a pair of rubber gloves and some wirecutters. The following Saturday, during the routine barracks and grounds cleaning, he hid the tools beneath some rocks outside his barracks. His plan was that, on the appointed night, four of them—he and Manya and another couple—would retrieve the tools, snip the wires of the electric fence, and make a run for it. Of course, they had only the striped clothes they wore, no further valuables to trade for help or food, no way to camouflage the telltale bristly heads of the men, and no idea where they would go; indeed, they were unsure of where they *were*. All that, they agreed, would be handled somehow when the time came. First they wanted freedom.

Lying in bed, waiting for the time to go to Manya, Meyer's neck tingled from the pressure of the clogs, so he moved the shoes to his side and curled around them protectively, resting his head on his arm. It was very dark now and very quiet except for a snore or a moan here and there. If he lived to be a hundred, he would never forget the smells that permeated the building, surrounded him at work, even seemed to season his food: smells of humans overworked and underwashed, clothing stained with urine and feces, bodies on fire with fever and disease, sliced with lash marks, swollen with infection, and flesh made raw by lice and the men's fingernails.

Meyer had been miserable in the ghetto work camp, but this situation brought a new level of suffering, and he felt that he had to get Manya and himself out before they resembled the hollow-cheeked, sunken-eyed people at the fence when they arrived. He didn't feel secure with the vagueness of his plan, but he eased his doubts with assurances that it was the only thing to do. He was worried about the fence, having seen careless, desperate inmates jolted by the wires, and he almost wished he had decided to try to escape while at work outside the camp. But he wanted the cover of darkness for their attempt. Besides, he believed the gloves and tools would get them through the fence safely.

Meyer eased himself to a half-sitting position under the overhead bunk and looked around. Adam lay fast asleep, undisturbed by his mate's movement. Meyer crawled to the barracks door and slipped out into the cool October night. Staying clear of the floodlight's beam, he scurried through slender shadows from building to building, then crouched low at the edge of the clearing that separated the men's side from the women's side.

How he hated that empty expanse! It was about forty yards across, in direct view of a watchtower, and cut through the middle by a barbed wire fence. Meyer scanned the perimeter of the open area, once again, then a third time to be sure—interrupting the sweep of his eyes only to glance periodically at the tower and to time the revolutions of the searchlight.

Then, he dashed across, teeth clenched, body doubled over legs and feet that moved with accustomed stealth. At the fence he dived to the ground and slid under, then rolled to his feet again and streaked for a patch of darkness that could hide him. Weaving his way among the buildings, he reached Manya's barracks, slipped through the door, and crept down the length of the room, counting off the bunks. He climbed in with Manya, hoping that the next time he did this would be the last.

The next night Manya lay in her bunk, still shaking. She had untangled her diary papers from her hair a moment ago while the waning shafts of light from the setting sun would permit her to write a phrase or two summarizing the day's events. But she was unable to capture the terror of this day. How would she put it all down? She composed it in her mind.

Dear Diary,
    Meyer came to see me again last night. It was such a thrill to

open my eyes and see his face close to mine. He said we were going to escape the next night—the four of us. I couldn't believe that would be my last night here. The plan had always scared me, especially the part about meeting Meyer on the men's side, because I'd never done that before, but he said the best place to go through the fence is over there. We talked and talked and ended up waking some of the other girls, but, God bless them, they didn't mind. A couple of them even doubled up so Meyer and I could share my bunk. I kept thinking about the first time Meyer sneaked over. We were afraid that the other women would report us if they found out he was there. But no one bothered us. In fact, those who saw him said they were happy for us that we had each other. Then I thought about the time Meyer was in my bunk with me and the guards came in unexpectedly. We lay very still and close. If there was ever a time when the other women could have reported us, that was it, for that would have saved them from being punished the same as Meyer and me. Nothing happened, though; the guards just stood there, shone a flashlight around, and left. I've made some good friends here. I'll miss them when I go. When the war is over, I'll look for them.

After Meyer left last night, I lay there a long time wide awake, and nearly jumped out of my skin when the wake-up siren went off. There was a lot of shouting, then pounding on the barracks door and we all rushed to get outside. It was still dark and quite cold as we lined up. Across the compound behind the fence, I could see the male prisoners in rows, facing us. We stood there and stood there, and still no dismissal to go to the toilet. I couldn't understand what was going on. It was daylight before we got an explanation. The Ukrainian sergeant appeared on his horse and trotted back and forth in front of us, staring. I never saw such hatred in anyone's eyes. Any moment I expected him to lasso one of us with the rope he always carries. Many times I've seen him throw his rope around one of the prisoners and drag his victim around to show his power over us. Whether for punishment or for fun, he takes great pleasure in his sadistic games. But today he didn't use his rope for that.

He looked over the entire camp of prisoners, then said he was going to teach us a lesson once and for all. He said none of us would ever leave Budzyn, that we'd never outsmart him. Then he gave a signal, and the guards led out some prisoners with their hands tied behind their backs. The sergeant pointed at them and explained their futile attempt to escape. Now they would pay the price. He said we were to watch them die so that we'd know what happens to Jewish pigs who try to run away. It was as if his words were directed right at me. I tried to find Meyer among the men standing across from us, but I couldn't see him. Off to the side, ropes were being tightened around the feet of the men who'd tried to escape. My skin was crawling; I wanted to run, hide, anything to get away. But the sergeant screamed a command for everyone to watch, saying he had plenty of ropes for the rest of us. The next instant the men were swinging upside down in the air. Their faces bulged with the rush of blood to their heads. A quick death wasn't good enough for the Nazi guards: they wanted the men, and us, to suffer. They left the bodies hanging there all day and all night. We had to stand in line the entire time.

When those people died, so did our plan to escape. So many thoughts and feelings went through my mind as we stood there in that horror. Those people were murdered, my senses told me. Do something: scream, run, fight back. I wondered how many others near me felt the same way, but there was only fear and shock on their faces. How many others had been plotting their own schemes for survival? So many of us standing in the clearing—surely we could overpower the guards. But who would be lost in the process? Me? The girl standing next to me? Meyer? I realized that as much as we tried to help each other in little ways—sharing food or tending each other's physical and emotional wounds—we couldn't think and act as a group. At some point, I don't know when, we changed, I changed. There isn't one of us who isn't sickened by what we saw today, and there isn't one of us, including me, who isn't thankful to be alive instead of dead. We don't spend time worrying about those who die. I heard comments like "one less" and "his troubles are over," and we go on. Perhaps it's because there are no families to com-

*fort; maybe we're just honestly relieved that it was someone else
and not us. I wonder sometimes if I'll get my old ways back when
all this is over. Perhaps that's one reason I wanted to keep this
diary, to have a record of my feelings as well as of the events. I
spend a lot of time trying not to think about what's going on
here. Maybe one day I'll be able to read what I've written without this feeling that I can't believe what my eyes see or my ears
hear.*

*Oh, I don't know, maybe the diary is silly, after all. Maybe
Meyer is right. I wish he understood, though; I wish I knew what
he was thinking now. I wish he were here with me. Last night
seems like a lifetime ago. So much has changed since then. The
gloves and wirecutters will have to stay put for now, but knowing they are handy gives me a little hope. We may not be free yet,
but Meyer will think of a way. Until then I'll be patient. Thankful to catch a glimpse of him now and then. Thankful to steal a
few moments together when we can. Thankful we're still alive. I
can feel good about that.*

The exhausted young woman turned over on her side and
curled up in a ball. The shaking had stopped, and she was very
tired. Thinking about that day had been almost like living it
again. If only she had the time to spend, the light to see, and
enough paper to chronicle it all just as she had thought it. But
she didn't. She'd have to stick with her habit of putting down
only a few words. Tomorrow, as soon as she had the chance, she
would write simply: "Jews hanged for attempted escape."

One day, Manya's group was taken to work in the fields. It
was sometime after lunch, and she was on all fours, digging potatoes out of the hard ground, when another figure knelt
down beside her and put his face next to hers.

"Meyer!" she cried. "What are you doing here?"

"We're working on the road on the other side of the hill," he
explained. "I thought I saw you marching along in front of my
group, but I wasn't sure. I slipped away as soon as I could, and
sure enough, here you are."

Manya looked toward the farmhouse—no sign of the farmer or the guards. It should be safe to talk for a while. They made their way from furrow to furrow until they reached the edge of the field, then found a little hollow and sat down under a tree. It was a raw day, but bright and clear, and it felt good to be shielded from the brisk wind that cut through the open field.

They huddled together, enjoying each other's warmth, talking and smiling. Meyer asked Manya about "the girls," as he called her group of friends, and she worried over how thin he was.

"How long do you think we'll be here, Meyer?"

"I don't know. Some of my friends have been in this place for a year. We just have to be careful and draw as little attention to ourselves as possible."

"I hope my family is in a better place than this. But if the men and women are separated, it must be very hard on my mother. Do you think she's able to see my father?"

"Even if they can't, they still have the children. Joshua would be with your father."

"Yes, and my sisters would be with Mama. That will help her a lot."

"I'm sure they're taking care of themselves. We have to do the same, so we can be with them when this is over."

They continued talking about their future and the good times before the war. They weren't sure what brought them back to the present, but suddenly Meyer jumped up. He told Manya to wait, then disappeared behind the hill. In a few minutes he was back, breathing hard.

"They've gone!" he exclaimed, wiping his hand over his face.

"Who? Who has gone?"

"My group. They've gone back to the camp. Look, I think your group is getting ready to leave too."

They stared at each other. For a moment Meyer thought about running away right then and there. But where would he go? He wasn't even sure where they were. And because the prisoners were counted on the way back to the camp, he would be missed within minutes and wouldn't have much of a head start.

"Come on!" Meyer yelled, grabbing Manya's hand.

"Wait! What are we going to do?"

"I'll have to go back with you. There's no other way."

"We could run away!"

"No. That's suicide. Come on."

They tumbled down the hillside and into the field. In a few moments the Ukrainian guards called everyone to line up. Manya and Meyer stayed as close to the others as they could. Meyer's mind raced to think of an explanation if he were detected. Some of the women had shaved heads, so his wouldn't give him away. Perhaps he could rely on the guards' usual attitude of ignoring the hapless crew they moved around. Maybe they would even skip the count this time.

They were just approaching the gate when one of the guards spotted Meyer and separated him and Manya from the group. The others filed inside while the couple was made to stand alone on the road.

"You!" the guard yelled at Meyer. "What are you doing here?" There was no time for an answer. Manya heard a whip whistle through the air; Meyer grunted from the blow and fell to the ground.

A second guard took up the challenge. "I'll tell you what the filthy swine is doing here: he was trying to escape!" The whip zinged again and again. "You're too stupid to understand, aren't you? You won't believe that you can't escape. You were even dumb enough to come back to the camp. Do you think we can't count? You should have made a run for it, Jew-boy!"

He punctuated each insult with another lash from the whip; then the other guard joined in the assault, pummeling Meyer and kicking him. Over and over the whip cracked. Meyer writhed on the ground. Manya dropped to her knees, sobbing. When the guard struck Meyer on the head with the whip handle, Manya screamed.

"Get up!" the first guard bellowed. "Get up!"

Meyer groaned, but he hadn't heard the command. He lay in a heap, nearly unconscious.

"I said get up!" the guard repeated. "If you don't get up, you'll die right here."

Manya crawled over to Meyer. Blood poured from his mouth and nose; his face was bruised and swollen. She tried to help him to his feet.

"Leave him alone!" spat the guard, waving his whip at Manya. "He is to get up by himself." He shoved Manya aside.

Somehow Meyer dragged himself upright. The guard took them through the gates and to an SS officer to explain themselves. Manya helped him along, wiping some of his blood away with her hand. Meyer had a faraway look in his eyes, and he moved with great difficulty. They were in the officer's presence only briefly. It was apparent that the man was annoyed by the interruption and by the blood that dripped from Meyer's wounds. They were dismissed and sent to their barracks without dinner.

For two weeks, Meyer's friends did what they could to speed his healing. In the morning they pulled him out of bed although he begged to lie there. They shoved him to the front of the washroom line so they could bathe his lash marks with cool water and rinse the blood and pus off his shirt. He leaned on them as they marched to work, and when they got there, they found a place for him to lie down while they worked. Then they helped him back to the camp at night.

When Manya told Tovah what had happened, she managed to sneak out extra bits of food from the kitchen. In the morning before the count, in the usual commotion of getting to the latrine, Manya would move close to the fence between the men's and women's barracks. She pretended to drop something or examine her shoe while she slid the food under the fence. Sometimes Adam was on the other side ready to scoop it up; sometimes it was Sol or Felix. A few times Meyer himself was there, especially after he had regained some strength. He had a different look about him now, thought Manya; he had seen death before, but this was as close as he had come to it himself.

Before too long, however, Meyer was sneaking into Manya's barracks again. It was a gradual process, starting with a hesitant "Maybe I'll come see you tonight." When Manya shook her head no, he seemed relieved and dropped the idea. Soon he didn't give up so easily when she told him it was too dangerous, and finally as the last marks faded, so did his reluctance to tempt fate.

The second time he picked his way across the compound to Manya, he appeared to be preoccupied and heard only half of what she was saying as they lay together.

"Meyer, something is bothering you. Tell me what it is— please."

"It's nothing, really. It's just that there's something I want you to do for me. Something I want you to promise."

"Of course. Anything."

"I've been thinking," he said. "If we are separated, I want you to promise me that you'll go back to Hrubieszow when all this is over. I'll meet you there. If for some reason you get there and don't find me, go to—" He paused, thinking of all the people who wouldn't be there: his family, Salki, maybe even Gorski. "Go to Josef. If I arrive before you, I'll leave word with him in case I cannot stay. You do the same. Do you promise?"

"To meet you in Hrubieszow?"

"Yes."

"I promise."

"And you'll remember to tell Josef where I can find you?"

"Yes, I'll tell Josef."

"Then, we meet again in Hrubieszow," he repeated.

"I promise," she whispered.

How many more people would she see die before it was her turn? New faces, brought from overcrowded barracks to hers, replaced those who were killed or who simply didn't wake up one morning. Manya was thankful that all her friends were still with her. She prayed to God every night to keep them alive and to watch over Meyer and his small group of friends. No matter what else happened, her belief in God did not falter. Some of her friends couldn't understand it at times, especially when she picked a day to observe Yom Kippur. Tovah and Hannah tried to talk her out of it, telling her it was foolish to fast and harmful to her health.

"God will understand your skipping it," Tovah said.

It was true, Manya knew. God would forgive her if she let it pass, but she felt it was important, even though the time she picked to observe the Day of Atonement was a random choice. The Nazis could deny her almost everything else, but they couldn't stop this expression of her faith. Although it was a small thing, it gave Manya control over something in her life. It reminded her she was still a human being.

So that day Manya had given her bread to Meyer and her soup and coffee to her friends. She was glad to be able to give something back to Tovah, who so often risked her life by smuggling a little extra food from the kitchen to share with the girls. It was amazing how that tiny bit more made them feel so much better.

Time was disorienting for the prisoners of Budzyn. Days flowed into weeks, weeks into months, under the rigid and endless routine, adding another dimension of futility to their existence.

Each morning when the siren screamed its announcement of a new day, Manya carefully tucked her diary into her hair, winding a few locks around to hold it secure. For the past few months she had kept the precious pieces of paper with her at all times out of fear they might be discovered if she left them in her bunk. The Nazis had begun conducting surprise inspections, especially when the barracks were empty. Patting the knot of hair that hid the diary, she bent over and carefully picked up her bread, catching also the crumbs that fell off.

She headed outside with Tovah and the others to join the race for the latrine and to get their share of the muddy liquid for breakfast. But today something was different. There was an extra contingent of guards outside. The count proceeded, but it took longer than usual. Manya kept looking for Meyer, hoping to see him before everyone went to work. But then something else caught her eye.

"Oh, no! This can't be," Manya whispered to Tovah. "Look," she said, pointing to the front of the camp.

The gates were open, and trucks were rumbling in.

"Please, God, not us," she pleaded.

Soldiers jumped from the back of each truck, taking their

positions. "Move to the trucks," an SS officer bellowed, motioning at the women's section.

The additional guards moved in and began pushing, shoving, and dragging women toward the waiting vehicles. Women ran in every direction, but it was no good—they were surrounded.

This time the guns were not just shot into the air. Manya saw someone fall. The trucks were filling; she was getting closer. Maybe there won't be enough room, Manya prayed.

Still she got closer. Screaming and yelling saturated the air, husbands shouting to wives, sisters bawling for brothers, boyfriends yelling for girlfriends, and Manya crying out for Meyer. Arms flailed the air and bodies crunched together. Manya saw men being beaten back by the guards.

Finally she saw Meyer.

"Meyer! Meyer!" she screamed, throwing her arms out in a vain effort to reach him. "Please God, please!"

She was thrown into the truck. She got up to look for him. He was still there, tears streaming down his face. She saw his lips moving, but she couldn't make out the words.

The truck groaned into gear. She leaned out, straining toward him, as a guard slapped her arms down again and again trying to stuff her back into the truck.

"I love you, Meyer, I'll meet you again in—" but the roar of the engine drowned out her words.

Manya stared out the rear as the truck shimmied away from the camp along the rutted road. A steeliness came over her. Despite all good intentions, she had kept a secret from Meyer. She had wanted him to recover from the beatings, so, for weeks she kept it to herself, as she lay in her bunk at night, feeling faint fluttering in her empty belly. Lately, the movements had grown stronger, and there was no doubt that she was pregnant. Under different circumstances the news would have been quite thrilling and she would be caught up in the moment. But not now. She had sworn her friends to secrecy, and without Meyer she would need their help more than ever.

CHAPTER ELEVEN

Konzentrationsläger (KL)

Throughout 1944, inmates were frequently moved from work camp to work camp as the Nazis shifted priorities among various projects to support their war effort and as advancing Soviet forces moved farther into eastern Poland. The camp at Budzyn, which had received Meyer and Manya and the other deported residents of the Hrubieszow ghetto, was about 150 miles northwest of Warsaw, near the German border. From there, Meyer and Manya were moved around to other camps in Poland. Mielecz, a labor camp that had about 3,000 inmates in August 1944, was in the southern part of eastern Poland, about eighty miles south of Warsaw. Plaszow, another forced labor camp fifty miles west of Mielecz, was a suburb of the city of Cracow. At Plaszow, which was headed by the infamous Amon Goeth, Oskar Schindler saved many Jews by employing them in his enamel factory nearby. During Manya's stay at Plaszow, she had no interaction with either of these men. The labor camp Wieliczka was also near Cracow, less than twenty miles to its southwest.

Since work was the purpose of these camps, the Nazis devoted much effort to regular "selections," at which those deemed weak or ill were taken away, usually to death camps. Knowing this, the inmates devoted much effort toward staying as healthy as possible, or at least appearing to be so, and doing everything they could to prevent themselves from weakening physically or emotionally.

The heat inside the cattle car was unbearable. Manya and the others were packed in so tightly they had to stand up to avoid suffocation. Some were lucky enough to be able to brace themselves against the sides of the car; the rest leaned heavily on each other. For hours and hours they were sealed up in the darkness with no food or water, little air, and no choice but to relieve themselves where they stood.

Finally, the train stopped, and the door was pulled open. Pushing and clutching at the same time, their hands reached out to each other as they descended to the platform. A late winter wind refreshed the sweltering prisoners with its first blast, then set them shivering as it turned their sweat-drenched uniforms to ice.

They tried to circle together for warmth, their backs to the wind, but SS guards ordered them into lines. Rifle butts cracked against ribs and heads to force the lines to move. Manya grabbed Tovah's hand as they walked, then glanced back to see that Hannah and Molly, her other friends, were following. The slush on the well-travelled road alongside the track was beginning to freeze as the temperature fell, but the tramping wooden shoes churned it to slush again. Muddy liquid splattered on the legs and into the faces of the dazed women.

They marched, slipping and sliding, for several miles. When they came to a farm, they were shoved headlong into a dark, drafty barn that offered little more room than the cattle cars. Manya and the others curled up together, seeking warmth. They slid out of their shoes and rubbed some circulation back into their freezing feet. Each time they heard a sound outside, they looked toward the barn door, expecting at least a ration of water. But the door didn't open, and no food or water appeared.

How long had they ridden? they asked each other. From sunup to sundown, someone replied. No—longer, insisted another, who had watched through the tiny window at the top of the car and had seen the daylight turn to dark, then to dawn again. More than thirty-six hours it had taken them to get here, but where were they? They weren't even sure if they were still in Poland. Soon it became too much of an effort to speak through parched throats, and they resorted to hoarse whispers, then finally fell silent.

They slept until they heard shouting and the barn doors swung wide. "March!" the guards shouted. The front of the line was being prodded on its way down the road before some of the women were even on their feet.

This time they trudged only a mile or two in the drizzly dawn. Manya could see the first rows of the column approaching a gate, then watched a wave of uniformed prisoners surge toward the newcomers and heard the clamor of voices desperate to match a name.

Ahead of her, Manya saw a chunk of the line break away and enter a one-story frame structure, which she now recognized as a barracks. Then a second group peeled off toward another building.

"Where are we?" one of Manya's group called out.

"Mielecz," a man yelled back.

"Mielecz," the woman replied. "Where is that?"

"Poland," came the reply.

Manya and her friends were propelled toward a third building. Inside, there was a general rush for bunks, but the four of them were able to find places together. Manya was inspecting her bunk when suddenly she remembered her diary. She hadn't given it a thought since leaving Budzyn! Her hand shot to her matted coil of hair, trying not to panic. The papers were still there. In a flash, she wrenched them out and slid them under the straw of the bunk.

A guard shouted for them to line up single file. They followed him to a large building and were handed, one by one, another striped dress, a cup, and a spoon. The shoes they had on now would not be replaced. They were ushered into a large room and told to strip off their ragged dresses and put on the new ones. A few voices pleaded for water. The guard cast hard eyes in their direction, then turned his back.

Manya and her friends hurried into the clean garments, the Germans watching coolly. Perhaps it won't be so bad here after all, she tried to reassure herself. We wouldn't be issued new clothes if we were going to die. Maybe, after we're dressed, we will finally get something to eat and drink.

The guards prodded the women into a column moving toward a door at the far end of the room. When Manya crossed the threshold, she peered one way, then the other, trying to see what was ahead. She caught a glimpse of the corner of a table and the sleeve of a jacketed man sitting down. Other officials bustled about behind him.

Even as she approached the table, she couldn't make out what was going on. A second man was sitting next to the first and checking items off in a ledger. The man in the jacket appeared to be writing something very slowly, and each time he paused and raised his head, the line moved up one.

Finally Manya was in front of him. Her eyes swept the equipment on the table. What was it?

"Hold out your hand," he growled.

Manya hesitated.

"Your hand, your hand," he said, pointing impatiently with an instrument.

She started to lift her right hand toward him, then changed her mind and held out her left.

"The other one," he instructed.

Her right hand moved toward him obediently.

He raised the instrument. Manya looked away.

"Turn around," he hissed. "Watch!"

She met his eyes, then blinked and looked down.

"Use your other hand to hold the skin," he instructed, demonstrating on his own arm. "Pull it tight."

With her left hand, Manya pinched the skin together on the underside of her right wrist.

He pressed the instrument to her skin. A needle pierced the flesh and deposited a blob of blue.

She tried to lower her face to her chest.

"I said, watch!" he yelled without looking up.

She obeyed, trying not to flinch as he used the needle like a sewing machine. Then it was over.

"Next!" he growled.

Manya cradled her hand as she moved away from the table toward another open door. Her arm throbbed and burned. Finally she held it up to look. In block letters it read: "KL."

Manya had been tattooed.

As the days and weeks passed, Meyer lost track of how long Manya had been gone. He knew it must be over a month, possibly closer to two. Images of her face and the arms she had held out to him were vivid in his mind. She's strong—she can make it, he would say to himself. There was only one thing *he* must do: stay alive, so that he could be with her again.

Conditions at Budzyn had gotten much worse. Now the lice were everywhere. Not a day went by that the inmates didn't have to have a sweeping when they first got out of bed. Each man would use his hands to sweep bugs off his own arms and legs. Then they took turns with their bunkmates to brush them off each other's backs. But there was no way to get rid of all of them, and those removed in the morning seemed to return at night.

In addition, the food had deteriorated, tasting more foul than ever. Beatings came more frequently and at the slightest provocation. And deaths were no longer sporadic.

The Ukrainian guards were the worst, seeming to take pleasure in the punishment they inflicted. Meyer couldn't understand this mad hatred the Ukrainians had for the Jews. Before the war, he knew some Ukrainians in Hrubieszow who had lived and worked with Jews under tolerable conditions.

But when the guards spoke to the inmates, they would say things like, "This war is your fault. Now you're getting your reward."

Or they would bait them with, "You should all go to Palestine. That's where you belong."

And a prisoner would answer, "All right, let us out and we'll go."

Always would come the same cruel response: "It's too late now. You're never leaving this place. You'll die here."

And so it went, day in and day out.

But not today apparently. A large group was separated from those being counted and was being led into waiting trucks. Meyer looked to see if all of his friends—Adam, Sol, Leon, Wolf, and Felix—had been selected along with him; for what, he didn't know. This time, there was little of the commotion that had occurred when the women were taken away. The men's attitudes had hardened with time: now, they thought mostly about themselves, staying alive, and helping those few people they were close to.

The ride on the trucks wasn't a long one. When they stopped, the canvas flaps at the rear were flipped up and the prisoners were ordered out. As soon as Meyer jumped down, he had a flashback to his and Manya's deportation from Hrubieszow. He saw the same waiting train of boxcars, the same SS guards lined up along its length. Jews were again being forced in at gunpoint, packed like fish in a can. Was this what had happened to Manya, Meyer wondered grimly as he entered the boxcar.

Clang! Again the familiar sound of the lock securing its human cargo. They were being shipped somewhere else. The men covered more and more miles, standing shoulder to shoulder in the cattle car with no food or water. It was cold outside, but the temperature inside rose steadily. Some of the men passed out. Some died where they stood. The train made numerous stops, but the doors to their car were not opened.

Then the train slowed again, slamming the occupants against each other as it came to a halt. The door slid open, and the command of "Raus! Raus!" was screamed in front of each car. It was all familiar: SS guards, pointed guns, snarling dogs, and harsh orders.

They were at another camp, this one smaller than Budzyn, but the environment was the same: watchtowers, guards, electric fences, barracks, and identical bunks. Adam and Meyer again teamed up to share a bunk, then waited in the barracks until the call for dinner.

Meyer hoped for something different to eat and a larger quantity, but he was disappointed. After his first taste, he would have preferred even the slop they served at Budzyn.

Maybe Manya made a stop here, Meyer thought as he lay in bed that night. Wherever you are, Manya, I love you.

The siren sounded in the morning, rousing him from sleep. What would today be like? The new arrivals were led away to a large building, similar to the one at Budzyn.

Once inside, they went through the same procedure: strip naked, take a freezing shower, receive an issue of striped clothes, have your head shaved.

But this time there was an additional room. It was bare except for six small tables, each with a chair on either side. The chairs on one side were occupied by SS guards, each holding some kind of pencil instrument in his hand. Meyer and the others were ordered to form rows behind each vacant chair. Everyone watched as the first six people took their places in the chairs.

"My God! They're tattooing us!" someone whispered.

Meyer couldn't believe his eyes or ears. We're being branded like cattle, he thought.

Then, it was Meyer's turn. He slowly sat down.

"Hold out your right hand, palm down. Now grab the skin underneath with your other hand and pull it as tight as you can," he was told.

The stinging needle pierced his skin. It burned. He watched as the blue ink began to form a letter.

Please hurry and get this over with, he thought desperately.

K

Meyer started to pull his wrist away.

"I'm not finished! Put your wrist back out!"

Again the sharp stings and the burning feeling.

L

"Now I'm finished," the guard said with a smile.

Meyer got up and rubbed his wrist in an effort to wipe the mark off before it dried. But it was on for good.

They were all taken back to the barracks, lined up, and counted. Then an SS officer addressed them: "Tomorrow you will begin work. You'll be taken out of the camp to a factory, where you'll be instructed how to make parts for airplanes. I advise you to do the best you possibly can. If you don't, what happens to you will be your fault, not mine." He turned and left. The prisoners were ordered into the barracks.

"Do you know where we are?" Meyer asked a group of people.

"A place called Mielecz," someone answered.

During inclement months, the women were issued light jackets that offered little warmth and they were given no gloves or socks. Many succumbed to the weather. Manya didn't know how she escaped frostbite.

The most horrible part were the daily lineups at dawn and sunset. They just stood there as the guards, dressed in gloves, boots, and heavy coats, slowly made their way up and down the rows. The Nazis would take their time, sometimes confusing the count on purpose so that they had to start over.

The morning counts were always the worst. Although the barracks weren't heated, they at least gave protection from the biting wind. Three or sometimes four girls would crawl into one bunk together to generate as much heat as possible. But the bit of warmth gained during the night dissipated with their first few steps on the snow-covered ground. From the bottoms of their feet, chills raced up their bodies and met shivers coming from the other end as the frigid wind scoured their exposed skin.

The lucky ones worked in unheated factories, but Manya's group worked mostly outside. By the time they lined up for the evening count, their bodies were like ice. When they finally got back to the barracks, they took turns rubbing each other's extremities to restore circulation to them.

But Manya fought more than cold on this day. She was racked with cramps every hour, then every half-hour.

The dull aches gathered into pains that came in faster and harder spasms. She moaned as she felt each one come on, and grunted through clenched teeth till it passed. Like human crutches, the women half-carried Manya back to the camp and stood for the count. The friends leaned against each other to disguise their own trembling and Manya's distress.

Finally, they were dismissed to the barracks. Tovah worriedly stroked Manya's brow, reassuring her, and making quieting noises to keep everyone calm. The labor reached a crescendo, and soon Manya's friends delivered a pre-term baby girl. The women cooed at the faint mewing coming from the infant as they wrapped it in a rag and nestled the bundle into Manya's eager arms.

They used scraps torn from their skirts to clean Manya and wipe the mess from the bunk. Exhausted, the new mother slept. Before dawn, Manya awakened, and the baby was gone. She was not told what became of the child, and never saw it again. There had been no instructions, no plan. Without saying anything, they all knew what had to be done. One person's transgression would kill them all.

As she wept, she wondered if she'd ever have a chance to tell Meyer. Coiling her arms around the empty space that had held her daughter, Manya thought about her diary but knew this night was emblazoned into her memory forever. She nuzzled closer to her bunkmates and closed her eyes. Somehow she had to find the strength to line up for the count in the morning.

After all she had been through, Manya thought she could survive anything. As each day passed, she was closer to being back in Meyer's arms. Like a teacher's instruction to write a phrase on the chalkboard, Manya repeated over and over, "I'll make it out of here. Meyer will be waiting."

Manya tried to calculate how long she'd been in the camps. She knew that they'd been taken from Hrubieszow in late August—no, September. At Budzyn, and then at Mielecz, they had seen the fall, winter, and some of spring.

Now, after yet another long ride, Manya and her friends had arrived at another camp. The sun was bright and patches of ground were green. It must be almost summer. How many months without Meyer? What difference did it make? There was only one thing that mattered: to make sure she survived this day so there would be a tomorrow.

"Manya, look how big this place is," Tovah whispered as they were marched in.

It was enormous compared to Budzyn and Mielecz. There were buildings and fences as far as her eyes could see. The sheer size made Manya feel more insignificant and frightened than ever. And there were thousands of women, all with identical clothes, haggard faces, and skeleton-like bodies. Manya and her small group of friends stayed close together, not wanting to be separated when they were assigned to barracks. But this time when they walked in to choose bunks, there was a difference: people were already there. The newcomers were asked lots of questions.

"Where did you come from?"

"Mielecz."

"How long were you there?"

"I'm not sure. Maybe two months."

"What was it like there?"

"Horrible, but smaller.. What's it like here?"

"The worst possible you can imagine."

"How long have you been here?"

"Over a year."

"Where are we?" Manya asked.

"In Plaszow."

"Where's that?"

"In Poland."

The light was very dim inside, but Manya's eyes were draw to a tiny girl standing in the very back. She had a small face and beautiful eyes that begged to be talked to.

"Oh, my God!" Manya cried, tears spilling onto her cheeks. "Make it be true, God! Yes! Yes!" She ran to the little girl, her arms opened wide. "Oh, Cyvia! Cyvia, you're alive!" It was Meyer's younger sister.

Meyer's three transfers to camps had all been conducted in the same manner: a truck ride to the train, hours or days in a boxcar, then disembarking on a siding, and a march to the gates of the camp. As they entered, it was always the same, too: wild-eyed figures pressed against the barbed wire of inner enclosures, shouting names of loved ones. By the time he reached the gates of Wieliczka, he knew the routine.

"Korenblit!" he yelled. "Korenblit!" His eyes scanned the crowd, his ears tuned into the chorus that answered him. "Korenblit!" he tried again.

A voice screeched "Kor—" and Meyer stiffened. But the voice finished with "—man!"

He searched the faces again. Hands reached through the wires. He panned the length of the fence. There were so may.

Then he said, softly at first, powerfully the second time: "Nagelsztajn! Nagelsztajn!" There was no answer.

Wieliczka was a name Meyer was sure he'd heard before. It was near Cracow, he thought. He'd most likely heard of it during his time riding the trains.

He tried to think how long ago that was. It had been summertime when he'd given up running to return to the ghetto, and he'd been there only a couple of months before he and Manya were deported to Budzyn. There he had spent the winter; then, just before spring, he had been transferred to Mielecz. Now it was summer again and he had arrived in Wieliczka less than a week ago. He had now been in the camps for almost one year.

It had been months since he had watched Manya reaching to him from the back of the truck that carried her away, and he'd stopped thinking about her so often. Perhaps it was because he couldn't conjure up positive images about where she was and what was happening to her. He couldn't bear the thought that she might now resemble the emaciated women he'd seen hauling rocks, favoring an untended broken bone, or nursing wounds from a beating. He preferred to picture her face as he'd last seen it, anguished though it was. But mostly he kept the thought of her locked away to be taken out and savored only when he doubted he could go on.

He felt lucky that his friends from Budzyn were still with him Sol, Felix, Adam, Wolf, Leon, sharing the same barracks, occupying neighboring bunks. They were friends, but not confidants; close, but not intimate. There was an unspoken but generally acknowledged barrier each erected around himself, a fragile shell that insulated each from the possible loss of the other.

Here at Wieliczka, Meyer worked in dank salt mines ten hours a day. There were about a thousand men on his shift; another thousand took up where his group left off. It was a 30-minute walk at a fast pace from the camp to the mines. Other work details marched in a different direction. What chores they performed, he didn't know.

Meyer remembered the first time he had entered the mines to work. The candles burning inside cast an eerie glow that flickered with the draft created by the passing workers. The walls of the cave glistened with drops of water that ran to the floor and made shallow puddles. The abundance of moisture made it difficult for him to breathe, and he had to adopt a rhythm of working that would allow him to progress with his task without wearing him out.

Tools meticulously accounted for, were distributed at the start of each shift and collected at the end. Perhaps that was why the actual work on a shift lasted ten hours instead of the usual twelve: it took a long time just to disperse and retrieve the equipment.

Meyer's job was to chip out blocks of salt. Others sacked it; still others loaded it on little trams. A whistle blast announced the 20-minute lunch break. The soup they received for lunch was sometimes spoiled; the bread was dry, sometimes moldy; but at least they were something to swallow. After the break ended, the workers filed back to the cave as another crew loaded empty soup kettles on a wagon. Meyer didn't know any of those men and had no way to get extra food, but he never saw those soup kettles without thinking of Tovah. He hoped she was still with Manya, somehow continuing to supplement their food.

Cyvia's face danced with delight when she recognized Manya, and the two fell into each other's arms. When other women in the barracks saw their tears of joy, they felt as if they were a part of the happy reunion too.

Manya looked sadly at the pathetic diminutive figure whose tiny hands clutched her. Cyvia had no hair, and scabs covered her entire head. The Nazis had obviously shaved her head in an attempt to get rid of the lice, but poor Cyvia had scratched herself raw. There were bites all over her skinny body as well, Manya had seen starving dogs that looked better than Cyvia did now. That she was still alive was a miracle.

That first night, Manya told Cyvia the whole story of what had happened to Meyer, Chaim, and herself after they left the haystack. The story revived sad memories for Manya, but just the mention of Meyer's name had given Cyvia more energy and hope. She wanted to hear about Meyer over and over again. If there was one thing that hadn't changed about Meyer's sister, it was her inquisitiveness.

Now many weeks had passed. As Cyvia slept next to her, Manya fumbled through the straw for her diary. A soft glow sifted through the windows from the floodlight outside the barracks, dispensing barely enough illumination for her to read and write. As Manya looked over the words on the torn pieces of paper, she thought of what she would like to say.

Dear Diary,

Cyvia is much better, but what a painful experience we've gone through. Thank goodness my friends were here to help. Every night I cleaned her scalp. At first I tore off little bits of my dress or hers; then others donated scraps. We managed to get a little water. Very gently I dabbed the sores with a piece of wet cloth. The hardest part was keeping her from scratching. I held her hands so that she couldn't attack the unbearable itching. Her cries turned to moans, then to whimpers. Finally she fell asleep, exhausted from the struggle.

Cyvia hasn't said anything about what happened to her mother and sisters or how she managed to avoid being shot along with them. She may have blanked it all out of her mind. I can't bear to think of her living with all that darkness inside, but I can't bring myself to ask her about it. Maybe she'll tell me in time.

For the first few weeks the extra food Tovah sneaked Cyvia to help her get her strength back. Yes, somehow Tovah again was assigned to kitchen detail. Now Cyvia's hair is growing out and I can see the tiniest touch of color returning to her face.

I have made a new friend, Marie Gaitler. She is a wonderful person, and we have become close. She has a boyfriend here and occasionally I sneak off with her to see him. Now I know how the other girls at Budzyn must have felt about Meyer and me: happy we had each other but a bit envious, too. I long for Meyer's touch, his companionship. The feeling grows even stronger when I see Marie and Herman together.

One morning I woke up to find that someone had stolen my right shoe. I was so mad—mad to have to walk to the fields with one foot bare, and mad to think that one of us would do such a thing to another. But then I calmed down. We have to take care of ourselves, and that's what that person was doing. The other girls urged me to do the same.

"You have to, Manya. You can't walk around like that. What if your foot gets cut?" Hannah said.

"But I can't. It's not right!" I argued.

"Was it right for someone to take yours?"

So, I gave in and that night I took—no, stole—one for myself. Unfortunately, things have a way of getting even with you. I now have two left shoes.

There are two very sick girls in our barracks. They say they have no strength to go on. They told us to just let them die. But instead my friends and I helped them up for roll call, then sneaked them back to the barracks. Tovah stole food from the kitchen and we shared our own rations with them. It has been a couple of days, and they're getting better. I think they want to live now.

One thing that's different at Plaszow is Sunday—at
least the day they tell us is Sunday.   On that day, we're
allowed to wash our dresses.   There's not enough water for
ourselves, just for our clothes.   They tell us we have our
chance to wash in the morning.   So they stand there and
watch to make sure no water is used for any other purpose.
Even if we could get away with it, we'd be denying water to
the next person in line.   They don't add to or change the
water very often.   We take our dresses off and rinse them in
the basin, then wring them out and put them back on wet.
The first time I did it, standing there naked was so
degrading that it really bothered me.   The next time I didn't
think about it as much.   I just told myself that everyone is
doing it.   At least my dress gets clean.   The summer heat
dries it quickly, but for a few minutes the cool cloth
refreshes my body.

That's what Manya would have written had there been
ample paper.   Instead, she wrote the words, "Cyvia, joy,
horrible condition, no hair, Cyvia better, new friend,
replaced shoe, washed dress, farmwork."   She rolled the
paper around the pencil and carefully tucked it into her
hair, closed her eyes, and drifted off to sleep.

The next morning she was standing in line for the
count, Marie on one side and Cyvia on the other, with the
rest of her friends close by.   The count was over, but no
order was given for their release to work.

"What are they doing?" Manya whispered to Marie.

"They're searching for the most unhealthy to send
away."

"Send where?"

"We don't know.   But we never see them again."

Manya eyed the women around her.   Did any of them
really look any better or worse than anyone else?

"Listen to me, Manya.   When they get closer to you, I
want you to pinch your cheeks as hard as you can.   No
matter how much it hurts," Marie instructed.

"But why?"

"To get color into them. If you have color, they'll just pass by. I'll tell the others on my side, and you do the same on yours."

When the guards in the row in front of them turned their backs, Manya and the others grabbed their cheeks and squeezed. The SS officers walked along the lines. They looked at each person, pointing to some and passing others.

"Please, God, make the color stay," Manya begged.

The SS inspector stood in front of her, his cold eyes examining every inch of her body. She waited for his hand to point at her, to select her as one of the unhealthy. Then it would be over, once and for all.

Without a word he moved to the next in line.

D eath and deportation had become as routine as the roll calls, the tasteless bits of food, the long hours of hard work, the short periods of restful sleep. Manya and her friends awoke to each day thankful only to be alive rather than dead.

Manya's hope of survival didn't diminish, but sometimes her confidence faltered. Then her thoughts would turn to Meyer and the day she would meet him at home in Hrubieszow. How happy he would be to see her standing there, hand in hand with little Cyvia! If only there were a way she could let him know that his youngest sister was alive. She prayed to God to give him a sign. She knew the smallest bit of information could give an inmate the incentive to make it through another 24 hours. Manya knew Meyer would never give up, his impulsiveness frightened her and now she wasn't there to calm him.

With Cyvia near, Manya felt closer to Meyer. Every time she looked at his sister, she saw him. Cyvia was also a link with the past; they could talk about the wonderful days before the war, and it was almost like talking with Meyer.

Now on this day, Manya stood for roll call. The count had been completed, but the usual selection of the unhealthy seemed to be delayed. None of the SS officers were taking their daily walk along the lines. The girls nevertheless pinched their cheeks just as they had done every time they expected a selection. The longer they waited, the more they pinched. Tovah had done it so hard and so often that there was a spidery blotch on her cheek from an injured vein.

Still they stood, and the Nazis continued to watch them. More guards arrived.

"Manya, something is wrong," Marie said.

"Maybe they're going to kill all of us here," said Hannah, giving voice to a common fear.

"Shh! They can't kill everyone. I've heard there are more than twenty thousand people here," Tovah added to reassure her.

But Manya wasn't sure. The Nazis had shown her they were capable of anything. She shuddered at the thought that murdering twenty thousand Jews would be as routine to these butchers as smashing a single baby against a wall.

"Maybe they're just going to send us away," Manya said, trying to convince herself as much as Hannah and the others. The thought of another camp terrified her. Here at least she was familiar with the procedures. She knew what to avoid and how to get away with little things that kept the spirit going. Here also, Tovah was able to supply the much-needed extra bits of food. What if she wasn't assigned to kitchen duty the next time? They all depended upon and helped each other. Each had times when they was ready to give up, but the encouragement of the others would pull them through. What if one of them was left behind?

The roar of engines filled their ears. A convoy of trucks appeared. Apparently the Nazis would remove a lot of people this time. As the guards began to move in, Manya reached down and grabbed Cyvia's hand. She made a split-second decision.

"When they start, we're going to run, Cyvia. Just follow me."

The gunfire and screams started at the same time. The prisoners took off. People scattered in every direction. More shots rang out.

Manya had to let go of Cyvia's hand to push their way through the scrambling crowd. Like a shield she and Tovah were side by side, their hearts pounded, their legs churned. Neither looked back. More shooting. They could hear bullets flying over their heads and saw them land on the ground around them. The women's barracks were just ahead. Although their own building was a bit farther away they knew they could hide under the first one they came to until this melee was over.

They got closer. The screams were louder. Manya tried to block them out. She didn't want to hear them. They meant death. Don't look back, she thought to herself.

"We're almost there, Cyvia! Hurry!"

Only a few more steps. Manya's chest was about to burst. The barracks were directly in front of them. One final push, and they made it.

Manya got down on her stomach and crawled under the building. "Hurry or they'll see us!" she yelled.

There was just enough room between the ground and the building for them to squeeze through. Had anyone seen them? The gunfire continued. Manya breathed in gulps, and she could hear the others trying to get their wind back.

"Cyvia, are you okay?" Manya whispered.

There was no answer.

"Cyvia!" Manya called.

"Manya, not so loud, someone will hear you."

"But where's Cyvia? She was right behind me!"

They scooted farther back under the building and waited. Manya had been so sure that Cyvia was right behind her. How could she have left Meyer's sister out there? Time passed slowly as Manya wrestled with the impulse to crawl out and look for Cyvia. "Oh, my God, please keep her safe," she implored.

Peeking out from under the building, Manya tried to spot Cyvia in the chaos they had just escaped. There was no sign of her. She had slipped through Manya's fingers and disappeared. Why didn't I look back? Her conscience asked. Because you don't look back, she answered, you just run.

Suddenly she saw black boots run by, then heard heavy footsteps pound the wooden floor above her head. The Nazis were searching the barracks. Would they look underneath? The girls held their breaths.

The guards came out empty-handed and left.

Manya could tell there was still a lot of commotion in the camp. The friends waited about an hour, then heard more footsteps. These didn't sound like heavy boots; instead they heard the familiar scuffling of wooden clogs.

"I think it's over. They've let some women come back to the barracks," Tovah said.

"Maybe we should go out," Hannah suggested.

But no one wanted to be the first. Finally they crawled out together and quietly stole their way inside. The women in that barracks warned them to go back to their own building.

"What happened out there?" Hannah asked.

"They took thousands away. It was terrible!"

"Was anyone killed?" Manya asked.

"Yes, some were, when everyone started running."

Manya's heart sank. She felt sick.

Tovah put her arm around Manya and led her out the door. "Maybe Cyvia's back at our barracks."

But when they returned, there was no Cyvia.

"She was probably taken with the others, Manya. She'll be all right,: Tovah said, trying to console her.

Manya hoped her friend was right. Even if Cyvia hadn't been killed, Manya knew one thing to be true: she had lost Meyer's sister, just as she had lost her own brother. And now it felt as if her link with Meyer had been severed again.

CHAPTER TWELVE

Crucial moments

*In time, Meyer and Manya were sent to camps
designed for both work — for inmates judged able to
perform back-breaking labor under the worst of conditions — and death — for those who were not. Flossenburg, one of the combined work and death camps, was
in mountainous south-central Germany near the Czech
border. Its inmates labored in the Messerschmitt airplane factory and in the German Earth and Stone
Works quarries. Although its small crematorium operated continuously, night and day, the bodies of inmates
put to death there still often exceeded its capacity.
When that happened, the bodies were thrown into pits
in the hillsides and burned there. Three hundred miles
east of Flossenburg, near Cracow, Poland, was the
complex of Auschwitz, made up of work camps and a
death camp, Birkenau, where at least one million people were put to death during the course of the war.*

*Among those who died at Auschwitz was a young
Dutch woman, Etty Hillesum, whose diary, written
between 1941 and 1943, included her clear vision of
what was to come for herself and so many others: "We
must accept everything as it comes and be prepared for
the worst. Don't brood and don't be afraid, but be
calm and think clearly. When the crucial moment
comes, you will surely know what you have to do."*

LATE SUMMER—FALL 1944

The trip had taken four days this time, or so Meyer thought. How could he judge for sure, cooped up like that in the boxcar? But the patchy stubble on his face had grown, and his body clock was becoming more and more adept at measuring time, so he thought he must be close. He'd try to catch a glimpse of the moon tonight; it would be another clue.

They'd been given food for the journey before being loaded up. That told Meyer that the Germans meant to keep them alive—perhaps only barely, but alive nevertheless.

Events during the transport and the arrival at this new camp had followed the usual pattern. But as Meyer marched with the others down the road and saw the camp up ahead, he noticed something he'd not seen before: thick columns of smoke billowed in the distance. He couldn't imagine why fires were necessary on such a hot day.

Crossing the compound, Meyer was eventually able to question an inmate and learned that the camp was called Flossenburg. The exchange was cut short by an impatient guard, preventing Meyer from asking the location. Flossenburg wasn't a Polish name, so Meyer took that and the long trip required to get there to mean that they were now in another country. It was at dinner that someone told him they were in Germany.

Meyer was pleasantly surprised by the condition of the camp. The grounds were tended and very clean. In the barracks, the bunks were covered with straw-filled mattresses instead of loose hay. Although the inmates were still assigned two to a bunk, Meyer felt the promise of more comfort. It looked like a large camp but how large he couldn't tell, for the boundaries of the fences were hidden for the most part by groves of trees, which in turn were ringed by mountains.

The new arrivals queued for an inspection, a shower, and a set of clothes. Heads and faces were shaved; tin cups and spoons were distributed as usual. The morning air was crisp and clean despite the season. As the day passed, though, the sun beat down on them and the temperature soared.

On the second morning, they rose, vied for the latrine, were counted, and then set off for work, following the typical pattern. But as they walked a longer distance than usual, Meyer looked from side to side, trying to get oriented. They should have reached the main gate by now; surely he couldn't have missed it. Yet they trudged on in the cool morning, passing more watchtowers and checkpoints, but still there was no fence. My God, he thought finally, we must still be inside. Wherever he looked, he saw buildings.

The dirt road they followed went into an incline and began to curve around and back, then around again. They were on the slope of a mountain. A short time later they stopped, and the group was pushed into a circle to receive instructions.

As the guard spoke, Meyer glanced around the area. The trees were thick below him, farther apart on his level, and even thinner above the clearing where they stood. Piles of rock were everywhere, and a couple of low-lying buildings sprawled several hundred yards to his right.

Meyer looked up. The mountain was bare and concave, its white face misshapen and jagged. He saw some soldiers busy at one side of the gutted area. They appeared to be making holes in the rock. Spools of wire lay at their feet.

". . . the stone quarry for buildings and roads," Meyer heard an officer say. He should have been listening more carefully.

". . . explosives, and loosen the rock," the officer continued. Meyer had missed it again. If he didn't pull himself together, he wouldn't know what they were expected to do.

". . . over there," the officer finished.

Where? Meyer thought, waiting for someone in his group to lead the way. But no one moved toward the mountain; in fact, they tightened their circle and retreated a few steps. What was going on? Meyer saw the soldiers pick up the wire and attach it to the mountain. They moved backward on the slope, unraveling the wire as they went. Then, he heard an "all-clear" shout. The group of prisoners moved away a bit more.

Suddenly, an explosion shattered the air, and a chunk of the mountain collapsed. Rocks and debris showered over the unprotected prisoners. When an order moved them quickly into action, Meyer took his cue from the others. Some scooped up canvas bags and bent over to fill them with broken rocks; some stooped to hoist the larger slabs.

"Schnell! Schnell!" the guards screamed at the struggling workers to hurry. Whips cracked in the air.

"Do it yourselves if you can go faster," Meyer muttered. Already his shirt was drenched with sweat, and the sun was barely an hour old.

It seemed forever until the whistles blew to signal the end of the day and the workers staggered away from the mountain. As they drew closer to the barracks, Meyer again saw smoke climbing into the darkening sky.

Later, in the barracks, Meyer described his work to Felix, then asked to what kind of work his friend had been assigned.

"The same, Meyer," Felix replied. "Everywhere I've been, it's the same. I'm still making planes."

"Planes?" Meyer asked incredulously. "There's a plane factory here? But where?"

"In a mountain."

"The factory is *in* the mountain?"

"That's right. There's a long tunnel, and the factory is at the end of it. We're making parts for airplanes, drilling holes for the rivets, you know. It's a pretty big place, too, and they're making it bigger every day. Another crew digs it out and loads the dirt in a string of tram cars that carry it to the outside."

"Do you realize how big this camp is?" asked Meyer.

Felix nodded. "And I'll tell you something else. The prisoners here aren't only Jews. Some are here because they were caught helping Jews. There are also Polish and Russian prisoners of war, as well as Germans and Austrians who were labeled as traitors."

They continued to compare notes, but Meyer was preoccupied with Felix's information about the plane factory. Not only was the stone quarry within the limits of the camp, but so was a plane factory—and both were in the mountains. He wondered if every mountain in his view housed its own industry. The size of the operation seemed staggering to him.

Some weeks later, Meyer's group felt the impact of death. It had hovered all around them for months—but for the first time it reached out and snatched one of Meyer's friends when Leon was led away to be executed. They were told nothing.

Leon's death forced them to recognize that their circle was not impenetrable after all. But Meyer grieved for more than a cherished friend. Because the two had been together since the ghetto in Hrubieszow, Meyer thought of Leon as a link with Manya. When Meyer lost Leon, he felt that he lost a little of Manya too.

About a month later, Meyer was given a new work assignment. He learned of this change not because it was explained to him but simply because he was steered one morning to a different route—one that led past the barracks area to the other side of the main compound.

As he walked, again he saw the smoke. His nose picked up an unfamiliar odor, a hint of which had hung in the air since his arrival. His group got closer to the columns of smoke, and the smell intensified. He was finally going to see what the fires were for.

Meyer looked at the crew that marched with him. Some were as curious as he, but most stared blankly ahead. Meyer's eyes moved to the trail of smoke and tracked it downward.

There, on his left, he saw naked bodies in a huge pile. They were on fire.

Which would happen first—she would run out of paper to write on, the war would come to an end, or she would . . . ? Manya didn't complete the thought. Many of her torn sheets had been filled by this time. Each sentence, each fragment, each word had meaning. She wouldn't forget the interpretation of a single one when she explained them to Meyer. His name rarely appeared in the diary, for she had no need to remind herself of a thought that was ever-present. It was Meyer's image that kept her going from day to day.

The conditions at Plaszow had deteriorated rapidly. Food had become worse and even more meager, while the work had grown harder and the hours longer. More and more people were sent away, endless others brought in to replace them.

Manya unrolled the diary and read the words "chosen, not taken." She and her friends had been lucky that day a few weeks ago. When all of them had been selected for the deportation, there had been nowhere to run that time, for the Nazis had surrounded them. Truck after truck had been loaded with people. Step by step, inch by inch, she and her friends had moved closer to the vehicles that would take them to an unknown destination: death at worst, another camp at best.

They had stood behind the final truck. It was half-loaded. They had moved closer. Five women had been in front of Tovah, who was the one of Manya's group closest to the vehicle.

"Stop!" the guard had suddenly yelled.

He had seen that the truck was completely full—not one more could be squeezed in. Manya and her friends had received a reprieve. But when they returned to the barracks, they knew it was only a matter of time before the trucks would have room for them.

Now Manya's departure day had arrived. Instead of going to the roll call, the women were led directly to the gate, where vehicles waited. There was little commotion.

Manya knew what to expect when they got off the trucks at the train depot. First they were packed into the boxcars; then the doors were shut. The train sat still. As the temperature rose, the car became stuffy and smelly, and the weakest soon succumbed. The women received no food or water. They prayed the ride would be a short one; that was a more immediate concern than whatever they would find at the other end.

But the trip took most of the day, and it was dusk when the train came to a rest.

The doors slid open, and the women jumped down, expecting the usual walk of some distance to the camp. Their first glance, however, told them that was not the case here.

The train had actually pulled inside the camp itself, and they had landed not on the ground but on a platform. Manya looked around. There were fences on either side, running along in back of her and intersecting with a long brick building with watchtowers on top. The wings of the building were one floor high, but in the center the structure grew to three stories. Heavy metal gates spanned the ground-level entrance. The train had entered the camp through those gates.

Dark clouds filled the sky, and there was a foul odor in the air. Manya felt a chill, but it wasn't cold.

Rows of buildings stretched as far as she could see. Behind the fence on the right were men with the same hollow faces as people she'd seen on entering other camps. Their shaved heads and striped pants and jackets made them all look the same. They were calling out names.

"Is there a Chaim Nagelsztajn?" Manya shouted.

No response.

She moved closer to the fence. "Is there a Chaim Nagelsztajn here?" she repeated at the top of her lungs.

"Yes!" she heard from somewhere in the middle of the group.

Was that yes for her or for someone else?

"Chaim Nagelsztajn?" she screamed again.

"Yes, Nagelsztajn!"

Oh, my God, someone was saying her name! A voice was saying her little brother was here!

"Chaim! Where are you? *Chaim*!" Please, God, let me see him! "Where are you, Chaim?"

She saw a hand wave in the air, and followed it down the arm until she lost it in the crowd.

Again she screamed his name. There . . . that was it! She saw the face. It looked terrible—no hair, sunken eyes, drained cheeks. No. Those were not Chaim's eyes or his round cheeks. This wasn't her Chaim Nagelsztajn. This ghost of a person was not her brother. She must have followed the wrong hand.

"Chaim Nagelsztajn from Hrubieszow!" Where was the voice that had called out to her?

"I knew Chaim Nagelsztajn." It was the same person who had responded to her before. It wasn't Chaim, but at least—

"You know Chaim? Where is he?"

"They took him away yesterday to—"

His words were drowned out as guards rushed in, yelling at the prisoners to hurry along. Manya was pushed and shoved from the fence although she fought to stand her ground.

She had missed the last of the man's message about her little brother.

When Meyer was transferred from the stone quarry, he was taken to the mountain Felix had described a few weeks ago. Not only was his assignment changed but his shift was also, so that now he worked nights.

At about the same time, word had gone out that the SS wanted volunteers for kitchen duty. Meyer had been in the right place at the right time and was one of the few who landed the job. Even though it would mean a double shift of work, he considered himself lucky to have the chance to do it. The more useful he made himself, the greater the possibility of survival. He believed such an opportunity was well worth the loss of sleep. He would make do with four or five hours.

The camp kitchen was hot, and the Jewish workers were kept busy preparing vegetables and tending kettles under the watchful eyes of the Nazi guards. The mandated procedures didn't allow for removing dirt caked on beets and carrots, but the workers rubbed it off on their clothes when the Nazis glanced away. Nor did the orders provide for paring away rotten sections of potatoes and turnips, but as often as possible the prisoners hid the spoiled pieces when the collection buckets were passed.

Meyer's job was to fill the huge kettles with water and hoist them to the surface of the wood-burning stove, ready to receive the few pieces of vegetables. If they could have managed it, the inmates would have added extra ingredients, but the supply for each meal was allotted grudgingly by the guards who held the key to the storehouse.

The kitchen workers didn't take their meals where they worked. They lined up at their barracks like the rest of the inmates. But somehow handling the food was a step toward satisfying their hunger, and the occasional morsels they were able to pop secretly into their mouths and pockets helped too.

Meyer went directly from his eight-hour day shift in the kitchen to dinner, then assembled with another work group for his night shift at the plane factory. At first he helped make parts for Messerschmitts. Then he was assigned to a crew enlarging the underground area to allow for expansion of the factory. Sometimes he wielded a pickax for twelve hours; other times he shoveled dirt and rock into the tram cars.

When the whistle announced the end of the shift the next morning, Meyer dragged himself back to camp. The only thing that kept him going was the thought of the lone slice of carrot he might be lucky enough to purloin in the kitchen after his nap.

One night, as his group stood ready to enter the tunnel, the SS guard asked if anyone knew how to drive, for they needed someone to operate the tram. Something inside Meyer clicked. His hand went up and caught the attention of the officer in charge. What are you doing? asked a skeptical voice in Meyer's head. You don't know how to drive!

The officer took a few steps in Meyer's direction. I know I can figure it out, Meyer countered to himself. It looks a lot easier than hollowing out the mountain.

The guard beckoned to Meyer. You're really in for it now, the voice warned. They'll see immediately that you don't know the first thing about driving! Meyer stepped away from the group. I can do it, he said firmly to himself, silencing the voice in his head and following the guard to the head of the string of cars.

The guard's explanation of the controls was confusing and peppered with "of course" and "you know." Meyer didn't know, but he nodded and muttered an occasional "of course" of his own to seem convincing, while his eyes and ears tried to absorb every detail of the steps. When the officer gestured toward the driver's seat, Meyer climbed clumsily aboard. His instructor eyed him warily.

There was a false start or two—a matter of confusing reverse and forward—but in a moment Meyer had it figured out and he was waved inside the tunnel. Moving along one of the two tracks, Meyer averted his eyes from those whose task he'd no longer share, making sure not to appear pleased with his new responsibility. He knew very well that the next week, the next day, even the next hour could find him back swinging a pick.

Meyer had thought that the less strenuous job of operating the tram would make it easier for him to continue working a double shift. But the motorman's position proved to be tedious and lonely. Back and forth, in and out of the tunnel he went, twelve hours a night, waiting inside for the cars to be loaded and outside for them to be emptied. And when he chugged out of the lengthening tunnel, there was no glare of sunlight to snap him out of his grogginess. The job consequently exaggerated rather than eased his fatigue.

It was probably his twelfth trip out of the tunnel one night when something happened. Everything had been routine: the humming of the tram's motor, the far-off grinding of drills biting into metal down another cavern, the chunk-chunk-chunk of the excavators deep within the shaft growing fainter as the car moved away.

But in a flash, a different set of sounds erupted. First a crash, then shouts, then a whirring of free-spinning wheels, a revving engine, and more shouts. Meyer opened his eyes; he was lying on the ground. He looked at the tram; it had derailed. He reached to the controls and pulled the throttle to neutral. The revving stopped and the wheels slowed, but the shouting got louder. What had happened? He knew there was only one possible explanation: he had fallen asleep and failed to apply the brakes at the unloading dock. The tram had run off the end of the track.

A guard yanked Meyer to his feet and punched him viciously. He called the foreman, who slapped Meyer and screamed at him to explain the accident. Meyer threw up his arms to fend off the blows, but his senses were dulled and he failed to anticipate where the fists would land next. The man shook Meyer from side to side, again demanding to know what had happened.

"The brakes," Meyer stammered. "They didn't work."

"This is the first time all night that you used the brakes?" the foreman asked sarcastically.

"No, but they didn't work this time."

The foreman made no comment as he shoved Meyer to the ground and bent over to inspect the tram. Out of the corner of his eye, Meyer noticed an SS major watching the scene. Two guards grabbed Meyer and hauled him to the foreman's office. Two more came in, and the four of them set upon Meyer again. They called him a nasty Jew and a swine. They said he had sabotaged the operation and they were going to shoot him like a dog, but first they were going to beat him so badly he would pray to die. After the beating, however, they walked out, leaving him bleeding on the floor.

A few minutes passed and another SS man entered the room. He told Meyer to take his clothes off. Meyer pulled himself over to a wall and used it as support while he painfully removed his shirt. Apparently he took too long to undress, for the German raised his whip before Meyer could pull off his pants. Meyer rolled on the floor as thirty lashes were delivered, his fingers clawing the walls, his feet executing a slippery crawl away from the stinging whip. He raised himself up only to be cut down again. His head crashed against the wall. He felt he was ready to die, just as they had predicted.

Then, seeing the young man was nearly senseless, the officer slapped him in the face with his leather gloves and stomped out of the room.

Meyer was left in a heap in the corner. Manya, he thought. His mind called to her. Manya. She wasn't there to help him get up this time, yet it seemed . . . yes, he could see her face. Perhaps she was with him after all. He tried to look around, but the room was spinning. Her image appeared, was lost, appeared again, then faded away. He focused on the thought of her, but couldn't get up.

The major who had been watching him earlier entered the room and sat down at the desk. He swung his squeaky chair around to face the young man. Meyer looked back at him through dazed eyes.

"You lied to the foreman," the major said in a low voice. "There was nothing wrong with the brakes. I checked them myself."

Meyer's eyes dropped to the jagged SS insignia on the man's collar. He didn't know what to say or even if he could speak at all. "The brakes," he managed to mumble.

"No, not the brakes. There's nothing wrong with the brakes. Why don't you tell me what really happened?"

The major's voice was calm, sympathetic even. It invited Meyer's confidence. Could he trust the officer? he wondered. Probably not.

The hesitation brought another question from the major. "What do you do when you leave here in the morning? Do you go back to your barracks and sleep like you're supposed to?"

Meyer eyed the major.

"Well?"

"Yes—mostly."

"Either you do or you don't. Give me a straight answer. Do you return to your barracks and sleep until it's time to go to work again?"

What the hell difference would it make to tell him, Meyer thought wearily. Could they kill him twice?

"No," he answered finally.

"No! What do you do then? You can't work if you don't sleep!"

"I take a nap, but . . . well, I work in the kitchen during the day."

"But why? Don't you work hard enough already?"

"The food," Meyer explained. "I . . . the food."

The major was quiet; then he sighed. "So what really happened tonight?"

"I fell asleep," Meyer began weakly. "I've been working two shifts for quite a while now. I guess it was too much."

"You lied to me when I asked you the first time."

Meyer didn't respond.

"You lied to me. But I lied for you. I told my staff the brakes were faulty. I'm going to save your life—or what's left of it."

There was another awkward silence as Meyer tried to believe his ears. The major looked at him expectantly.

"Danke schön, Herr Oberführer, danke schön," Meyer whispered in the fragile air.

"You can thank me by not letting it happen again."

"Yes, Herr Oberführer, thank you."

"I won't be able to help you again," he warned. "I shouldn't have this time. You'd better give up the kitchen work."

"Yes, Herr Oberführer."

"No more kitchen," he repeated to be sure.

"Yes, Herr Oberführer."

"The shift is almost over. I'll see you tomorrow night, if you don't die on me. Now get out of here," he said, swinging his chair around to his desk.

Meyer got to his knees and picked up his shirt. He pulled himself up and limped toward the door. As he opened it, the major spoke again. "You forgot your shoes." Meyer hobbled back for them.

M anya and the other women from Plaszow stood in a row along the length of a platform, having just arrived at this new camp. Manya was still trying to recover from the news that Chaim had been here before her, but now had been taken away.

The door of a small one-story building close by opened, and three men stepped out.

Seeing a selection coming, the women pulled themselves a little straighter, tried to smooth their matted hair, licked their dry lips, and pinched their cheeks pink.

The SS officers ordered them to form several lines, then faced the women at the head of each line. Appraising eyes evaluated the female prisoners one by one. A hand signal communicated the judgment to guards who carried out the sentence. The waiting lines shrank as people were sent off in two directions.

Manya neared the front of her line and pinched her cheeks again. She was next.

The SS officer looked her up and down, then gestured his decision, and Manya was waved to a path on her left that led through some gates and inside a fence. Most of the women had been led in a different direction. She was going with the smaller group. She didn't know if that was a good or bad sign, but she took heart when Marie and Tovah caught up with her. At least they would be together to face what was ahead.

Manya looked around as she walked. She gasped at the vastness of the grounds within the barbed wire. Plaszow had seemed enormous to them, but this—this was impossible to describe. Every bend in the road they followed gave a new and more overwhelming perspective of the gigantic enclosure.

Off in the distance, smoke oozed across the darkening horizon. Manya watched it, thinking that night would come soon; she hoped they hadn't missed dinner.

After walking for about ten minutes, they were delivered in bunches to several barracks. Manya heard a woman's voice in the back of her building as she entered. She was curious, but she had something more important to do. She reached into her hair to remove the tattered roll of diary papers, then buried them in the straw of her bunk before joining the others.

Seeing more faces come up to the group, the woman started over. "This camp is called Auschwitz," she began. "It is a very bad place. Part of it is a death camp. The path you took from the train was the path to life, at least for tonight. The other road went to the gas chambers and crematoria. Tomorrow you'll be inspected again, and some of you may not come back here. But even if you do, that isn't the end of it. Every day they make selections. Every day."

Her voice continued, but Manya had heard enough. Had she listened, she would have gotten a description of the size of the camp and the daily routine and the kind of work there was to do. But Manya couldn't get past what the woman had already said. Now she thought she knew what the man at the entrance gate was going to say about Chaim when he began, "They took him away yesterday to—" In this place there was only one way the sentence would have ended: "—the gas chamber."

Manya retreated from the group and pulled herself along the bunks, then fell into the middle berth. She covered her face with her arms and sobbed. Then, she numbly drew out her diary and unrolled the paper. Her hands shook as she wrote: "Auschwitz. Chaim dead." Then she collapsed against the straw and slept.

The next morning, Manya woke with the first whine of the siren and stumbled outside with the others. Thirty minutes later, they were led to another building. SS men with guns at the ready lined both sides of the huge hall inside, and a staccato voice shouted instructions over the wails of panic that filled the air.

"Strip and line up!" the shrill voice directed, bringing a new chorus of cries from the women, but no compliance with the order.

"Achtung!" the voice screamed, but they paid no attention. Then another command was heard, and shots were fired into the ceiling. There were screams as wild eyes searched for safety and the women huddled together around the room.

"Strip and line up!" the voice directed again. This time the women complied, removing their clothes quickly and letting them fall at their feet.

The crew of inspectors pushed into the throng and looked over each of the naked women. There were signals of thumbs up or down.

When they came to her, Manya stood quite straight and still. Then she saw a thumb point to the floor, and she was directed toward one of two groups forming in the chaos.

She looked at the faces around her in the group. Some were old, some young. But they were all strangers. She looked across the room. There were her friends, but they were on the other side of the room, in the other group of women. She had to get over there; she wanted to be with them. But she was trapped in a tight circle; more women were added every second.

A string of guards snaked through the middle of the room, trying to cordon off one group from the other. She didn't have much time. The swirling thoughts in her mind suddenly parted, and everything became sharp and clear.

Dropping almost unconsciously to her knees, she used her arms to wedge her way through the frenzied crowd.

Sometimes she was able to crawl a few steps. More often she

resorted to clawing her way across the floor and between pairs of legs and feet. Despite her exertion, Manya was cold—shivering with fear. At any instant she expected to be trampled or to be lifted upright by a uniformed arm. But the women paid no attention to her, and the Germans must not have noticed her in all the confusion.

At last she stood up. She peered around frantically to see where she was, then breathed a long sigh: there were Tovah and the others. Manya was only a few people away from her friends.

Still not sure where this group was headed, Manya followed them as they were led into another room. When she saw what was happening there, Manya knew she was safe—for the guards were passing out the usual camp issue of clothes and a cup.

Without really knowing what she was doing, she'd managed to escape the group headed for death and joined those allowed to live. Once again, Manya thought of how God was still looking out for her.

Still in a daze but more confident now, Manya followed the others along to the next inspection station. There, an SS officer eyed her hair, turning her around to get a better look. Then, a guard guided Manya and a few others into a third room.

When she came out, there wasn't a hair on her head. She walked, staring at the ground, trying to hide her baldness with her hands. Her fingers fanned protectively over her bare scalp, incredulously stroking the smooth skin. She patted the top, then the sides, then the back of her head, fascinated by the strangeness.

The next time Manya looked up, she was at her barracks door. She rushed in and threw herself onto her bunk.

Relieved that Manya was back with them, the girls formed a circle of comfort around their friend. They had been spared the barber's razor, but their hair had already been short. Manya's had been long—long enough to hide her precious diary. What would she do with it now? The friends gathered closer to the weeping girl. She'd lost her hair, but she was still alive.

Some time later, a bucket of soup was brought to the barracks. After the women drank their lunch, they were called outside. Line after line of women stood facing a bank of tables. As the columns inched forward in the autumn afternoon, Manya's knees buckled when she saw the tattoo equipment. She turned fearful eyes to Tovah, who stared back, then nodded her confirmation.

All too quickly, it was Manya's turn. The arm she held out this time lacked any fatty tissue, the muscles atrophied from inadequate food. The needle made its first inky puncture, then continued. Manya read an upside down A, then 2, 7, 3, 2, 7.

As she walked away, her throbbing arm pulsed a message to her. She was prisoner A27327 of Auschwitz.

Despite what she'd gone through that day, she felt a sense of relief. Surely they wouldn't go to all this trouble if she was only going to die.

As Meyer stood in line for the lunchtime count, still at Flossenburg, he thought about his near-encounter with death. It had been two weeks, and he was still in bad shape from the beating. There were marks all over his body, and the pain in his ribs was a nagging reminder of the kicks he'd suffered. He was unable to turn over in bed, get up, or lie down without help, and at work he used his arm to support his aching side whenever he could.

The beating had been even worse than the one he'd received in Budzyn. As they had on that occasion, his friends shared their food with him. But other than an extra bit of food, they had nothing but encouragement to give their friend to aid in his recovery. And Meyer knew the consequences of not getting up for work two mornings in a row: his body would join the others at the ever-burning fire.

He had no idea why the Oberführer had spared his life. Maybe the man had killed his quota for the day. Or maybe he had believed Meyer's story. What Meyer wanted to believe was that he had found another decent human being in the midst of all this horror.

At least he had been allowed to keep the job of driving the tram. The men who worked in the quarry were in increasingly weakened condition from the harsh physical labor. Had he been reassigned to that pit with his injuries, there would be little chance of survival.

Meyer spooned through his soup hopefully, but found nothing more than a few shavings of vegetables. One time they actually had had meat in their soup. Allied airplanes dropping bombs in an attempt to hit the plane factory and adjacent facilities had killed some horses. The Germans ate their fill, then allowed the leftover meat to be given to the inmates.

As he ate, he felt someone staring at him. Cautiously, without moving his head, Meyer glanced to his left. He *was* being watched. With nervous hands he continued to eat, never taking his eyes off the cup. One of the first things he had learned in the camps was not to draw attention to himself. He wanted to look over again, but forced his face down, avoiding the penetrating gaze.

After finishing, Meyer started to walk away. Then he heard a command: "Halt!"

He stopped but didn't turn around, preferring not to see whatever blows might follow. The guard approached and stopped in front of the frightened young man. Meyer was trembling. He hoped the man wouldn't notice.

"Tell me, what is your name?"

"Meyer," he answered. "Meyer Korenblit."

"Meyer. That's Polish, isn't it?" the guard inquired.

"Yes, it is."

"Well, I'll call you Max. Yes, in German that would be Max," he said in a friendly voice. "My name is Hans-Wagner Gerber. Tell me, Max, how old are you?"

"Eighteen or nineteen, I'm not sure."

"You don't know how old you are?" the man asked.

"I'm not sure how many months I've been in the camps."

"I see," he responded with a look of understanding on his face.

The inquisitive guard seemed to want to learn as much about Meyer as he could, and he kept asking questions. "Where are you working? What shift? What is your hometown?"

With each question, the man became more friendly, but Meyer was wary of his intentions. If this Nazi was treating him like a human being, it must be some kind of trick. Meyer offered no more information than was necessary, but it was difficult to keep from responding to this unexpected friendliness. The guard's next words made that even harder.

"Where is the rest of your family?"

"They were killed—near my home town."

The man's face showed deep dismay. "I'm sorry," he responded sympathetically, then quickly changed the topic. "Do you get enough to eat?"

"The only time I've had anything substantial was when the bombs killed those horses. We had meat in our soup then," Meyer answered.

The guard reached into his pocket and pulled out a package. "Here, take this," he said, handing it to Meyer.

Meyer hesitated, not sure what to do.

"Take it, it's all right," the man insisted.

Meyer's shaking hand reached out to the mysterious package. He unfolded the paper. Inside were a few small hunks of sausage. Meyer's eyes darted back to the man.

"Go ahead, eat it."

Meyer didn't need further urging. He downed it quickly. "Thank you, Herr Gerber."

"Call me Hans, or Hans-Wagner," the man instructed.

"Thank you very much, Hans-Wagner."

"How did you get those nasty marks on your body?" he asked.

Meyer explained the accident with the tram.

"And you're still alive? You don't know how lucky you are. Even a hint of sabotage means death."

Meyer nodded his acknowledgment, then finally got up the nerve to ask a question. "Why are you doing this?"

"Doing what?"

"Being nice to me. Giving me food, treating me like a human being."

The man paused for a moment, as if he wanted to choose each word carefully. A faraway look came into his eyes. "Because you look like my son," he finally said sadly.

Meyer was dumbfounded. "Like your son!" he repeated. "But you see the condition I'm in."

"When I first saw your face, it was from the side," Hans-Wagner explained. "But when you turned, I saw his eyes in your eyes, his face in your face." He sighed and went on. "He's only twenty-two years old. He is fighting on the Russian front, and I haven't heard from him for a long time. If he is shot or captured, I just hope someone will do for him what I'm doing for you."

It was difficult for Meyer to imagine trusting this man, but for the next few days Hans-Wagner searched out Meyer to furtively give him more food and to continue their conversations. Meyer began to drop his distrust and even went so far as to mention his friends in the barracks.

One day Hans didn't find Meyer at work as usual, so he went to his barracks. He located Adam and gave him two small packages: one for Meyer's friends, the other for Meyer himself. Inside each was bread and meat. At first Adam and the others were suspicious of the guard's motives, but Hans-Wagner's generosity had by then convinced Meyer that the man was a friend, and he soon laid his companions' fears to rest.

The older guard and the younger prisoner talked frequently. They discussed everything.

"Germany is a beautiful and good country," said Hans, "with many fine people."

Meyer couldn't hide his horror. "Hans-Wagner, don't you know what the Germans are doing to people right here? They are killing them and then burning the bodies! In some cases, they don't even wait to make sure the prisoner is dead, so that many of those burned are still alive!"

"Not everyone does such things, Max. I don't, although there is nothing I can do to stop it," he responded, his voice rising.

Meyer had not intended for his accusation to extend to his new friend. He had never heard Hans-Wagner insult the Jews or blame them for the war, as most Germans he'd known did. And he didn't want to lose the man's help and friendship.

Hans looked angry, and Meyer hoped that he was only showing his rejection of the Nazis but was afraid to voice it. Meyer changed the subject. "Hans, I've noticed that you limp. Is there something the matter with your ankles?"

"It's my leg. I was wounded fighting the Russians. That's why I'm here. I didn't want to come to this horrible place, but this is where they sent me to serve my country," he answered sardonically.

"Do you think this war should be going on?" Meyer asked.

"No! It's terrible, especially what they are doing here. Hitler should never have started it. He did many good things for Germany. Before he came to power, there were millions of Germans out of work. People couldn't buy enough food to live. He changed that. He created jobs, and people had plenty to eat. But this war is no good. If we don't stop, there will be no more Germany. When it began, everyone thought it was all right, especially when we were winning, but we are no longer winning."

Meyer tried to contain his excitement at hearing this last admission. For months the inmates had heard rumors, but there was never any way to confirm them. Now a German was saying that the Nazis were losing the war. Meyer didn't know which to be more grateful for: the extra food or the news that lifted their hopes of getting out.

He wondered if Hans's friendship was based partly on the fact that Germany was losing. But if his superiors caught Hans helping to keep a Jew alive, he'd be severely punished—probably even killed. Meyer felt that the overriding reason Hans helped was because it was the humane thing to do.

To be able to tell his friends the wonderful news made Meyer feel good. Anything that gave them encouragement helped them get through the long days and nights.

As the weeks wore on, there were times when either Hans-Wagner or Meyer would be assigned to different shifts. When that happened, Hans would hide the food at a designated site. Meyer was glad it didn't happen often. He didn't want to be caught retrieving the food, and he also didn't want to miss an opportunity for conversation with the older man.

"I long for this to be over, Max," Hans said one day. "I want to go home to see my wife. It's been quite some time since I've seen her. What about you, do you have a wife? No, of course not, you're too young," he said with a smile.

Manya's face flashed before Meyer's eyes. "Well, no, she's not my wife yet, but we've been together for many years—even before the war. Her name is Manya Nagelsztajn, and she is a beautiful woman, with long dark blonde hair that's soft, just like her skin. We were separated after the first camp. I have no idea what has happened to her or if she's still. . . ." He stopped, refusing to finish the sentence. "From everything I've seen, it's very difficult to survive. Maybe someone is also helping her. In Budzyn, her friend worked in the kitchen and was able to sneak out some food." His voice trailed off.

"Listen to me, Max," Hans-Wagner said firmly. "You must hold on. The war will be over soon. Then, you'll be free to go back to your hometown to find your Manya."

Meyer didn't know whether Hans-Wagner was telling him the truth or only saying it to make him feel better. He wanted to believe it was true, that he would make it through this horror, that someday he would be free and would hold Manya in his arms again.

But as weeks turned to months, Meyer couldn't help but wonder what "soon" meant to Hans. Again and again his friend repeated his assurances: "Hold on, Max. It will be over soon."

As circumstance or maybe luck would have it, Hans did even more to help Meyer and his friends when he was assigned to march Meyer's group to the plane factory. As they went each day, Meyer noticed an apple orchard on the way. After a couple of days with Hans-Wagner as their guard, Meyer finally asked him, "Do you think we might . . . ?" He pointed to the trees.

"Max, there are lots of people with us. If we're caught, it would be bad for all of us."

"No one will tell, and we could do it quickly while no other guards were around," Meyer begged.

Somehow, Hans-Wagner arranged for their group to be last in line, and for a few minutes allowed the prisoners to eat as much of the fruit as they could stuff into their skinny bodies. The agreement was that they wouldn't try to take any with them.

The extra food for several weeks now, along with Hans's insistence that the war was coming to an end, gave Meyer hope that they would soon be free.

Considering that, it was a devastating shock one day to be led again to waiting trucks. Meyer didn't even get to see Hans again before they were taken.

Meyer knew why the man had befriended him—partially because of the resemblance to his son but more importantly because he disagreed with what the Nazis were doing. Meyer was sure of that. After all, he could have helped Meyer alone, but instead he'd done what he could for many more at great risk to himself. When this is over, Meyer thought, I'll try to find him and thank him.

As Meyer was packed into the train for an unknown destination, his thoughts flashed back to another man to whom he owed his life. There were certainly differences between the two men, but he couldn't help but think he had just been separated from his German John Salki. Wherever he was going next, he would have to figure out a way to get along without that help.

CHAPTER THIRTEEN

"The power to refuse

our consent"

On June 6, 1944, the Allies landed on the beaches of Normandy in northern France and began crossing the European continent to liberate it from Nazi control. From the other direction, Soviet forces moved more deeply into Poland. Caught between these advancing armies, the Nazis accelerated the pace of killing within the camps and of moving prisoners from camp to camp. Meyer and Manya were again among those moved, one or the other of them spending time in each of the following: Leitmeritz and Lichtenwerden in Czechoslovakia; Mauthausen, in Austria; Dachau and Kaufering (a satellite of Dachau), in Germany; and Auschwitz-Birkenau in Poland..

In the face of worsening conditions, what were prisoners to do to increase their chances of survival? Primo Levi described the credo of some Auschwitz inmates: "... precisely because the Lager [camp] was a great machine to reduce us to beasts, we must not become beasts: [we must believe] that even in this place one can survive, and therefore one must want to survive, to tell the story, to bear witness. ... We are slaves, deprived of every right, exposed to every insult, condemned to certain death, but we still possess one power, and we must defend it with all our strength for it is the last—the power to refuse our consent."

"Initiation," page 36, from IF THIS IS A MAN (SURVIVAL IN AUSCHWITZ) by Primo Levi, translated by Stuart Woolf, Copyright © 1959 by Orion Press, Inc., ©1958 by Giulio Einaudi editore S.P.A. Used by permission of Viking Penguin, a division of Penguin Group (USA) Inc.

JANUARY–MARCH 1945

For the third time in less than two months, Meyer was on the train again. From Flossenburg he had entered Leitmeritz; then a three-day ride to Mauthausen; and now, after hardly more than two weeks, deportation to yet another place—where, he didn't know. He wondered if Manya's time in the camps had been as hard as his. He had kept her safe in his dreams all these months. But now, weak as he was, he had to admit the possibility that she hadn't endured the horrors as well as he had.

He knew that he now looked as haggard as the living skeletons that greeted him in every camp. The only questions were whether he fell into the category of the worst of them and whether his next destination would be his last. "Hold on," Hans-Wagner had told him, and he was trying. But the words predicting the end of the war that had been so encouraging ten weeks ago rang hollow now.

Once every so often he would hear distant explosions. Maybe now, he'd think. But each time no rescue came, he lost a little more hope.

In Leitmeritz there had been another plane factory, seemingly modeled on the one in Flossenburg. Meyer was taken to the assembly area and handed a drill. As the parts came along the conveyor belt, his job was to drill holes for the rivets. In Flossenburg, Felix and others had waged an undercover battle against the Germans by making extra holes in parts they handled. Meyer had listened to his friends talk about the satisfaction they'd gained from this sabotage, but his work assignments there had not offered such an opportunity.

In Leitmeritz, drill in hand, it all came back to him. Here was his chance. Almost gleefully he picked up the first piece and saw twenty scored marks where the holes should go. He didn't know anything about planes and couldn't be sure his action would have any effect, but he didn't care. He drilled twenty-three holes. In the next one he made eighteen. If nothing else, his actions would delay the eventual assembly of the fighter planes. He had liked that job in the Leitmeritz factory, even though the noise was deafening and he was stiff with fatigue from the tension of each twelve-hour shift.

However, his small opportunity to undermine the German war effort had been short-lived. Only a month after arriving, he was moved on.

The feeling in Mauthausen, the next camp he'd been in, had been strange. Trouble and death had lurked everywhere. Meyer was assigned again to the back-breaking work of the stone quarry—a chore with no beginning, no end, no sense of purpose. He spent every hour of the long work day lugging blocks of stone from the carved-out mountain to a pile that never seemed to change in size. This perception was due, no doubt, to another crew of workers who carried the stones from there to a new pile. The process concluded with the hapless group that dragged the blocks up 186 stone steps built by prisoners who had preceded them. Meyer had heard stories about guards taking inmates who were working too slowly and throwing them from the top of the quarry, betting on which prisoner would hit the bottom first. As much as Meyer hated the dirt, sand, and exhaustion of his work, he was grateful that he wasn't assigned to work on those steps. Perhaps this relief helped him project an impression of diligence as he trudged back and forth, hour after hour, day after day.

Now, he'd been sent somewhere else. The Germans couldn't seem to make up their minds where they wanted him, he thought ruefully.

After the train stopped, the doors of the cattle cars opened. Meyer and the others jumped out, and the familiar march toward the fences began. This time, a new set of gates swung wide. At their top, letters spanned the wire: "Arbeit Macht Frei." "Work makes you free," Meyer translated to himself.

The grounds were clean here, and trees lined a fastidiously

raked gravel road. The initial inspection of the newcomers was marked by a soft-spoken, almost considerate attitude on the part of the Germans.

Meyer's old clothes and shoes were replaced, and he was shaved, then fed; the food was surprisingly good. Hans-Wagner's words—"Hang on, the war is ending"—surfaced again, mixed with "work makes you free." But the prediction contrasted with the conditions. If the war was ending, why did this place look so free of disaster? Meyer felt he could only do two things: believe that his German friend's words would eventually come true, and interpret the words on the camp's gate as a promise. If there was a future for the inmates of the camp, one beyond what he had known for so long now, he wanted to be alive to see it.

As Meyer marched toward his new barracks, he called out to a passing group: "What place is this?"

"Dachau," was the answer shouted back to him.

Dachau, he muttered to himself. Where was that?

There was no need for Manya to record the tattoo in her diary, for it was permanently implanted on her arm. Had Chaim been numbered as well? "Yesterday," the man had said, "they took him away yesterday." That was so long ago. If only she could have seen Chaim, cradled him in her arms as she had when he was small. The picture of him in her mind was of a shy, loving little boy whose eyes sparkled with excitement when he and Meyer played together, whose cheeks dimpled with happiness at the affection she and Meyer showed him, and who tried to mask his fear with courage when he acted as her guard in the ghetto. Yes, that was the Chaim she would carry with her forever.

There were over a thousand women in her barracks here at Auschwitz. The bunks held not two or four, but six scrunched together on each level. Manya's was on the back wall, directly across from the door. It was a good location because there was no other bunk in front of her to obstruct the view if anything happened. Manya always slept on the outside edge. She felt safer there, maybe because she could get out quickly. Being on the outside also meant there was nothing to block her path when the food arrived. What food they received here, every single drop and crumb, was even more important than before, for Tovah wasn't assigned to the kitchen this time and could no longer slip them stolen food.

At this camp, there wasn't just one latrine building but a whole row, each of them as large as Manya's barracks. A large concrete block with holes cut out for toilets stretched the entire length of the structure. There was no laundering as there had been on Sunday at Plaszow. What little water went into the washbasins disappeared with the first wave of women to enter each morning. Even though the facilities were much larger and more numerous than those of other camps, there were thousands more people desperately trying to get in. Seldom did Manya or her friends make it to the toilets. Most women resorted to relieving themselves outside on the ground.

When they were taken to work, the march from their barracks to the outside of the camp was very long. They passed building after building on either side of them. The first time they were led out, Hannah whispered, "If those barracks have as many people in them as ours, there are many, many thousands more people here than there were in Plaszow."

It was a frightening thought, but it was nothing compared to the terror they felt at not being sent to work regularly. At this camp, they were taken to a farm or factory only once or twice a week. They all knew that working meant they were still useful to the Nazis; without it, all the inmates did was occupy space. Also, the monotony of being in the barracks constantly was as stressful as the work they had performed at the other camps. Minutes seemed like hours, hours like days.

It was with mixed feelings that Manya would pull herself out to the three roll calls each day. She wondered that the Nazis had nothing better to do than count people. She estimated she spent at least three hours a day being counted. But the roll calls did serve a function for her. They meant that somehow time had passed and she had managed to survive a few more hours. Would they be her last? she would ask herself as she watched the unhealthiest waved out of the lines.

The weather always seemed to be wet and muddy, and a constant haze covered the camp. It was as though even the sun had given up on them. When she had arrived and seen chimneys on top of the barracks, she had looked forward to the warmth they would provide. But it had only been an illusion: there were no fireplaces inside, only coldness.

Manya's barracks was near an electric fence, behind which she could see a row of trees. The buildings she could just make out beyond the trees had chimneys, and when she first arrived, she had thought that at least those chimneys seemed to work for she could see smoke rising from them. Later, she learned the meaning of the words the woman had spoken when they had arrived: death camp, gas chamber, crematoria. They were new words in Manya's vocabulary, but these alien terms had taken on increasing significance as survival seemed less and less certain.

Manya prayed to God to let her live; to let Meyer live; to let Tovah, Marie, Hannah, and the rest of them live. Make it be over, she begged. But the evidence before her was strong: Chaim . . . death . . . smoke. She feared that would be her fate if she didn't get out soon.

Dachau, Meyer had been told, was a model camp, subject to inspections by something called the Red Cross. He didn't know what that was and never witnessed their visits, but the name of the organization was spoken with such respect that he knew he should be impressed and relieved.

On the one day of the week that he didn't go to the nearby factory to work, he summoned energy from somewhere to perform his camp cleanup duties. It wasn't a new task; he'd done it everywhere. But here, he did it differently. Thinking of the phrase on the gates as a means of self-preservation, he took great care in the duties he performed: instead of sweeping dirt into a crack in the barracks floor, for instance, he picked it up; scattered gravel was rounded up carefully now. The feeling of satisfaction for a job well done boosted his self-esteem and, he told himself, helped keep him from the crematoria that smoked day and night on the other side of the camp.

The routine at Dachau was little different from the six other camps he'd been in. The workday was just as long, if a bit more civilized. But the faces in the group that marched off with him each morning changed constantly, as someone with him one day was often gone the next.

In the bunks at night, while the inmates waited for sleep, they talked. Some shared rumors about the war ending; others doubted that the rumors were true. A few spoke of what they would do when it was over. But always a cloud of doubt and fear hung over them, and no one could deny the ever-present threat of the smoking chimneys.

Winter turned to spring while Meyer was there, and the constant rains of the season soaked him to the bone, often twice a day.

One cool morning, under an overcast sky that would keep the sun from drying them out, Meyer and his bunkmates had just taken their positions in the lineup. Thunder sounded overhead and a preamble to rain misted the air. The count proceeded. Then there was a delay and a conference of uniforms.

An officer joined the military huddle, and they began the count again. Drops fell from the sky. Still they were counting. Ah, finished. Another military parley. The officer cursed and swung around to address the prisoners: "There is one missing," he yelled. "One missing. You'll stand here until we find him."

Now the rain was coming down in torrents. Puddles formed around the feet of the inmates. All but the lowest-ranking Germans sought cover.

No reprieve, though, for the prisoners. Striped uniforms that had hung in folds now took the form of the bony frames to which they were plastered. Slices of bread turned to paste in their pockets. Gravel washed into the grass beside the road.

Still they stood—through lunchtime and dinnertime and all night long. A change of guards was the only variation in the scene. Every so often there was a spongy thud as a weak prisoner keeled over. They were left where they fell.

At dawn, soldiers with clipboards took their usual posts, and the familiar count proceeded. No explanation was given, no announcement made. The whole incident was ignored. When the lines were dismissed, morning coffee was doled out, and work groups tramped off through the mud. A new detail was formed to collect those whose bodies had not survived the ordeal.

Later that day, Meyer found out what had happened. The missing man had been found in his bunk—dead.

The day in Auschwitz started the same as all the others for Manya. She scraped away the straw from the crack between the boards where she kept her diary at night. Her hair had grown some, but it still wasn't long enough to conceal the roll of papers. She prayed the Nazis wouldn't cut it again so that Meyer would never see her with a shaved head.

She pulled the diary from its hiding place, then fumbled for the piece of thread she had pulled from the hem of her jacket to tie around the papers. Finally, she poked the roll through two tiny holes she had made in her dress. She never left the precious papers in the barracks untended.

When that morning's roll call was over, women all around were released for their work assignments. But Manya's group continued to stand in the bitter cold. The guards stood watch. A couple of SS officers walked toward the group of freezing women, looked them over as a group, and then started to slowly check them individually. Selections, thought Manya. Please, God, let us make it through.

But the Nazis weren't conducting this inspection as usual. Instead, they ordered the women to hold out their hands and examined each pair carefully. Now the officers were in Manya's line. Hundreds of women had already been chosen. She clenched and unclenched her frigid fingers.

"Turn them over," an officer yelled at one of the girls. He gave her a withering look and moved on. They never touched a single hand, as though they would contract a disease even through the gloves they wore.

"You, out!" one of them shouted, pointing to a woman.

"You!" Another was gone.

"And you!" Oh, no, it was Tovah being sent away.

Manya held her hands out to the officer. She could feel them quiver inside, but kept them as steady as possible.

"You! Join the others."

He said it so matter-of-factly! Her heart stopped; her entire body shook. Her selection had been determined by the condition of her hands!

Hannah and Marie soon followed. At least all her friends were there. They had gone through so much together; now they assumed they were to die with one another.

After a few more selections, the Germans had their desired number. Manya heard one of the officers say, "Three hundred." They didn't even look at the rest of the women.

Manya and the others selected were led away. But after a few steps, they suddenly turned right. Manya's heart pounded with relief against her chest, for the gas chambers and crematoria were in the opposite direction. The women were being led to the front of the camp instead. Perhaps they were being taken to work?

The Germans gave each woman a slice of bread. "Make it last," they said.

Last? For what? Then Manya saw the train. They weren't to die, not today anyway, and not at Auschwitz.

The women were divided into three boxcars. When the door slammed shut, the whispers started: "Where could they be sending us now?" "Does it matter? We're out of that death camp!" "Maybe it's just a trick and they're sending us somewhere else to die." "But they must be sending us to another camp: they gave us bread." "What if it's a place even worse?"

Worse or better was not at issue in Manya's mind: she was just relieved to be leaving this most horrible place. She knew she would make it through this day to see another.

Their bread lasted the women only the first day of the trip. On the second day they were given water—a single bucket for about a hundred women, but they shared so each got at least a sip.

"We're slowing down," Marie finally announced. "Maybe this is where we get off."

The train screeched to a halt. The door slid open. "Raus! Raus!" came the command.

The women jumped to the hard ground, and Manya glanced around. They weren't far from the camp. Snow covered the ground wherever she looked, making the scene appear quiet and peaceful. There was a serenity about this place. Compared to the camps she had come from, this looked like heaven.

The women trudged along the road toward the gates. As Manya looked ahead, she was struck by something different. No endless fences this time; she could follow the perimeter of the enclosure with her eyes. And there were fewer buildings inside the small compound. But that wasn't it either. Then it hit her: there were no prisoners inside, no clamorous greetings for the newcomers. Their arrival was quiet, marked only by the sound of scuffling clogs on the rutted dirt road. She looked for smoke. There was none. She searched for a scaffold. Nothing in sight. What was this place? There was no one to ask. Our hands, she remembered. The Nazis examined our hands. What did that have to do with this solemn little place?

"This is Lichtenwerden!" a guard finally announced.

Then, the processing began. With so few to handle this time, it was over quickly. Two large female guards led the women to empty barracks. Manya thought wryly that lack of food was obviously not a problem for them. She couldn't remember if she'd seen female guards at the other camps, but if they were Nazis, she expected that they would be as mean as their male counterparts.

Hurrying to find bunks together, Manya and her friends gasped at what they saw. Thousands and thousands of names had been carved in the wooden frames—names collided and intersected; letters spaced out at first and crowded at the end; crude letters shaped by flattened-out spoons.

Where were all those people now? The names that stared at them gave the barracks a haunted atmosphere and contradicted Manya's first impression of more peaceful surroundings. This camp was not that different from the others, she thought; it too was full of despair.

The women were called out for the evening count, but when it was finished, they were led to another building with long tables and benches. It was a dining hall. They sat down to eat, hoping for more substantial food than they'd had before, but the same watery soup was dished out as grudgingly as ever.

The two female guards were joined by male guards, who paced in and out of the rows of tables. Suddenly Manya felt Tovah's elbow in her rib.

"Look!" she whispered, pointing with her eyes and head.

"Oh, my God! Is it really him? Is that really Schnauzer?"

Soon the girls who had come together from Budzyn were all aware of his presence.

Manya smiled at Tovah. "Maybe he'll remember you."

After dinner, the women were allowed to walk around outside their barracks.

"Go ahead, Tovah, it can't hurt," Manya encouraged.

"Do you think I should?"

"Yes. He won't do anything. He liked you."

"Only if you come with me," Tovah said.

The two friends walked over to where Schnauzer was standing. He was alone.

"Excuse me, sir," Tovah began. "I don't know if you remember me . . . us. You were in Budzyn while we were there."

He eyed them carefully. "I have seen many thousands of people. Why should I remember you?" he finally asked.

"You assigned me to work in the kitchen," Tovah reminded him.

He stared at her some more. Then a glimmer of recognition crossed his face. "Oh, yes. I think I remember you. We used to talk, didn't we? The last time I saw you was well over a year ago, close to two. I see you've made it this long. I'm surprised. Not many do."

The conversation halted when the women were ordered into the barracks for the night. Tovah repeated the story to the others. They felt good about his being there.

"Why are you glad he's here?" Marie asked.

"I don't know," Manya answered. "I guess it's because we started out with him and now he's with us again. Maybe it's a good sign."

"But why do you call him 'Schnauzer'? Is that his name?"

The friends from Budzyn began to laugh.

"Oh, no. It's because of his long nose. We gave him that nickname at Budzyn," Tovah answered.

It was the first time they had laughed about anything in a very long time.

The next day, when work assignments were given out, Tovah was assigned to the kitchen again. Manya and the others found out that their hands had been checked because they were to work in a textile factory. The Germans wanted women with the smoothest hands, so work could be done quickly. Women with rough hands might snag the cloth they were weaving on the looms.

They had to march to the factory in freezing weather. Except for the lint-filled air they breathed, the work wasn't difficult, especially compared to what they had done before in Budzyn and Plaszow, but the hours were long and monotonous. It made little sense to Manya that the Germans had taken such care to choose women whose hands would be right for the job and then put them in a building with no heat. Their already cold fingers grew numb, making work difficult and the chance of mistakes greater.

Whether it was the freezing cold weather or her near-starved body, sickness finally caught up with Manya. Tovah and Marie helped her to the camp infirmary, a small building with a dozen cots. It was much warmer there than in the barracks or the factory, and a Jewish inmate acted as a nurse.

Manya had a high temperature and kept vomiting up what little she was given to eat. The nurse thought she might have the flu, pneumonia, or possibly typhus, and told her that she needed rest, a warm place to sleep, and some good food. Unfortunately, the only thing the nurse was able to provide was a somewhat warmer place to sleep.

"People brought in here are only allowed to stay for twenty-four hours," the nurse explained. "The guards will come in and check after one day. If you're still here after that, they'll send you to another camp." Manya feared what would happen if they took her out of the infirmary before she could work.

The nurse took care of Manya as best she could. She kept cold compresses on Manya's forehead throughout the day, but the sick girl's temperature stayed high. Manya's stomach and throat hurt from gagging, although there was nothing left to come up. When she did eat, it was the same soup as the rest of the camp received, but at least here it was hot.

The next day, Manya was still too weak to work. But she knew she must or be sent away. She had no intention of coming so far only to die in this place. She struggled to get up, but another wave of nausea swept over her and she fell back.

The nurse leaned over Manya and whispered in her ear. "Just rest here until the others go to the latrine. I have an idea."

She helped Manya to the washhouse after the other prisoners had gone, then whispered again. "Stay in here and hide until after roll call and after they've checked the infirmary. Then I'll come back for you."

"Hide? Hide where?" Manya said weakly.

"In there," the nurse answered, pointing to the cut-out holes in the concrete slab that served as toilets. "There's no other place."

The nurse helped her patient climb down inside the toilet area. Manya gripped the inner edges of the concrete slab with her fingertips and braced her feet against each side of the hole. The smell was nauseating. She tried to hold her breath. She felt she would pass out, but instead she turned her head to one side and threw up the food she'd eaten only a few minutes before. She prayed to God not to let her fall. "Hold on," she kept repeating to herself. "Hold on tight!"

When she thought she could not hold on any longer, she heard a familiar voice. "Manya, I'm here!"

Hands reached down into the dark hole, grabbed her arm, and helped Manya slip through the narrow opening. When she returned to the infirmary, she passed out.

But the extra day of rest saved her. The next day Manya had recovered enough to drag herself to the barracks and back to work.

This was a place that reflected a faltering army and a rotting system, thought Meyer. No proud, pristine Dachau was this. This was Kaufering, with its rotten food and dilapidated barracks. The next stop on his journey.

The officers in charge here were pale and tight-lipped, their faces furrowed with anxiety and etched with the experience of seeing too much death. They stringently administered the basic routines, but there were sloppy lapses.

The guards were in a hurry, dipping cups into scant bucketfuls of sour soup and ignoring the cries when the line of prisoners outlasted the supply. Sometimes, they even skipped a meal altogether. While the work schedules were carried out faithfully, the tasks were random and disorganized—the workers might sit idle at factory assembly stations but the mandatory number of hours was filled no matter what. Something considered important one day was immaterial the next.

Explosions in the vicinity were louder and more frequent, and sometimes Meyer heard gunfire. Once in a while he saw a plane up in the sky. There was no doubt that the war was getting closer. Although rumors of German losses swirled through the camp, there was no way to confirm them. When the sounds of war erupted, Meyer looked to the guards for their reaction, anxious to read some sign, some affirmation that they could see the end too.

Meyer still had his friends; they had made every transfer with him. The warped life they had shared for so long had created an unbreakable bond among them. But now the friends spoke more and more of escape.

"It's the only thing to do," one would say.

"But where would we go?" asked another.

"We can hear the guns, but we don't know whose guns they are," admonished a third. "What if we do manage to get out of the camp and then run right into German machine guns?"

"It's a chance we have to take," insisted the first.

"We would have to go at night, that's for sure. Even if we're lucky enough to avoid the German troops, there's no guarantee that the other side would hold their fire if they saw us coming.

But let's say they spot our uniforms. How can we be sure they will know we're no threat to them? What if they think we're Germans in disguise?"

"It's no good to try it now. There are too many risks," someone would caution.

"But every hour we spend here is risky," another would counter. "We could be killed next week, tomorrow, this afternoon. We don't know what the Nazis are planning. They are more desperate than ever. We've seen the shortages in materials; half the time we can't do what we're supposed to because we don't have the supplies. They're just marking time. If we wait, one by one, we'll all go up the chimneys. I say we make a run for it."

"But I don't want to be shot while escaping. I've made it this far, and I want to be here when those gates are opened for good. I can make it another day, another week, another month if I have to. What about you, Felix? Sol? Everyone?"

They all nodded.

"Then we will stay."

Some opened their mouths to begin the debate again, but they were too tired. Besides there were no new points to raise; they had rehashed it again and again. They wanted to stick together on this, patiently waiting and hoping for their freedom.

Word was passed along as Manya and her group returned from work in single file. One woman leaned forward to whisper the signal to the one in front of her, and so on. They had talked about it for days, feeling each other out, noting the importance of banding together. The food was vile, they agreed. Because it was like eating nothing, what would they really miss if they refused to eat it? What could the guards do? Would they decide to feed them better if they feared the workers might die?

They let the idea sit for a while to be sure no one would change her mind. If some did, the rest would be undermined. But everyone was willing, so tonight there was going to be a food strike. Manya couldn't wait to write about it in her diary. It made her forget how sick she'd been a few weeks ago.

They were led in to the tables and benches, and the soup was dipped out. The room grew silent as the women stared at the food before them but made no move to eat. It took a few minutes for the guards to notice. Manya glanced around her table to see if anyone had weakened. So far no one had.

A female guard, riding crop tucked under her arm, paced slowly from table to table, eyeing the prisoners. Her footsteps echoed in the room. She looked over at another, similarly uncertain guard, who raised her eyebrows in surprise. They walked around a few more tables. Not one of the women took a bite.

The first guard angrily accosted one of the inmates. "What's the matter?"

The woman's body stiffened with fear. She squirmed a little, then felt the shoulders of those beside her pressing against her in support. The prisoner shrugged.

The guard wheeled around to another striped dress. This one spooned contemptuously through the liquid in the cup and stared at the guard's uniform.

The guard decided a more general form of address was in order. "Why aren't you eating?" She spoke to all of the women at the table.

There was no answer.

"I order you to eat!"

No one touched the food. Many women crossed their arms in front of them, perhaps to show resistance, perhaps to stifle noisy stomachs, perhaps to arrest the impulse to relent. But no one ate.

"Very well, then," the angry guard shouted. "Back to the barracks!"

The group rose and filed out without a backward glance. Reaching her bunk, Manya pulled out her diary and recorded the triumph, amid a chorus of jubilant whispers.

Again, here in Lichtenwerden, Tovah had been assigned kitchen duties, and she told them as they lined up before dinner the next night that a few extra potatoes and a bit of meat had gone into the kettles for the evening meal. The food did seem to the women a little more substantial when it was served. They had done it! That night, there was excited chatter and more than a few grins over the women's small but significant victory.

Every day the prisoners at Lichtenwerden were marched through the snow to the unheated factory where they worked. Winter seeped through every crack in the building, prolonging the frigid condition of the fingers that operated the looms. As terrified as Manya had been when her hands were inspected at Auschwitz, she now thought of the action as a sign that she was still useful. If the Nazis thought so, she should too. It helped to answer a question that was ever more present in her mind: Will I make it to the end?

The cold weather seemed to drag on. Manya thought that spring would never come. Trudging back to camp after work one day, she drew her cotton jacket tighter around her and thought of suggesting that the girls triple up in the bunks this evening. Then they would stay a little warmer during the freezing night.

They reached the camp and lined up, but something was wrong. Instead of heading for the dining hall, the women were marched off to their barracks. The buxom female guard with the riding crop accompanied Manya's group inside. Running the crop along the bunks as she strode to the rear of the building, she let the prisoners wonder what was about to happen.

Finally, the guard turned around and pointed to one of the bunks with her whip. She surveyed the faces of the prisoners. "Whose bunk is this?"

The prisoners looked at the floor.

"I want to know who sleeps here," the guard repeated. The group shifted uneasily. The guard bent down and fished in the straw. Manya's eyes closed. A roll of papers was held up for all to see.

"Whose is this? Who writes on paper here? Tell me now, or everyone will be punished."

Oh, God, why had she chosen today to leave her diary behind? There was nothing for Manya to do but step forward.

The guard nodded. Her threat had worked. "This belongs to you?" she asked Manya.

"Yes . . . it's mine," Manya admitted.

"Come with me!" the guard commanded, leading the way. Marie reached to touch Manya's arm as she followed the guard out and across the compound. They entered a building, and a guard at Manya's back shoved her inside.

"What is written here? What language is this?" the guard demanded, waving the diary at Manya.

"It's Polish," Manya answered. "I—"

"What does it say?" the guard interrupted. "And you'd better tell the truth. I can find out another way."

"It's nothing," Manya began, "Just a few words . . . it's nothing important—only things that have happened to me since—"

"What were you planning to do with it?" the guard cut her short again.

"Nothing . . . truly . . . just a diary, just things I wanted to remember."

"I don't believe you," the guard screamed, throwing the papers in Manya's face. She raised the whip and cracked it, crisscrossing Manya's body with blows.

"You are not allowed to have such things," she went on, puffing with exertion. The leather loop bit into Manya's body—face, arms, back, legs, chest, neck. She tried to cover her head with her arms; then the whip would land again, and an involuntary flinch would cause her to lower her defense. Finally she collapsed on the floor. Another guard dragged her outside and threw her to the snowy ground.

"I promise you, no diary will be needed to remember this night—*if* you survive. Now, kneel!" the guard commanded, yanking Manya's arm upward. "Kneel!"

Manya stretched her fingers on the icy terrain, seeking the traction to obey.

"You will kneel here all night," the guard ordered. "Both knees on the ground. No sitting, no use of hands. I will be watching. You'd better not cheat." She turned and went back into the building.

The cold was even more intense close to the ground. Manya shook with pain and exposure. A biting wind cut through her thin garments, and she wrapped her arms around herself. It got darker and icier; she couldn't feel her knees anymore.

She looked toward the barracks. The floodlight at the top of each door cast its illumination on routes of escape. A searchlight inched along in its sweep across the compound. She had to close her eyes against its glare when it came to her.

The shivers were violent now, coming in spasms that threw her off balance. She put a hand down to steady herself, then snatched it away in case the guard was watching. Again the wind, and another spasm. The hand touched the snow. This time it stayed longer; there was no shout of discovery from the guard. She shifted some weight to it. A touch of relief for her cramping thighs.

The searchlight was making another pass. She lifted her hand from the snow and returned to the required position. On it went. She might as well risk it again. She rocked to the side and lifted one knee. Ahh, better. Now the other side. The guard couldn't be watching. Manya leaned back and sat on her feet. Blessed relief! Wait—the searchlight! She raised herself back up again until it passed.

She continued to alternate her position, timing the movements with the progress of the searchlight. As the hours passed, she tried something else. As the circling beam approached, lit her up, and went on, she got to her feet. At first her knees wouldn't unbend. She shook her legs and rubbed some blood into them. They tingled, then burned like fire. They were coming back to life. But that cursed beam was only a building away. Back on her knees she went. An incredible fatigue came over her. She couldn't keep this up.

Another kind of trembling took hold—the kind that comes from within and starts with a howl. With the loss of her diary, she had been stripped of the last record of herself, just as surely as the Germans had stolen years of her life. She was going to die—not by fire, or gas, or even beatings. Oh, Meyer, she whispered, is it all going to end like this?

In the middle of the night, after hours had passed, Manya imagined the guard looking at her from the window, watching the freezing girl, alone but resolute, kneeling in the snow.

CHAPTER FOURTEEN

Liberation

In the final months of the war, soldiers from Allied and Soviet armies gradually moved around Germany from camp to camp, discovering unimaginable horrors as they went. At some camps, the Nazi guards simply fled before the armies arrived, seeking to save themselves and leaving their former charges behind in numb confusion. At other camps, news of approaching liberation armies provoked German officers to lead their nearly starved captives on "death marches" around the countryside. These frantic attempts by the Nazis to elude the liberators led to hundreds of thousands of additional deaths.

For those inmates who survived, liberation ended the most desperate time of their lives. However, after years of suffering and numerous instances when fiendish tricks had been played and hopes of war's end dashed, the period immediately before liberation seemed among the hardest of times to get through.

APRIL–MAY 1945

It took some weeks for Manya to break the habit of reaching for her diary at night. Each time her hand came up empty, it brought the whole incident back to her with a renewed sense of loss. She recalled kneeling on the frozen ground, then after what seemed an eternity, blinking her eyes and realizing that the sky was getting light and that she had endured the punishing night. She had closed her eyes and listened: it was quiet. She had tried to hear and then feel her heart: it was beating, slowly. She had looked at her hands and felt them. They had been white and hard and felt like wood when she rubbed them together, so she had tucked them under her arms.

The wake-up siren had sounded, and across the compound guards emerged from their quarters and readied their duty sheets. She had heard noises from the building just behind her. The door had opened, and leather boots strode into her view.

"Still alive, eh?" said the female guard who'd left her there the previous night.

Manya looked down. The guard took it as a nod.

"Well, then," she continued, "it's time to get to work." She lifted Manya's chin with the end of her riding crop. "Get going."

Somehow Manya had struggled to her feet. The riding crop was pointing toward the lineup area. The guard had watched Manya's struggle with relish, wanting to punish the young woman for surviving the night. While she seemed to have trouble deciding whether to prolong the agony or end it, Manya had read the challenge on the guard's face and limped toward the line.

After the loss of her diary, Manya often tried to recall the words she'd written, in order to lock them in her mind. Many things she would remember no matter what: even if she wanted to forget, she couldn't. Chaim dead, Cyvia gone, Meyer who knows where?

Tovah comforted Manya as best she could, finally discovering that humming songs seemed to soothe her. Little by little others joined in the singing, and eventually Manya did as well. It became a ritual for the women of their barracks. First a few familiar songs as a group, perhaps a duet or two from Manya and Tovah, then usually Tovah would be prevailed upon to conclude with a solo.

Sometimes the guards who checked the barracks each night at curfew were late and interrupted the program, but normally the women waited to begin until after the guards were gone. The singing helped to alleviate the desperate loneliness of those cold days.

At this time, in most of the camps, desperation had set in. The Germans were edgy and unpredictable, but the realization that the end was near didn't stop most of the guards from continuing to inflict cruel treatment on their prisoners.

Kaufering, Meyer thought, had become a morgue. More and more men died from diseases. The Nazis did nothing to help the sick, letting them suffer a slow, agonizing death. Others fell because of the near-starvation diet, and a few just no longer had the will to last until the next day.

The prisoners existed under the most hideous conditions. The general filth and smell of decomposing bodies in the barracks was an incentive to those who could still walk to go out for work. Getting out at least allowed them to fill their lungs with air that didn't nauseate them.

If Manya was in the same kind of camp under the same kind of conditions, Meyer thought, what chance was there that he'd see her again?

In spite of these circumstances, Meyer and his friends continued to encourage each other. They silently cheered when they heard gunfire and explosions in the distance. They grew ever more hopeful as they read the news on the faces of the guards.

One morning, the wake-up call came, and Meyer pulled himself from the dilapidated bunk. The roll call was done in a hurry, almost too quickly. The inmates were given coffee and then were handed food.

"You'd better ration it wisely," the officer told them. "You won't get any more for a while. We're leaving this camp and taking you with us. Those who can't walk will be left behind."

A light drizzle was falling when the prisoners, led by SS officers, walked out through the gates. Men who could barely stand tried bravely to put one foot in front of the other, knowing they would surely die if they were left behind. Many didn't have the strength to even attempt the journey, and gave up. Others were too weak to travel far but forced themselves anyway, assuming they'd have to walk only a mile or so to meet the trucks or train bound for their next destination. But there were no trucks and no trains.

The drizzle turned to a cloudburst. The men were ordered to march faster. Some couldn't go on, fell to the mud, and were shot. There was no stopping to bury them, no slowing down to help those who stumbled. The guards simply fired on them as they staggered.

On they trudged. The rain didn't let up, and the dirt road turned to slush. Meyer's feet got heavier and heavier as his clogs collected more mud with each step he took.

"Faster, you filthy Jews!" came the command.

At the end of the first day, they stopped and were allowed a few minutes to eat the bread in their pockets. Although it had become mush, Meyer carefully ate all he had. If tomorrow was the same as today, he knew he would need every ounce of strength he could muster.

The men were then ordered to lie face down on the wet ground. Guards climbed into the trees to watch them.

"Don't look up! If you do, it will be the last time you do, I promise you that," the officer in charge shouted.

Meyer heard the officer order the posted guards to shoot if anyone so much as moved his head.

The next day was the same, only there were fewer of them

stumbling along the road. Those that had succumbed during the night were left where they lay.

The rain reverted to a drizzle. Throughout the day, the men heard shots and explosions. On they walked. The sounds of fighting grew closer. More people fell. It was the end of the second day, and they were ordered to the ground for the night. There was no more food to put into their growling stomachs. They were running out of time and life.

"Meyer, wake up." It was Sol whispering to him.

"What is it?"

"Adam and I think we can sneak away. Do you want to risk it?"

"Yes, of course!"

"Tell Felix. I'll tell Wolf."

There was no argument from any of the friends. They agreed that the Nazis might kill them at any moment and believed that it was better to die trying to escape than to be shot as they walked.

One at a time, Meyer and his friends began to crawl through the wet grass. Slowly, inch by inch, they moved away from the makeshift camp. There was no moon to illuminate their escape, and the rain covered the sound of their bony frames slithering along the ground.

They had gone about a hundred yards when Adam sprang to his feet. "Come on," he whispered. "Let's make a run for it."

The body said no, but the mind said yes. They all jumped up and took off. Legs that had been too weary to function a few minutes ago now sprang to life.

After a few minutes of running, Wolf spotted a barn and flagged the others to the ground. "Should we hide there?" he asked.

All the men answered yes, for it would soon be light and they didn't know where they were or who would be around the area.

They made their way to the rickety structure. It was empty. They threw themselves into the soft, dry hay, each one breathing hard.

Finally someone asked, "What now?"

"We should take turns at guard duty while the others sleep. After everyone has rested, we'll decide what to do," Felix suggested.

They knew they weren't safe. The war wasn't over, and they were somewhere in Germany, wearing striped clothes. They had no food and looked like skeletons. Soon they would surely be missed from their group.

After what seemed only a brief sleep, Wolf awakened them all abruptly. "Everyone get up!" he whispered. "Someone's coming."

"Bury yourselves in the hay!" Meyer commanded, his instincts for hiding coming back to him.

Each dived into a thick pile. The door creaked open.

Meyer heard footsteps walk past his mound of hay. He held his breath, fearing that his heaving chest was causing the hay to move up and down. He detected some kind of activity—a scrunch, swoosh; scrunch, swoosh. Something was being thrown through the air.

Suddenly there was a loud scream. Five piles of hay went flying. Five scared faces fixed on one scared farmer with a pitchfork in his hand. They all stared at each other. No one moved or spoke.

Wolf was holding his leg. Blood was oozing onto his shoe. The scream had come from him when the farmer stuck his pitchfork into the pile Wolf was hiding in and pricked the young man's leg.

Finally, Meyer spoke. "We've just escaped from the Nazis. We need a place to hide!"

The farmer looked at the young men before him with sympathy in his eyes. "I thought so. They're on my farm now, saying they're looking for escaped Jews. They had dogs sniffing out the whole area. Well, you can hide here for now. I'll try to lead them away." He turned and walked out.

"He could be going straight to the Nazis to turn us in!" Adam said nervously.

"We don't have any choice but to wait," Sol responded. "If the Germans are out there with dogs, there's no way we could get away from them."

"And besides, did you see his face?" Felix added. "He looked truly concerned."

Meyer agreed. "We have to trust him. Besides, Wolf can't run with that leg."

They kept watch through cracks in the walls of the barn. Hours passed with no visible movement. It became late afternoon.

"I see someone!" Adam called out to the others. "It's the farmer. He's alone, and he's carrying something."

Everyone scooted over to look.

In minutes the farmer had joined them. "You were worried I would turn you in, weren't you?" he asked. "I can understand that, with all you must have gone through. It took me longer than I expected because I thought you might need this."

He held out a large basket. Inside were fruit, bread, eggs, and chicken. The young men's eyes nearly popped out of their sockets as they looked at the food, then the farmer, then the food again. It took them only seconds to recover. They quickly devoured the basket's contents.

"I don't think you should stay here," the farmer said after they ate. "It's too dangerous for you. And it's dangerous for my family too. If the Nazis should find you here—well, you know better than I what they would do. You can stay for a while; then you must leave. I'll check the area to make sure it's safe."

"How can we thank you for your help?" Sol asked.

"I'm only sorry I can't do more," he responded. "Rest now. I'll be back soon."

The fugitives nodded gratefully and settled in to wait.

It took the farmer about an hour. "It's clear, but you must be careful. The German patrols have just left."

They thanked their new friend over and over.

"Good luck," he responded, "and may God go with you."

The five young men headed for the trees. Luckily Wolf hadn't been hurt too badly and was able to walk on his own. But after the barn was out of sight, they stopped and huddled together.

"There's a chance we'd be putting the farmer in danger if we went back, but I think that barn is the safest place to stay," Adam said.

"I agree," Meyer echoed. "The Germans have already looked in this area, so it should be safe for a while. We'll keep an eye out for the farmer and be sure to hide in a place where he can't find us."

That night, they took turns again keeping watch. It was a peaceful night.

They woke up to a beautiful day. A bright sun shone down on the barn and the fields surrounding it.

The young men were discussing their plan of action when they heard the sound of engines. Sol went to the door.

"What is it?" asked Felix.

No one moved.

Sol turned around, and tears were streaming down his face. He opened his mouth but no words came.

Meyer went running to the door and looked out. His eyes scanned the scene, then froze on a colorful banner flying from one of the military vehicles. There was no mistaking it. He had seen a picture of one in a school book long ago: a pattern of stars and stripes on a field of red, white, and blue. He turned to face his friends.

He too was crying, but his lips formed a smile.

"It's the Americans. We're free."

Spring took hold at last in Lichtenwerden, melting the ice and snow and bringing a bit of cheer to the daylight hours as the singing had uplifted the nights. With the change of weather, Manya could guess that Passover had come and gone, but she was too weak to give up her morning bread for the customary eight days. They were all weak and sick, but no systematic selections had reduced their ranks and no new contingent of prisoners was brought in.

After dinner one night, the women were lying in their bunks talking. The guards should have checked them already, but they must have been delayed. The women waited, preferring not to begin their songs too soon.

Still the guards didn't come. It grew quiet in the barracks. A few women fell asleep.

Suddenly, the place erupted with sound and activity. There were airplanes, ear-splitting explosions, machine-gun fire. The women dived to the floor, crowding together under the bottom bunks. The gunfire went on and on; moans erupted into wails.

"They're going to kill us all," whispered one woman.

They first pushed closer to the walls; then, sensing that bullets might burst through, scrambled in the opposite direction. Rifle shots spat in the distance, joined by muffled shouts and racing motors.

"What's happening out there?" someone whispered.

"Look outside," another pleaded to no one in particular. All were too frightened to do as she'd asked.

Ten or fifteen minutes later, the guns were quiet, but the shouts outside were louder. One woman crawled to the barracks door and peeked out. "I can't see anything," she called to the others. A few more women inched along the floor to join her.

"The searchlight is out," one announced her discovery. They didn't know what to make of that.

Then, boots scrunched rhythmically along the dirt paths outside. Those at the door dashed under nearby bunks.

The women lay there crowded together and trembling all night, listening to noises they couldn't explain and missing the silence of earlier nights, when at least they had known what to expect.

Finally, morning came. They heard footsteps approach, then the squeaky hinges of their barracks door. A uniform stood sideways, using the door as a shield. A rifle barrel panned the interior.

The women crammed their fists into their mouths or buried their faces in shoulders next to them. Anything to keep from screaming.

The uniform moved to the doorpost and took another sideways stance. Then the rifle was lowered and the soldier stepped in.

"You're free!" he yelled. No one moved.

"You're free!" Eyes squeezed shut now peeked open.

My God, Manya thought. He's speaking Russian! She scooted noiselessly to the center aisle until she could see the man's boots, then drew forward slowly. Her eyes rose from his boots up to his pants and then his shirt, until they reached his helmet. He *was* Russian!

"You're free," the soldier repeated. "You can come out." He turned and left the barracks.

The women, accustomed to cruel tricks and afraid to believe that good news had finally come, were too frightened to move or to follow the man out. They clutched one another nervously and sobbed. "You go first," they begged each other.

Finally, they couldn't stand it any longer and crawled out of their hiding places. What began with fearful and halting steps ended in a stampede. But once out, the women stood confused, waiting for directions in the lineup area of the camp. They stared toward the main entrance as the gates were swung open, but they didn't move.

"I don't believe it!" Tovah cried, throwing her arms around Manya. "I don't believe it!" Still they didn't move.

A Russian soldier yelled out instructions. "If you're hungry, take what you want," he said, pointing toward the kitchen, where other men in uniform were wrenching doors wide open.

"If you want clothing, help yourselves." Now he pointed toward the building that had housed the German guards.

"Whatever you want, take it. We'll go with you to town; it's not far. There's plenty more there."

There was another moment of uncertainty, followed by absolute pandemonium. Some of the women ran to the dining hall. They took bread, tearing off chunks and tossing the loaves back and forth to each other. Hands scooped sugar and salt out of bins.

Another few made for the guards' barracks. Drawers were upended on the floor. Underwear flew in all directions; slacks that had belonged to the heavy guards were held up against emaciated waists; belts twice too large were tied instead of buckled. When the supply ran out, strips of cloth were torn from anything handy and threaded through belt loops or wound around waists to secure a skirt or to hitch up a too-long dress. Insignias were ripped from uniform jackets; socks were pulled over feet misshapen by bunions and lost toes.

The Russian soldiers threw open the gate. As Manya and Tovah approached it, they clutched each other, half expecting their exit to be stopped by the soldiers on either side of them. But when the women streamed through the gate, clusters headed freely into town and in all directions.

Manya and Tovah followed the soldiers into town, and as the

Russians stood with them, joined the women who were taking
nightgowns, robes, slips, sweaters, boots, shoes. They marveled
over face powder, cologne, combs and brushes, soap, cigarettes,
and fountain pens. They stroked fruit, cheese, sausage; someone
held up a bar of chocolate; they downed mugs of milk, pressed
their ears close to radios, and asked civilians for directions.

Manya tore off her striped dress and found a skirt and blouse
to put on. Then she and Tovah, also in new clothes, stepped into
the street.

"What should we do?" Manya asked her friend.

"We're going home," Tovah answered. She wrapped Manya's
arm tighter around her own.

"But where are we?"

"We'll find out."

"Which way do we go?"

"We'll ask along the way."

With each step, Manya heard Meyer's voice, ringing in her
ears: "*. . . there's something I want you to promise me. When all
this is over, we meet in Hrubieszow. . . .*"

CHAPTER FIFTEEN

Reunion

"Home is where the heart is."

—Anonymous

JUNE-AUGUST 1945

As he looked out the train window, Meyer couldn't help but reflect on the thousands of miles he had traveled the last three years: all over Poland as a fugitive from the ghetto, in cattle cars as a prisoner, going from camp to camp and country to country—Poland to Germany, Germany to Czechoslovakia, Czechoslovakia to Austria, and finally from Austria back to Germany.

But now he didn't have to worry about where the train would make its next stop or whether it was full or empty. He could stretch out his legs and be comfortable without concern for who was riding in the next seat or the next car. And he could stare out the window and enjoy the beauty and peace of the countryside as it passed before his eyes.

It had been ten weeks since that April day when Meyer and his friends were liberated. Their debilitated condition hadn't kept them from rushing out to greet the soldiers, from cavorting in circles and dancing about, or from pounding their glee on the backs of the Americans.

The soldiers had given them food and water and listened to their stories about Kaufering and the death march. The friends had hoped that the soldiers could send someone back to the camp to save any of their fellow prisoners who might still be alive.

Then, before the Americans had loaded Meyer and his friends into a truck to take them away, the newly freed young men had explained to the soldiers how the German farmer nearby had helped to hide and feed them. They said they wanted to do something to thank him.

While the soldiers had been a little surprised by the request, they had had an idea for a way to help out. They told the young men there was a shoe factory not far from the German's farm. Together, they went there and carried scores of shoes and boots to the truck.

The farmer had been very surprised when the American truck pulled up and out jumped the five young men he had hidden. His face immediately lit up when he realized they had not been caught. Then, Meyer wished they had a camera to catch the farmer's expression when they started dumping shoes at his feet.

"What are these for? What am I supposed to do with all these shoes?" he had asked.

"We wanted to do something to repay you for your kindness and courage," Meyer had explained.

"The shoes were the only things we could find," added Felix.

"There are probably lots of people who will need shoes, now that the war is over. You can sell or trade them," Sol had suggested.

They had left the farmer, thanking him a hundred times over, and watching as he waved to them from the pile of shoes and boots at his feet.

The Americans had then taken Meyer and his friends to the German town of Eggenfelden, where they received medical attention. Hotels there had been turned into living quarters for Jews being liberated from camps in the area. They were given three hot meals a day, although the doctors had warned them against eating too much all at once. They had seen freed prisoners die because their emaciated bodies couldn't tolerate the sudden abundance of nourishment.

The Americans had repeatedly told Meyer how lucky he was to be among the small number who had survived. They had related stories from camps where newly released inmates had taken their revenge on the disarmed guards while the liberators had looked the other way. The soldiers had hinted at allowing Meyer and his friends a similar opportunity, but they had declined. Had they done so, they explained to the soldiers, they would be no different from their former captors.

As many camps as Meyer had been in, as many people as he had seen in the camps, he had been stunned to learn that his own experience represented only a fraction of the horror that had taken place. Did the slaughter consume Manya? Did she somehow survive? He rode a pendulum that swung endlessly between despair and hope.

There were many nights when sleep refused to come as he thought of the missing pieces of his life. He could mourn his father who had been beaten to death, and his mother and sisters who had been shot, and John Salki who was executed in front of his family. But there were others whose fate he could only guess: Josef Wisniewski, Franiek Gorski, Isaac Achler, Antonio Tomitzki, his brothers Shuyl and Motl, Chaim, the rest of the Nagelsztajns, and his precious Manya. One moment he was sure they had to be dead, and the next instant he felt that one or even all of them still lived. He was determined to find and thank those who had helped him and his family, and full of unrelenting grief for the family he'd lost.

But there was something else just as important. Meyer felt thankful that Avrum was his father. From him, Meyer had learned courage and will and self-reliance. As a boy, he had imitated his father's example. Later—perhaps because Avrum entrusted the Korenblit family to his son's willing legs, perhaps to help himself and others—those qualities had become part of Meyer's own character.

Meyer knew that he was alive, in large part, because of luck. He was lucky he'd been young and healthy when the war started, lucky he knew Poles who were willing to risk their lives to help a Jew, lucky the Gestapo pursuing him were transferred out of Hrubieszow, lucky that Hans Wagner Gerber singled him out for help, lucky he'd made such good friends in the camps, and lucky that he had the hope of being with Manya again as his ultimate incentive.

Again and again, he tried to convince himself that Manya was alive; wanted desperately to believe it. Yet images of violence crowded out that hope: babies tossed in the air for target practice, piles of burning bodies, corpses swaying fron nooses, hordes of walking skeletons and others who lay cold in their bunks on any given morning. Still, he couldn't shake the memory of her arms reaching toward him from the truck that carried her away from Budzyn.

Maybe later, when he was stronger, he could go home. But not now. It would be too painful to return and learn for certain that Manya had not survived.

His thoughts were interrupted by the train whistle. They were pulling into Munich.

Meyer was trying to go forward with his life, and the first thing he wanted to do was find work somewhere. It would help get his mind off the past and plant him firmly in the future. He had come to Munich to find a man whose name and address he'd been given with the suggestion that this man might be able to help.

As he walked down the street, he thought he heard his name called, but no one knew him here, so he assumed he'd heard wrong. Then a hand grabbed his shoulder and spun him around.

"Meyer! Meyer Korenblit, it *is* you!" the man cried.

A little bewildered, Meyer stared at him. He looked familiar. Then, Meyer remembered him from Hrubieszow: he had done business with Avrum but left for Russia when the war began.

The two men grabbed each other.

"It's good to see you are alive, Meyer."

"I'm glad to see you too," Meyer responded warmly.

"But what are you doing *here?*"

"I'm living in Eggenfelden, and I came to Munich on business."

"No, no! I don't mean that! Haven't you been back to Hrubieszow?"

"No, I've thought about returning many times, but I don't think there's anything left for me there. Only bad memories."

The man took hold of Meyer's shoulders in a firm grasp.

"But listen, Meyer. Manya Nagelsztajn is in Hrubieszow! She and Tovah are staying with Motl Reese."

It took only a second for the words to sink in.

"My Manya's alive? Manya Nagelsztajn is alive? She's in Hrubieszow?" he yelled.

Now Meyer was hugging the man wildly, jumping up and down and laughing.

His mind travelled back to Budzyn:

"*Promise me, Manya . . . when all this is over . . . we meet in Hrubieszow.*"

It took several days for Manya and Tovah to reach Hrubieszow. Much of the journey was made on foot. Once a truck driver gave them a lift. And finally they caught a train.

How they got there mattered little. They were out! They were free! The nightmare was over. Manya was going home—home to Meyer, home to her family. She would walk into town and head for the marketplace, go past the baker, turn right, then past the shoemaker, the tailor, the dressmaker, all shops in the brick building that was her home, that had belonged to her family for generations. She'd tiptoe up the flight of stairs from the street to their apartment. Yes, that was it; she'd surprise them. Of course, they'd all be there. Let's see: her mother would probably be in the kitchen, and her father home after work, unless Ely had a soccer game. Her brothers and sisters would be sitting around the table doing their studies. She would just walk in casually. Imagine the looks on their faces! She couldn't wait!

But there was no family awaiting Manya—indeed no house to return to. There was no Josef Wisniewski, no Police Chief Gorski, and no Meyer.

One by one the hopes that had nurtured her splintered away. Maybe she didn't belong in this town anymore; it had taken little notice of her return. There were no familiar arms to welcome her or cheer her survival. Her homecoming was marked instead by bitter reality.

When she stood in the marketplace, the streets were the same and the storefronts hadn't changed. But when she looked in the direction of her house, it wasn't there.

She and Tovah got funny looks from the townspeople. They heard whispers behind their backs that seemed to say, "What are *they* doing here? Did you see? They're Jews. Just look at them!" Manya knew she looked ill; she weighed only about sixty-five pounds.

She wandered through the streets, hand in hand with Tovah, looking in shop windows. Suddenly, one day a man inside the butcher shop looked familiar. Wanting to be sure, she stared at him another moment or two. Yes, it had to be him. They went inside.

At first the man didn't recognize Manya, but then his face broke into a wide grin and he hugged her. It may not have been her family, but it was close to the kind of greeting she had dreamed about all the way home.

The man explained to Manya that he hadn't been back long himself. He'd been relieved that, on his arrival, the people who had run the shop under the Germans had returned it to him. He told her he'd been in a camp with Meyer, but that had been long ago. He had no idea where Meyer was now.

"What are you going to do now?" he asked Manya finally.

"I don't really know. I have no place to live. My friend Tovah and I would like to stay together and maybe find some work to do."

"Why don't you come live at my house?" he suggested. "There are two other men sharing it with me. You and Tovah could take care of it for us—help to clean, do the laundry, and cook. I'll give you money to buy food. It's a good arrangement, don't you think?"

"You're very kind," Manya answered happily as Tovah nodded her agreement. "We'll do it!"

And so the two young women moved in and began putting their lives in order. Manya thought frequently of leaving, but had no money to travel and didn't know where to go anyway. Besides, Josef Wisniewski was not there for her to leave a message with, so she felt she had to stay in Hrubieszow in case Meyer showed up.

Her hometown was a mausoleum of memories, reflecting happy times and sad times and, worst of all, the end of both. Everywhere she looked, the past taunted her: the marketplace where her mother had shopped, the houses and buildings her father had built, the streets where her brothers and sisters had played.

Weeks passed before Manya found out what had happened to the rest of the Nagelsztajn family. They had been discovered in their basement hideout, as Manya had feared. Then, the Nazis had taken them to the foxholes outside the city and killed them.

"Maybe one of us will survive," her mother had said when they parted. Well, that was just what had happened. Manya was the lone survivor. She resolved that although her family was dead, their faces and her memories of them would live forever inside her heart.

About three weeks later, Manya was out shopping for food, when the next thing she knew she woke up in a strange place. She felt a hand on her shoulder.

"Meyer?"

"No, I'm a nurse, miss. You're in the hospital."

"What's wrong . . . I can't see you. Where are you?"

"Shh . . . you're all right. You collapsed in the street and were brought here."

"But I can't see. I'm blind," Manya whispered.

"Please, lie back now. You're going to be fine. We're going to take good care of you."

Manya fell back against the pillows. She was blind. Had she survived the camps only to spend the rest of her life feeling her way around rooms and being led down the street? It was a cruel trick, for now, even if Meyer returned, she would never be able to see his face again.

Manya stayed in the hospital for a week. The doctors told her they could find no physical damage. They attributed her loss of sight to the terrible conditions she had lived through in the past several years, compounded by the trauma of learning of her family's death. The doctors gave her medication, but all they could do was wait and hope, and they told her to do the same.

Finally, she returned to the butcher's house. Every day she prayed, and though she lay in bed helpless to move about without assistance, unable even to distinguish night from day, in her mind she walked through the park and the fields with Meyer. In her thoughts, she strolled hand in hand with him under the stars. In her dreams, she saw him walk through the door and take her in his arms.

Tovah was her constant companion, helping in many ways, listening patiently as Manya recounted a jumble of memories and dreams. Tovah even seemed to know when it was better for Manya to be on her own trying to break through the dark barrier.

The pattern continued for three weeks. Then, one morning the others in the house were readying themselves for the day as Tovah clattered dishes in the kitchen.

Manya woke up and opened her eyes. The room seemed blurry, but the hazy images were the most she'd seen in weeks. When she saw light, she realized her sight was returning.

"Tovah! Tovah! I can see! I can see!" she yelled.

Manya went to the park that morning, despite Tovah's protests that she should stay in bed. But Manya had to go. For hours she walked and sat, looking at the sights and watching couples strolling, sitting, talking, and kissing, just as she and Meyer had done long ago. She refused to believe it wouldn't happen again.

Gradually she again took up her tasks in the house—cooking, cleaning, shopping, settling in to the rhythm of her new life. But every few days she made a point of walking in the park, for it was there that she felt closest to Meyer.

A few more weeks passed. It was a hot August day, and Manya spent the afternoon in the park. When she returned, she didn't feel like cooking. She didn't want to add to the heat by lighting the stove. But it wouldn't be long before she'd have five hungry people to feed. She sighed and picked up some matches.

Suddenly, a voice boomed on the floor below and echoed in the hallway.

She jumped when she heard it.

It called again, and now there was a thundering of feet climbing steps by threes.

"Manya! Manya!"

There was no mistaking that voice. She ran to the other room as the door burst open.

She was in his arms as soon as he came through the door.

"Oh, Meyer, I knew you would come back. I just knew it! I love you, I love you."

"I got you back," Meyer cried, holding her tighter and tighter. "Oh, God, I got you back! Don't let go, Manya. Don't ever let go."

"I never did, Meyer. I never did!"

Epilogue

Manya Nagelsztajn and Meyer Korenblit were married in January 1946 in Eggenfelden, West Germany. Meyer's friends Sol, Felix, Adam, and Wolf were in attendance. The newlyweds took a small apartment in a hotel and started building a life for themselves. On July 18, 1947, their son Sammy (named after Manya's father) was born.

In 1948, through a lucky set of circumstances, Meyer was reunited with his brother Motl in Eggenfelden. Motl told Meyer that he and Shuyl had been forced to join the Russian Army. Shuyl was killed during the liberation of Berlin shortly before the war ended. Motl married and moved to Israel in 1948. In 1956, he immigrated to Chicago.

Little by little, Manya and Meyer's friends left Eggenfelden, and there was much talk of immigrating to various countries, among them Australia and the United States. Meyer and Manya were on the verge of filing papers to go to Australia when they learned that no couples with babies would be accepted. Meyer was reluctant to apply for immigration to the United States, for he had seen others wait with no luck for years after applying and he didn't want to be disappointed.

Without telling Meyer, Manya went to the authorities and applied for immigration to the United States, thinking that if they were accepted, they would have at least a year to decide whether they wanted to make such a move. It was quite a surprise when they received word two months later that their application had been approved and that they were to report to the USNS *General W. C. Langfitt* in Bremerhaven. It was with some reluctance that Meyer agreed to go. In the five years since the war had ended, he had settled into their new life and was leery of making another new start. He spoke no English and had never heard of the destination chosen for them by their HIAS sponsor.

With the help of B'nai B'rith, Manya and Meyer settled in Ponca City, Oklahoma, in April 1950. On July 30, 1951, their second son, Michael (named after Manya's mother), was born. There, Meyer and Manya learned English and ran a tiny drive-in restaurant called the Dixie Dog. They became American citizens in April 1979. Sammy is married to Diane Fraley and has three children. Michael is married to Joan Bravo; they have two children.

As part of their research for the first edition of this book, Michael, Joan, and Manya attended the World Gathering of Jewish Holocaust Survivors in June 1981 in Jerusalem. It was also an opportunity for Manya to visit cousins on her father's side, who had moved to Palestine. There too she would see her friends Tovah, Hannah, and Molly. Tovah had visited Manya in the United States in 1979. But it was the first time Manya had seen Hannah since being liberated from Lichtenwerden, or Molly since they had left her behind in Auschwitz.

In August 1981, Michael, Joan, Meyer, and Manya traveled to Poland and West Germany. The decision to make this trip had been very difficult for Meyer and Manya, for they would be reliving the nightmare they had experienced thirty-nine years before.

The four visited Hrubieszow and as many of the concentration camps as they could find. In Hrubieszow, they found out that Josef Wisniewski had been killed in 1944 when he was hit by a train. They found Isaac Achler in Mislavitch. In an emotional reunion between Meyer and Isaac, both men cried as the Pole talked about the love and respect he had for Meyer's father.

And they found Henrik Gorski and his sister, children of the police chief. Henrik explained that his father's activities in support of Jews had been discovered and he had been sent to several concentration camps. He was killed by the Nazis in Gusen (a subcamp of Mauthausen) for helping the underground and for hiding Jews. On the day his father was taken away from the house, hidden in the attic were three Jewish girls; Henrik is not sure if they are still alive.

As the Korenblits were leaving, Henrik said one last thing to Meyer: "I want you to know, Meyer, my father did the right thing. I have no regrets. Knowing the outcome would be no different. I would want him to do the same thing again."

As for Cyvia, Meyer's sister, neither Meyer nor Manya can explain how she could have appeared in Plaszow concentration camp when they thought she had died with her mother and sisters. From Plaszow, camp records indicate that Cyvia was transferred to Auschwitz and then to Stutthof, but the trail leaves off there.

In December 1981 and January 1982, Manya and Meyer travelled to Israel to visit Meyer's elderly aunt, who had immigrated there in the early 1930s. The trip would also allow him a long-overdue opportunity to see some of his friends from the camps.

During the trip, Manya became aware that a cousin on her mother's side lived in Israel. She contacted him and, in the course of the conversation, said that she had lost all her immediate family during the war. The cousin told her she was wrong: he had received a letter from her brother Chaim after the war, postmarked from Scotland he thought. Manya was stunned: could Chaim really still be alive? Even if the letter was authentic, it had been thirty-nine years since it had been sent, and anything could have happened in that time.

When Meyer and Manya returned to the United States, Mike enlisted the help of the British embassy in trying to track down Chaim. They finally, miraculously, came up with a Nagelsztajn, C. As told in this book's preface, Mike's phone call that day confirmed that he was indeed Manya's long-lost brother. Chaim, like Manya, had thought that the rest of his family had died during the war.

Chaim, Manya, and Meyer had a reunion on the telephone that day. Manya learned that when Chaim left her that day in the Hrubieszow ghetto, he was deported to Majdanek and from there on a death march, ending up in Auschwitz. From there, he was transferred to Ebensee concentration camp in Austria.

Chaim had indeed been taken to the gas chambers in Auschwitz, as Manya believed she was told when she arrived there, but by luck that can never be explained, the Nazis had overestimated the available capacity for that day. A group of inmates—including Chaim—was marched back to the barracks area to wait their turn. In the confusion, Chaim's group was instead escorted to barracks whose inmates were scheduled for transfer. A week or so later, he was moved out of Auschwitz. During his two years there, he worked building roads and landing strips.

When he was liberated from Ebensee, he went to Italy, where he was told he could find a way to immigrate to Palestine. However, the refugee centers were so crowded and the wait so long that he joined the Polish Army in Italy instead and later immigrated to England. It was then that a faint memory surfaced and he wrote a letter to a cousin in Palestine—the same one Manya saw during her second trip to Israel. After some weeks, Chaim was taken in by a family in Newcastle, the Abrahamses whose daughter Sonia and her husband Bernard Lewis remain close friends today.

After the war, Chaim searched for Manya through the International Red Cross, but her name was not listed with that organization because she had never registered in a displaced persons camp. He went back to Hrubieszow in 1968, but when he found no information there, he was finally convinced that she had been killed.

Chaim ran a small construction business in Newcastle for many years. He married and raised four children with his wife, Cecilia: David and his wife Marion have two daughters; Pola and her husband David Charlton have a son and a daughter; Julie and her husband John Metcalf have two daughters; and Michael and his wife Judith have two sons and a daughter.

Four days after Mike located Chaim's telephone number, a joyful reunion occurred at the foot of a ramp of a British Airways plane at the Newcastle airport. In the face of overwhelming odds and unspeakable horrors, Manya, Meyer, and Chaim were together again.

Many later called it a "fairy tale" ending. Of the 8,000 Jews of Hrubieszow, these three were among the fewer than 200 who survived.

ACKNOWLEDGMENTS

We thank the staff and associates of the Close Up Foundation, who put their energy and their hearts at our disposal; Joyce Golding, for being our friend; Chris Schillig; Ann Buchwald; Lynn Pate Whittaker, who believed the story should never be lost; Chaim, for giving us all hope; and Meyer and Manya, who did everything possible to help us write their story, especially for having the courage to relive it.

--Mike Korenblit and Kathie Janger

Shahnaz Mehta, for her support and enthusiasm; Vikki Bravo, who gave me advice and encouragement when they were needed the most; and my wife, Joan, who is as much a part of this book as I am, an inspiration who was always there for me.

--M. K.

My husband Steve; my children, Margi, Jay, and Andrea; my grandmother; Ruth and Harry Janger; Joan Korenblit for having the idea in the first place and for her constancy; Bill, Kristin, and Matte for the pleasure they bring our family; Hayley, Will, Brian, Megan, and Sadie for grins and infectious giggles; and my mother, for reasons I am still discovering.

--K. J.

SOURCES

This book is based on interviews conducted by the authors in 1980 and 1981. For verification of places and events, preparation of chapter headnotes, and general context of the Holocaust, the following were consulted: Martin Gilbert, *The Holocaust: A History of the Jews of Europe During the Second World War* and *Atlas of the Holocaust;* Lucy S. Dawidowicz, ed., *A Holocaust Reader* and *The War Against the Jews;* Elie Wiesel, *Night;* Thomas Keneally, *Schindler's List;* Primo Levi, *Survival in Auschwitz* and *The Drowned and the Saved; An Interrupted Life: The Diaries of Etty Hillesum, 1941-43;* Anne Frank, *The Diary of a Young Girl;* Abraham Eisen, "Chronology of the Holocaust in Hrubieszow"; Nakhman Blumental, "Jewish Hrubieszow in the Years 1939-45"; Art Spiegelman, *Maus I: A Survivor's Tale;* Konnilyn G. Feig, *Hitler's Death Camps;* Gordon J. Horwitz, *In the Shadow of Death: Living Outside the Gates of Mauthausen;* Jon Bridgman, *The End of the Holocaust: The Liberation of the Camps;* Richard C. Lukas, *Forgotten Holocaust: The Poles under German Occupation, 1939-44;* and Yisrael Gutman, et al., eds., *The Jews of Poland Between Two World Wars.* Thanks go to Gordon Horwitz for assistance with historical details, and to the Holocaust Memorial Museum in Washington, D. C.

Index

MICHAEL KORENBLIT

The son of Manya and Meyer, Mike is the president of the Respect Diversity Foundation, a nonprofit, 501(c)(3) educational organization. RDF was created to foster understanding and acceptance for people of all races, nationalities, religions, sexual orientations, and ability levels. A graduate of the University of Oklahoma, Mike was the executive producer of educational documentaries and an award-winning public affairs series on cable television for the Close Up Foundation. He is a resident of Edmond, Oklahoma.

Call 405/359-0369 or message rdfrdf@cox.net to book a speaking engagement with Mike, or to interview him via FaceTime or telephone.

Topics: Diversity, tolerance, the Holocaust, school shootings, bullying, and genocide.

Audience: 5th-12th graders, university students and faculty, religious communities, civic groups and government conferences.

KATHLEEN JANGER

Helped create the Close Up Foundation's government studies program for students and teachers. She also co-founded and directed a national writing competition for first through eighth graders. She authored two other books and numerous essays and enjoys freelance writing and editing. She is a resident of Houston, Texas.